SHOT AT & MISSED

Vietnam October 1967 to November 1968

Neal E. Morgan

Table of Contents

WEBSITE: www.shot-at-vietnam.com

Dedication

I would like to dedicate this book to my incredible family. They have always been there to help me enjoy each and every day and have without hesitation offered their support whenever it was needed; I cannot envision life without them. Each one of them and their families have told me I should write this book, and it is their confident encouragement that has helped me finish this work.

To my understanding wife for her tolerance to my many quirks and for her love and companionship. Her dedication to make sure this book is easier to read and is grammatically correct has proven to be an invaluable asset. And I know that without her support and guidance there would be no book – and quite possibly no one to write it.

To my daughter for her love and support and to her family for brightening my day every time I see them. I see great promise in her children and know with the tutelage of her and her husband, the kids will do very well. I have always been so very proud of how well she has lived her life and for her dedication to her family. She is a gift I will always treasure, and I know how very lucky both my wife and I have been to have her be a part of our lives.

To my step-daughter who throughout her life has proven to be successful at everything she has tried. Her many endeavors, love of the arts, endless enthusiasm, and dedication to her friends and family have always been the mainstays of her life. Both her mother and I are very proud of her many triumphs and love her strength of character.

To my sister for her strength of spirit, kind words, and her "I can do it" attitude. She has always proven to be a true friend and has dedicated her life to help others improve their circumstances. She has survived many trials; and each time she has not only triumphed but has become a stronger person and an inspiration to everyone who knows her. To know her is to love her.

To my younger brother and his family for always being there whenever or wherever help was needed. He and his wife have empowered their children to live happy, God-loving, successful lives. He too has overcome many of life's hardships but still puts every other person's needs before his own. He and his wife are the salt of the earth and the kindest people I know.

To my youngest brother and his wife for their friendship and never-ending willingness to offer comfort and aid and to him for his constant support and companionship. He too has always been successful at his endeavors and has proven to be a loving and generous soul. His dedication to every member of his family knows no bounds, and we can always count on him to be there whenever needed. He is my best friend.

To my parents, although both have passed away, I would like to honor their memory and thank them for giving me their love, making sure I got a good education, giving me the skills to make my way, and for always being there.

To my friends, thank you so very much for making my life such a pleasant journey and for everything you have all done to help us along the way. To my dear friend and former colleague for his friendship and support and to his family and children. And especially to my ex-neighbor and his wife (he is another Vietnam veteran), for their friendship and support. I know I owe them a debt I will never able to repay. I hope each and every one of our many friends will always be a part of our lives.

And last, but certainly not least, I dedicate this book to all of those who have served our nation in the military. It is their service and sacrifice that have ensured our country's constitution, our ideals, and that our way of life will always be there for future generations. Perhaps in some small way this book will help provide the impetus to the leaders of our nation to better support the needs of these selfless veterans and active duty personnel, and I pray our leaders will endeavor to find more peaceful resolutions to our conflicts. And most of all, with my respect and gratitude, may everyone who has served our country receive the recognition, esteem, and admiration they all so very much deserve.

Special Tribute

It still seems unbelievable to me now, but one day as I exited the Kansas Laundry, located at the 1st Infantry Division's basecamp in Di An, Vietnam, I literally bumped into my former Drill Sergeant "Doug Meier" from my Basic Training days at Ft. Knox, Kentucky. Mistakenly I thought maybe I had outranked him; I didn't know his rank because he had no sleeve or collar insignia, but I was wrong. His seemed to be in a hurry, and after I introduced myself he wished me well, shook my hand, smiled, and walked slowly away without another word.

I really didn't know what was going on at that time, but I somehow felt very lucky to have known him. I never saw him again, and now I never will. Sadly, I recently discovered his name is now inscribed on the Vietnam Wall Memorial in Washington D.C. He was 6 months my junior and died 2 days before his 24th birthday on June 6th 1969, 7 months after I had returned home, close to 5 decades ago.

Although I said I would not refer to any real names, I feel you should know his name in truth was Duane H. Landwehr and that he had attained the rank of Second Lieutenant. He was awarded both the Silver Star and Purple Heart medals which makes him a hero by anybody's standards. Maybe on occasion he had been my nemesis in basic training, but the lessons I learned from him served me well both in Vietnam and for all the years since. I am truly very sorry to offer this tribute way too many years after the fact. So far, he is the only person I have discovered from my stateside training days who died in Vietnam. I'm truly saddened by his loss and so with honor, respect, and condolences to his family, I offer this humble tribute. He served his country well and his tragic loss of life at such a young age will be something I will always remember.

Whenever there are desperate times and dire circumstances and common sense tells you to run away, most will heed the warning and go. Then there are those chosen few who will always run toward the danger. You will find their names chiseled into the black granite walls of the Vietnam Memorial in Washington, D.C., and never doubt each and every one of them is a hero.

Foreword

I always wanted to title this book "Shot at & Missed," but thought that name was already taken. The other book is actually titled *Shot at and Missed, Recollections of a World War II Bombardier* by Jack R. Myers. His book is an account of his exploits over most of Europe with the Second Bomb Group, Fifteenth Air Force. I'm sure Mr. Myers' experiences were much more intense than mine but firmly believe we shared the same thoughts whenever we heard the unmistakable sound of a bullet or shrapnel cutting through the air.

When I was overseas there was a popular military phrase: "Shot at & missed" (usually followed by: "Shit at & hit"), and this is something I've repeated all too frequently since 1968. So far my research has failed to conclusively identify the original source of "Shot at & missed." Right now, my best guess is that it came into use shortly after the discovery of gun powder. Winston Churchill has been quoted as saying "The greatest thrill a man can experience is to be shot at without result," and this is almost now always 'translated' as "shot at and missed." Not so sure if thrill is the correct emotion, but I couldn't agree more there are certainly feelings of exhilaration and happiness, but for me there was a lot of anger tempered with revenge.

The next title that came to mind was *A Skewed Perspective*, but that was a book concerning oil paintings 1991 to 2000. Then I came up with *A Reluctant Witness*, but again, there is a book copyrighted 2008 with that name that was also titled: *Robert Taylor,*

Hollywood and Communism. After several more unsuccessful attempts I thought maybe "An Unlikely Perspective" or "Fateful Witness" might possibly be a couple of candidates, and, although true enough, to me they lacked the punch of "Shot at & Missed." So I kept the title decision as a work in progress because the more I thought about it, the better I liked my original title. So, if it doesn't get rejected by the publisher's lawyers or the copyright process (if it ever gets that far), so be it. In hopes of getting it published, I decided to title this book: *Shot At and Missed – Vietnam – October 1967 to November 1968.*

My book was never even a thought -- that is, not until I received a startling email on October 16, 2011. It concerned the tally of all those heroes who have been immortalized on the Vietnam War Memorial in Washington D.C. I had actually seen this email once before, but seeing all those sad, tragic statistics again really had an impact. I started to write a reply shortly after receipt of that message, but it took until December 7th of that same year for me to actually send my email.

The following is an edited excerpt of my thoughts as they appeared in my December 2011 email reply that ultimately was the impetus for this book:

> The work at the Vietnam Memorial began on March 16, 1982 and it was dedicated on November 13, 1982. The statistics provided by the unknown author of the original email message herald the tragedies of a war that have impacted all of us in one way or another.
>
> I have amended the contents of this dissertation countless times and could probably do so forever; so, for no reason other than I think I've said what I wanted, it's time to pass this on. The personal facts and figures are based solely on my memories from 43 years ago (now 48) and the balance of the history and statistics have been researched. I

am solely responsible for this information and apologize for any errors but firmly believe the following to be true. And perhaps it is somewhat fitting I pass this on to you on the anniversary of the Pearl Harbor attack 70 years ago.

The Vietnam conflict has been referred to as "The Ten Thousand Day War" after the title of a Canadian documentary released in 1980. The French Indochina War began on December 19, 1946 and ended on August 1, 1954. At that time it had gone on for 7 years and 7+ months, or 2,782 days. For a year and 3 months (457 days) there was no declared conflict, although hardly a day passed without an angry shot being fired. America formally became involved on November 1, 1955; however, we had already been a presence in Vietnam for a long time, supporting the French in their efforts and had even provided American advisors since the early 1950's. The American involvement mercifully ended on April 30, 1975, close to two decades after the U.S. 1955 declaration, for an additional 7,121 days. So in all reality the conflict in Vietnam (which started shortly after World War II) went on for 28 years, 4 months, and 11 days for a total of 10,360 days. By far, most of those who were lost enjoyed life for a much shorter time.

A total of 9 other countries joined America and also had troops on the ground in country: Australia, Khmer Republic, Kingdom of Laos, New Zealand, Philippines, Republic of China (Taiwan), South Korea, South Vietnam, and Thailand. This coalition was engaged in the conflict eventually known by the politically correct term "Police Action" in an effort to halt the progress of communist aggression in Southeast Asia. Most of the combat took place in South Vietnam, but North Vietnam, Cambodia, and Laos were also battlefields. The communist forces consisted of North Vietnam, NLF (National Liberation Front), Khmer Rouge, Pathet Lao, and

North Korea, and there were Russian and mainland Chinese "advisers" who also had a significant presence.

I arrived in Vietnam the middle of October 1967 and departed at the end of November 1968. Due to the intensity of the times I was a reluctant witness to the statistics (as noted in that October 2011 email 44 years later) as they were tallied. Although trained as a combat engineer and a squad leader, I was a fortunate victim of circumstance and reassigned to be a finance clerk with 1st Admin Company, part of the 1st Infantry Division also known as the "Big Red One." I ended up on a base named for a local township named Di An (pronounced Zeon) which is about 19 miles northeast of what was then Saigon but is now known as Ho Chi Minh City.

We spent 7 days a week in the "office" for 8 to 12 hours each day but less on Sundays if we attended morning church services (something most of us said we did "religiously"). We produced pay vouchers; updated records; processed people coming into, transferring, and leaving country; and, sadly, audited the payroll files of those killed in action (KIA). My responsibilities changed as the troop strength kept increasing, but my primary job was maintaining the payroll records for the Combat Engineers and Military Intelligence. Each month I produced hand-typed pay vouchers, starting with 350 and increasing to more than 500 people by the end of my tour of duty.

It was a very eventful time because the North Vietnamese had launched a countrywide offensive during the Lunar Tet celebration late in January of 1968. This dramatically increased the fighting and the casualties and almost resulted in the takeover of Saigon and the U.S. Embassy. Due to the increased activity, I found myself on guard duty many days and nights for most of the duration of my active service. Although I was involved in several skirmishes while on guard duty, the majority of my time was pretty much uneventful. During my 13-1/2 month tour, I had a total of 8 days off for R&R (Rest & Recreation) consisting of one three-day vacation "in-country" at Vung Tau, and one five-day trip to Taipei in Taiwan.

My best guess is that during my tour of duty, I processed well over 100 KIA records which is significant because I shared this chore with about 25 others. Not all of us worked with combat troops, and it is important to note that 80% of all of those in the armed services were actually support personnel. However, everyone there experienced ready alerts of potential attack and most could easily identify the near and faraway sounds of war: machine gun fire, mortars, rockets, artillery, napalm, bombs, their AK47s, and our M16s. Countless numbers heard the close angry buzz of bullets or shrapnel cutting through the air and way too many felt the horrific impact of those terrible noises. Whether we accepted it or not, we were all in harm's way.

When I started this essay, President Obama had just announced the end of the Iraq war and soon our troops will be home. I applaud the end of another meaningless conflict and am sorry it ever started. Perhaps one day we will stop the chest-beating and finally acknowledge there is no such thing as a good or just war; the final tally will always prove there were no real winners. The losses to both sides outweigh any gains, and all too often only prove to be the fodder for the next confrontation (and even now is still evidenced by the current conflicts peppered throughout Asia and the Middle East).

I was very fortunate and left Vietnam pretty much as when I arrived, but to this day still recall the terrible times I witnessed. I offer this remembrance as a humble tribute to all who have given of themselves since 1776 and especially to those who sacrificed everything serving our country. Whether it was 235 (now 240) years ago or today, and regardless if it was right or wrong, we need to honor all those who rose to the cause and offered their service with a sense of duty and patriotism. The United States has always inspired and provided a militia to do whatever was necessary to defend the principles and freedoms which are the foundations of our country. The October 2011 email statistics are testament to that resolve.

Well, apparently I hadn't said everything I needed to say. My email reply noted above is offered to help clarify the horrific history that plagued the 1967 to 1968 era. This book is a semi-biographical account which allows for more than a touch of poetic license to incorporate other experiences. Besides, I just can't tell a tale the same way twice anymore, maybe because the memories have started to fade a little; but please know the impact of each event will always be with me. Although never shot, even now there is the occasional faint feeling of still being a member of the walking wounded, as are far too many others.

While researching the events I had witnessed, I found I actually knew very little of the history that led up to the Vietnam War, nor the consequences of America's involvement, that escalated out of control for far too many years. To avoid making the same mistakes again, it is always important to understand what prompted a horrific event and there is nothing more tragic or ironic than human beings trying to kill each other in the pursuit of peace, independence, and freedom of choice. You would think by now our species would have learned how to transcend the tragedy of combat. I firmly believe there must be something in our nature and DNA that demands we occasionally cull the herd for our own preservation, regardless of the consequences. Perhaps human evolution is not everything it's cracked up to be.

When I was overseas, the culture allowed for very crude language. Everyone's speech was liberally sprinkled with an assortment of obscenities which, when you returned home, could transform you into a pariah and social outcast. Everybody swore including officers, enlisted men, doctors, nurses, chaplains, etc., etc. Of course the most popular obscenity is the acronym for "Forbidden and Unlawful Carnal Knowledge." We even used it in the middle of words ("in-f'n-credible" and "un-f'n-believable" immediately come to mind).

One of my favorite comedians, George Carlin, had a comedy skit titled "The seven words you can't say on television," which was featured at the 1972 "Summerfest" event I witnessed in Milwaukee. As George jested, this word is the most versatile in the English language. It can be used as a verb, adverb, noun, pronoun, adjective, modifier, etc. and can be placed almost anywhere in any sentence or word. His soon to become famous comedy routine was stopped and he was promptly arrested on obscenity charges and then unceremoniously briskly escorted off the stage. A short time later the charges were dropped. Today, most of those seven words can and are being used daily on regular network television shows (all except that special one, but "freaking" and "frigging" are rapidly gaining in popularity). Surely one day the "F-word" will transcend the censors (if they still exist) and become acceptable speech. Hollywood long ago gave up on holding back on this word and at times has used it liberally to earn the coveted "R" rating. This all said, I have made the decision to not color this story with an abundance of obscenities, but there are a number of exceptions to this rule.

The names in this book are all fictional and are not intended to refer to any one person. This story revolves around the perspective of a payroll clerk, doing a mundane job in insane circumstances that metamorphosed into a lifetime of memories, all in the short span of only 13-1/2 months in country. If you are expecting an action-packed battlefield diary or intense accounts of heroic exploits, you will have to look elsewhere. My memories often summon the well-known military acronyms FUBAR (F'd Up Beyond All Reason, or Recognition, Repair, etc.) and SNAFU (Situation Normal: All F'd Up) both attributed to World War II and celebrated in Joseph Heller's classic book "Catch 22."

There are things in this book that I've tried to repress all these years, but the memories return whenever I'm reminded and I can't help but to think back. Perhaps this book will prove to be a therapeutic journey. We all hide behind carefully crafted masks meant to project the persona we aspire to, and it has always been incredibly difficult for me to drop the façade and unveil my true self to the world. It is not my intent to vent forlorn memoirs or cry on anybody's shoulder. This is an attempt to understand what happened and perhaps find answers for all the unasked questions. When I started this book, I simply wanted to tell my story; but once the writing began, it transformed into the history of how and why the United States became involved in the genocide of a country. Undeniably, it is this incredible history that is the most important story of all.

Anybody who knows me has probably heard more than they ever wanted to concerning my Vietnam experiences; still, it is some of these very same people who encouraged me to write this story. My family and friends have always been the strength and fuel that keeps me going, and without them there would be no story to tell. My experiences are far from unique and I know that every combat era veteran has his or her own storied history. I sincerely hope that the need to offer my perspective and the incredible history of Vietnam has finally found an appropriate outlet.

I have actually written two "last" chapters and I consider each to be the completion of this work. The first "last" chapter chronicles the end of my experiences in Vietnam and concludes my personal history as I return home. The final "last" chapter is a continuation of the history of what happened in Vietnam after I left the country and how we finally terminated our contribution to all the madness. My original plan was to tell the story of what I had seen and experienced; however, as I started to write, I soon realized the real story was not what I remembered but what had happened to thrust the youth of America into harm's way and our country into turmoil. So please consider my story to be simply a vehicle intended to provide insights into the Vietnam era, and, more importantly, the lunacy our country demonstrated in its orchestration of chaos.

An unedited copy of the original 2011 email follows this forward.

The Original 2011 Email

The Wall Statistics

A little history most people will never know.
Interesting veteran statistics off the Vietnam Memorial Wall.

- There are 58,267 names now listed on that polished black wall, including those that were added in 2010.
- The names are arranged in the order which they were taken from us by date and within each date they are alphabetized. It is hard to believe it is 36 years since the last casualties.
- The first known casualty was Richard B. Fitzgibbon, of North Weymouth, Mass. Listed by the U.S. Department of Defense as having been killed on June 8, 1956. His name is listed on the Wall along with that of his Marine Corps son Lance Cpl. Richard B. Fitzgibbon III, who was killed on Sept. 7, 1965.
- There are three sets of fathers and sons on the wall.
- 39,996 on the Wall were just 22 or younger.
- 8,283 were just 19 years old.
- The largest age group, 33,103 were 18 years old.
- 12 soldiers on the wall were 17 years old.
- 5 soldiers were 16 years old.
- One soldier, PFC Dan Bullock was 15 years old.
- 997 soldiers were killed on their first day in Vietnam...

- 1,448 soldiers were killed on their last day in Vietnam…
- 31 sets of brothers are on the Wall.
- Thirty one sets of parents lost two of their sons.
- 54 soldiers attended Thomas Edison High school in Philadelphia. I wonder why so many from one school.
- 8 Women are on the Wall. Nursing the wounded.
- 244 soldiers were awarded the Medal of Honor during the Vietnam War; 153 of them are on the Wall.
- Beallsville, Ohio with a population of 475 lost 6 of her sons.
- West Virginia had the highest casualty rate per capita in the nation. There are 711 West Virginians on the wall.
- The Marines of Morenci – They led some of the scrappiest high school football and basketball teams that the little Arizona copper town of Morenci (pop. 5,058) had ever known and cheered. They enjoyed roaring beer busts. In quieter moments, they rode horses along the Colorado Trail, stalked deer in the Apache National forest. And in the patriotic camaraderie typical of Morenci's mining families, the nine graduates of Morenci High enlisted as a group in the Marine Corps. Their service began on Independence Day, 1966. Only 3 returned home.
- The Buddies of Midvale – LeRoy Tafoya, Jimmy Martinez, Tom Gonzales were all boyhood friends and lived on three consecutive streets in Midvale, Utah on fifth, sixth and seventh avenues. They lived only a few yards apart. They played ball at the adjacent sandlot ball field. And they all went to Vietnam. In a span of 16 dark days in late 1967, all three would be killed. LeRoy was killed on Wednesday, Nov. 22, the fourth anniversary of John F, Kennedy's assassination. Jimmy died less than 24 hours later on Thanksgiving Day. Tom was shot assaulting the enemy on Dec. 7, Pearl Harbor Remembrance Day.

- The most casualty deaths for a single day was on January 31, 1968 ~ 245 deaths.
- The most casualty deaths for a single month was in May 1968 – 2,415 casualties were incurred.

For most Americans who read this they will only see the numbers that the Vietnam War created. To those of us who survived the war, and to the families of those who did not, we see the faces, we feel the pain that these numbers created. We are, until we too pass away, haunted by these numbers, because they were our friends, husbands, wives, sons and daughters. There are no noble wars, just noble warriors.

Please pass this on to those who served during this time, and those who **DO Care**.

1

Drafted and Not

It was snowing lightly on that Thursday back on January 26, 1967 when I arrived mid-afternoon at the Ryerson Steel plant in Melrose Park, a working-class neighborhood and industrial suburb just west of Chicago. I was employed as a second-shift timekeeper computing incentive bonuses for the mostly Polish welders.

After parking the car, I opened the hood, removed the air filter to access the distributer, detached the rotor and lead wire, and put them in my pocket. Since I shared the 1958 Chevy Impala with my younger brother, it needed to be disabled. He would often hitchhike from our home in Oak Park after I started work, take the car, drive to see his girlfriend in Des Plaines, and would be nowhere around when I got off at 1:00 AM. Sometimes he didn't show up for another hour or two. I had to be a little creative and vary the disabling, as he had started to bring spare parts. Sometimes I removed a tire and took the jack and tire iron to my office; other times, 3 or 4 of the spark plug wires were removed. This sounds extreme, but it worked to my advantage (most of the time).

I said "Hi" to Hal, the security guard at the gate, got a laugh when I told him to say hello to my brother for me, then walked almost a city block to my office. The Ryerson Steel Plant was enormous. It had to be – they fabricated huge bridge support I-beams 90 feet long or more. Whenever they shipped one out of the plant, 25th

Avenue would be closed around midnight, and it would take several hours to get it out of the yard before heading out on its carefully plotted course.

The plant was actually a safe place to work and, the fact is, I know of very few accidents. Still, with a half dozen 100-foot-long bridge cranes flying overhead carrying huge I-beams and dangling chains with links 4- to 12-inches long, all moving about fifteen miles per hour, single and teams of wall cranes sometimes lifting loads beyond their capacity, and huge forklifts always in a hurry, there was the constant potential for serious consequences. I only saw the aftermath of one horrendous accident and afterward never had to be reminded again to wear my hard hat and steel-toed shoes whenever in the plant; unfortunately, I also knew they wouldn't help much if ever needed. I told my friends that Ryerson didn't have any first-aid kits – only tourniquets and stretchers. Actually, there were first-aid kits everywhere, but I thought my description drove the point home.

Business was so good there were three work shifts. I had chosen the second-shift opening when I started in August because it worked well while I was going to college. I had subsequently dropped out of college and told myself I was trying to find myself (funny, I only looked in places with beer and girls).

After receipt of a notice from the draft board, I had taken a physical for the Army at the end of November, then was mailed a rubber-stamped approval dated the same as the exam. I had heard nothing since then and it was of no concern that day. We were supposed to get about six inches of snow, but accurately forecasting the weather was just as elusive of an art form then as it is today. Even the revered Chicago iconic weatherman P. J. Hoff, with all his hand-drawn forecasts and famous cartoon character "Vice President in charge of looking out the window," didn't predict any particular concern. Hey, we lived in Chicago and in the winter it snows.

The shift that night was pretty uneventful and as usual I headed home a little after 1:00 AM. The parking lot had been transformed into a sea of cotton; guess the weather forecast had been a little un-derestimated. Instead of the predicted 5" to 6", the snow was still coming down and already up to the bottoms of the windows of the Chevy. It was so surreal and quiet, and through the eerie silence, I swear you could hear the snowflakes as they gently settled on their predecessors. The car looked like a weird igloo with wrap-around windows.

Luckily it was a very light powdery snow. All I had to do was brush off the top of the car, reassemble the distributor, then I gave it a try and, without any problems, proceeded to slowly drive through the parking lot like a road-grader through popcorn. I made my way onto 25th Avenue and headed north about a half mile through fading tire tracks up to North Avenue (a major artery heading east to my home in Oak Park and then continuing on to Chicago and the lakefront). There were three lanes in each direction separated by a wide ditch, but you could switch from the eastbound to the westbound lanes at every intersection. This was a very good thing because I used every lane that night to get home.

There were groups of bunched-up traffic stalled everywhere in-cluding every car model known to man as well as huge pick-ups with snow blades, road graders, heavy-duty jeeps, semi-trucks with trail-ers, dump trucks, etc. They were all trapped by a mixed-up mess of cars that had half skidded off the road, were in crashes, facing the wrong way, or stalled with their hoods waving in the wind. I followed a pathway that snaked back and forth between the stalled masses. I never stopped, not even at the red lights. It had to be about 10 miles or so to my house. On the whole journey I never saw another person in or out of a vehicle. It took an hour and somehow I made it back to within a block of my house, inevitably getting stuck right in the middle of our street.

I knew Oak Park would be plowing the snow first thing come morning and, since parking on any street was never allowed after 1:00 AM, I had to get that car off the street. I walked to the house, got a snow shovel, and shoveled two tracks from the car to the next door neighbor's double driveway. By then the snow was much heavier than when I started, perhaps because I was closer to Lake Michigan. So I skidded first to one side and then the other, from one curb to the other, the total length of the block. The noise of the spinning tires and smell of burning rubber summoned help from family and neighbors, and after another hour or so the car was off the street. I and everyone else were completely exhausted. Oh, and of course, our street wasn't plowed for another four days.

The entire Chicago area was crippled by the blizzard of 1967 and the long-term Mayor of Chicago, Richard J. Daley, pleaded for civilian help to untangle the mess. The official count was 23 inches of snow, but that didn't include the countless drifts 3- to 4- feet high.

I camped out at home for the next couple days, only going out to make a run to the grocery store which luckily was only a block away. The first mail delivery was the following Wednesday, February 1st. Just my luck, Uncle Sam hadn't forgotten me after all and this time had thoughtfully sent a very special summons. It was titled: "ORDER TO REPORT FOR INDUCTION" and stated: "GREETING: You are hereby ordered for induction into the armed forces of the United States, and to report at 7520 Madison Street, Forest Park, Ill. on February 23, 1967 at 7:00 AM."

At first I was in shock. Nobody I knew had received this special invitation, and I really didn't want to be the first on my block to go. I knew just enough about Vietnam to know I really didn't want to be there. On occasion, I had watched the TV news reports but hadn't paid much attention. It was the first televised war and I thought we were holding our own and doing pretty well. After I started watching the news broadcasts with newfound personal interest, my naiveté quickly evaporated.

Yes, I had heard about the draft dodgers who were leaving the country (most went to Canada at first); they claimed political or religious differences – but, to me, most were simply cowards. The thought of running away was never a consideration for me. No, I was not a glory hound or super patriot and really didn't like the idea of either shooting someone or being shot at. I just figured I was an American and had an obligation to serve my country.

The Vietnam Conflict was very unpopular and it seemed like most nights there was more TV news coverage of the protests than of the war. Still, I just couldn't run away. One more thing, at that time the news media never called it a war because "Police Action" was the popular politically correct nomenclature of the day, and for whatever reason that term still pisses me off.

I fretted for another week and then got a real surprise – another notice from the Selective Service System: "Dear Mr. Morgan, Your induction order is hereby cancelled and your file will be considered for reclassification at the next local board meeting. Very truly yours, FOR THE LOCAL BOARD (Mrs.) Rosemary Jones, Chief Clerk." My relief was legendary.

Things at work were going well and, after a couple of co-workers left, I found I was able to do the night shift all by myself and was up for a promotion. The week flew by and I thought everything was coming up roses. The following Monday was March 19th and guess what? I got another greeting card from my pals at the Selective Service. This time I was to report on April 20th. Unbelievable but true, yet another induction cancellation letter from that dear Mrs. Jones was delivered on the 22nd. I'm not psychic, but the handwriting was on the wall in clear bold type – I was going to be drafted. I called the Local Board and found out they still showed that I was in school and had a deferment, then I assured them I was not in school. So on the 24th of March, they sent my third and final draft notice and I once again was to report on April 20th. This most likely was not a unique experience, but I'm the only person I know who was drafted three times. Much later I learned that my dear and very worried mother had been in a letter-writing frenzy contacting every politician she knew or could find to get me a deferment. She never said anything about it to me and I never knew.

The only precaution I took prior to induction was to have all my wisdom teeth pulled, a decision I never regretted. When that fateful day finally arrived, I said my goodbyes to family and friends and was dutifully driven to the Selective Service System offices at the American Legion in Forest Park on April 20th, 1967 at 7:00 AM sharp. I saw quite a few guys I knew from the neighborhood and high school and we all nervously chatted and speculated about the days to come. At least I wasn't going in by myself and would be with some people I had known for years.

Before boarding the bus, once again I was told to go home due to that phantom deferment and then explained I was not in school so there was no deferment. They agreed and after the coffee, too many donuts, and a couple dozen cigarettes, we were off to the downtown Armed Forces Examining and Entrance Station on Van Buren Street in Chicago.

When I arrived downtown, you can probably guess what happened – you got it, they told me to go home! After I explained the situation, they had to send a runner to pick up my paperwork in Forest Park. By the time he returned, everyone I knew had been processed and were on their way to various posts around the country. I never saw any of them again until long after I was out of the service.

To this day I firmly believe that never in the history of the Selective Service has one person been told to disregard two draft notices, then told twice to go home after he had persisted and showed up for the third notice, and after that had elected to stay and be inducted. As I write these words, I have to admit I must have either had an incredible unknown patriotic streak running head to foot or was as dumb as a post (I'm inclined to believe the latter). I can assure you that my responses would have changed dramatically not very much later.

With a little research, I later found that April 20th is a date with quite a bit of significance:

- *In 1939 Billie Holiday had recorded the first Civil Rights song titled "Strange Fruit."*
- *It was Adolph Hitler's birthday and also the last date he was seen above ground out of the bunker in 1944 before committing suicide on the 30th at the end of the war in Europe.*
- *In 1961 America suffered the embarrassment of the "Bay of Pigs" Cuban invasion.*
- *In 1967 NASA's Surveyor 3 Probe successfully landed on the moon.*
- *Also in 1967, and most significant for me, this was the date the U.S. first bombed the port of Hai Phong in North Vietnam.*
- *In 1968 my future step-daughter was born on April 20th.*

Of course, at the time, I knew nothing of these milestones. I did know the next day, on the 21st, Illinois had suffered the impact of 10 powerful tornados stretching across the top of the state to the south side of Chicago that killed 58, injured more than 1,100, and caused 80 million dollars in damage. Needless to say, 1967 witnessed some very turbulent times both at home and abroad.

After my paperwork from Forest Park was delivered, I started to be processed. There was another physical to endure; but it seemed like the only real requirement was that you were able to stand up and breathe and, if successful, you passed. Although many inductees had doctor's notes, even some with x-rays, very few "dodged the bullet" and almost all went on to be sworn in.

I do remember one lad who tried to fail the color-blindness test. There was a spiral-bound book with large block letters and numbers printed in various mottled pale shades of gray, green, red, orange, and yellow. Page after page, this young man could see nothing. I guess it is very rare for any one person to have trouble with every color variation; so the doctor was pretty skeptical. He turned to the last page which was all gray and black with a bold letter A in the center, but again the draftee said he didn't see anything. The doctor then held up two fingers and asked how many the "crafty dodger" could see, and he replied "two." With that, the doc rubber stamped his examination with a large red "PASSED."

There was more paperwork to fill out and we were given a short orientation on the protocol of the swearing-in procedure. Then we were ushered down a long hallway to a large room with windows on two adjacent walls. The room was painted an unattractive light pea green with dark green trim, but cigarette smoke had long ago dulled every surface including the glass panes in all the windows. Even the empty wood floor was missing most of its original finish. There was no furniture – just a small platform simply adorned with a chrome microphone on an adjustable pole. On the wall behind the platform a brand new American Flag was hung, sagging on a row of hooks. It really was a depressing room, much more so due to the purpose than the appearance.

The inductees were instructed to stand in a straight line in front of one of the three walls and face the podium. The sergeant numbered each wall, put three pieces of paper in his upturned campaign hat, and had one lucky recruit pull a number out. It was the number two. That recruit and I were on wall number one but we didn't know what to expect. The suspense was short lived. We were told for the first time since World War II, the United States needed to draft for the Marine Corps due to recent heavy losses and that today two was the lucky number. If they passed a more intense physical, they would be off to Camp Lejeune in Jacksonville, North Carolina. I always respected the Marines but didn't think I was tough enough to be one. For the first time in all my 22 years, I thought I now knew what it was like to be shot at and missed – but I was very wrong. I watched as the worried number two's left for yet another physical exam. As they exited, their shocked and bewildered faces reminded me of the "Bataan Death March" I'd seen on TV in old World War II documentaries.

Afterward we were all dutifully sworn into the U.S. Army without complaint, and you could have heard a pin drop. Some of the potential Marine Corps draftees rejoined us later, and it took days for their smiles to disappear.

Another Sergeant gave a brief discussion what being in the Army really meant to us. We had no rights and were literally "property" of the Armed Services. For instance, if we hurt ourselves accidentally or otherwise, we could be punished for damaging government property. If we disobeyed any order from an NCO (Non-Commissioned Officer) or from an (Commissioned) Officer, we would be subject to either an Article 15 (Non Judicial) hearing for a minor violation or a full-blown court-martial which usually resulted in jail time or worse. Oh, and we couldn't sue the government or any military individual for damages or injury, regardless of the cause. You have no idea how much I missed that timekeeping job at that particular moment.

We were assigned to Ft. Knox, Kentucky for more intense evaluation and basic training, then escorted over to Union Station, boarded a special chartered train, and given vouchers for dinner. First we were lead to our Spartan 3-level berths (6 to a suite) and assigned a bed. As the train started to roll, we tried to find the dining car but were told it needed repair and consequentially had not been connected to our train. I believe this was the first time I heard the term FUBAR.

Simply said, I was a little dazed and confused myself but too tired and hungry to worry about it. My main concern at the time was that somehow I had been assigned the top bunk which didn't fully accommodate my 6'2" frame. We shot the bull for a while then decided to get some sleep. My bunk was perpendicular to the outside wall and, being the top, was even more cramped due to the curve of the sleeper car roof. Although apprehensive, I soon fell asleep in the good ol' reliable fetal position but hit my head on the ceiling 3 or 4 times every hour. Each time we passed a noisy street crossing with bells ringing loudly and bright flashing lights, I sat up startled. Guess I was a slow study, but I have not traveled by train any distance anytime since.

I realized that being inducted into the U.S. Army certainly wasn't a difficult task, but then again it certainly wasn't very uplifting either. The only thing I was still certain of was that I had just lived my longest day.

2

Basic Training

April to July 1967

It was a gray, damp, cheerless, and chilly morning when the train pulled into Union Station in Louisville, Kentucky around 7:00. Most of us were blurry eyed after our shaky journey and stark accommodations (not to mention hungry and a tad cranky). Billows of cigarette smoke followed as we disembarked the train, each clutching our one bag of personal possessions.

Some nice folks from the local VFW greeted us and offered the obligatory donuts and coffee which were gratefully accepted. The donuts evaporated in a couple of seconds flat. A drill sergeant dressed in heavily starched khakis, topped by a "Smokey the Bear" broad-brimmed campaign (drill sergeant) hat, grouped us in rows two across and quietly lead us to three waiting Greyhound buses.

As each recruit boarded the bus, he paused a moment and looked around, instinctively appreciating civilization as each knew it before being transported to our unknown destiny with an alien reality. After we were boarded and the bus was moving down the road, everyone stared blankly out the windows at the panoramic views of Kentucky's rolling countryside. Looking but not seeing; just like a scene I imagined was from *Voyage of the Damned.*

Our busload of young men ranged in age from seventeen to the early twenties; all reflecting a mixed bag of emotions. Most looked like they belonged in high school and maybe at best were juniors. Some were quite visibly shaken, just like a frightened caged animal. Others laughed and joked, masking any concerns. A few sat with mouths slightly open, comatose as a corpse. Some were angry. Still others simply looked out the window without emotion as the bus traversed the endless hills. I'm not exactly sure what I looked like, but I felt numb, confused, and somewhat doomed. Norman Rockwell would have had a field day.

Just as every person's demeanor was different, so were the reasons each of us sat on the bus. Quite a few had joined the Army on their own for a three- or four-year commitment and were known as RA (Regular Army), and this is the designation which preceded their service numbers. They had joined as patriots, for family tradition, to learn a trade for a job, or to honor someone who had been lost. Several had simply been given a choice in juvenile court – jail or the Army. About 75% of us were draftees which meant we had a US preceding our service numbers. I'm not sure what the US actually stood for but "Unfairly Selected" or "Unfortunate S.O.B.'s" were my guesses. The only definition my research has revealed is the US prefix was used to identify all conscripted enlisted personnel. I contemplated the reason I was sitting in that bus and wondered if I had perhaps made one too many bad choices the day before.

The trip south to Fort Knox only took half an hour but somehow seemed longer. We finally passed the gold depository vaults, and at first it didn't look like a very impressive site to me. Then I remembered Ft. Knox was the armor training facility and that a couple of hundred tanks were waiting at the ready so I concluded the compound was actually pretty well situated; and that was the last time I ever saw the depository building.

The bus rolled to a stop in the reception area after passing countless well-kept, sterile-looking, bright white barracks with charcoal gray roofs. We were met by a cadre of drill sergeants each cloned to look exactly like our sergeant from Louisville. As we stepped down out of the bus, everybody started yelling at us, even our mild-mannered escort had gone from Dr. Jekyll to Mr. Hyde. We were called every name in the book as we were herded into three platoons of four squads each.

There we were, standing equally spaced in very straight rows, dressed in our civilian garb, just like sheep to the slaughter. Someone behind me was quietly humming "You're in the Army Now" and it was so hard not to laugh. Lucky for him there was so much yelling going on only a few of us heard it. One recruit in the next platoon nervously lit a cigarette and was immediately besieged by two Tasmanian Devils. He was ordered to put it out, field strip it, stick the butt into his pocket, get down in front of the formation, and do 20 pushups. He readily complied but couldn't complete the task. When he said as much, one of the drill sergeants kneeled next to him and quietly told him he understood and to take all the time he needed to complete the chore. He quickly stood up, bent over, and yelled in the man's ear "and when you're done, give me another 20!" Apparently, failure was not an option.

Sometime later I figured this was all part of the U.S. Army's basic motivational and training technique. First they mentally break down the new recruits and at the same time build them up physically; and then mold these crazed and confused, semi-physical specimens into whatever best meets the current needs of the Army. Incredibly easy and extremely effective; but then again, so is torture.

A master sergeant addressed us, of course first noting smoking was a privilege only permitted when we were told it was OK to do so. Then he started his well-scripted welcoming speech listing a few do's and don'ts, and then told us to be proud of being members of the world's greatest military force. He noted we would be in the reception area for several days for physicals, immunizations, and issues of clothing and equipment. We would also be tested to see how we could best serve the U.S. Army and our country. He concluded by welcoming us to the Fort Knox Basic Training Facility and knew we would all be good soldiers. Well, only speaking for myself, at that particular moment, I didn't exactly feel all that welcome.

One of the drill sergeants instructed us to pick up our bags and follow him and two of the guys also picked up the totally exhausted pushup victim. We marched to a nearby white-framed supply building and were given bedding and towels. We carried our supplies and personal baggage to a reception area barracks and were assigned a bunk, after which we were quickly shown how to make our beds.

We were taken to the mess hall for our first Army meal served on divided aluminum trays with a well-worn scratched patina. We could take as much as we wanted but had to eat everything we took. The mashed potatoes tasted funny and some guessed it was because they were made from dehydrated spuds. However, the more popular theory was that they were infused with saltpeter, the thought being the Army didn't want any raging adolescent hormones interfering with our training. Regardless, we ate everything and turned in empty trays.

Next came the inevitable haircut. Some of the guys had especially long hair in anticipation of this little festivity. Most of the barbers had a tired little joke asking how you wanted your hair cut and styled, then proceeded to scalp you until maybe 1/8" of stubble survived the encounter. I was talking to a couple of people before the great transformation and afterward couldn't find them again; nobody looked the same any more.

Sporting our new demeaning, hygienic haircuts, we were marched to another supply depot to get our first clothing issue of fatigues, skivvies, shoes, boots and socks, plus a duffle bag so we could carry everything. Fitting the pants took a lot of time as did printing and sewing of our names on the fatigue shirts just above the right-hand pocket. We lugged our new wardrobes back to the barracks and were shown how to fold and store everything in our foot and wall lockers, then we packed up our civilian clothing after first changing into our new very dark army green fatigues. Training manuals were distributed which explained in a proper military manner the finer details of behavior, rank and insignia, dress codes, chain of command, guard duty, and way too many protocols to list here.

Dinner was next on the itinerary, and then we were told we had the rest of the evening to ourselves but not to get used to such privileges. A dress code had been posted and the sergeant suggested we read it carefully, strongly advising that reading our manuals would also be a good idea.

The next morning, all dressed in the proper manner, we were treated to a delightful breakfast at our new favorite restaurant, the mess hall. The menu consisted of gritty oatmeal, watery scrambled eggs, burnt toast, sinewy ham, mystery sausage, pancakes similar to rubber *Frisbees*©, mashed potatoes (available at every meal), and apricots, and I hated canned apricots.

After our little culinary adventure, we were off for an in-depth physical that picked and poked at every conceivable nook and cranny. This was followed by a professional eye exam and dental evaluation. Quite a few of our group had to return to pick up glasses and/or to keep dental appointments. One trainee, Bob Bamfeld, had to have a tooth extracted. After they knocked him out, they discovered a bad case of gingivitis and pulled every tooth in his head. He must have freaked when he woke up. It would take at least eight weeks for his mouth to heal before he could be fitted for dentures. He had to endure basic training surviving on oatmeal, mashed potatoes, creamed vegetables, and milk. I was so glad that I'd already had my wisdom teeth removed.

Immunizations came next and became a ritual repeated frequently during basic training. Most shots were given with a pneumatic injector that looked just like the ray gun Flash Gordon used to defeat Ming the Merciless. We were told not to move or tense up when receiving a dose of whatever. The strapping young man in front of me was the picture of health and worthy of being on the cover of any muscle magazine. However, he flinched when the doctor pulled the trigger of the air gun which neatly cut a deep ¼" long slice in his arm. The cut immediately started to bleed. When our Mr. Healthy saw the blood, his eyes rolled up into his head and he was down for the count. According to my "Certificat De Vaccination" or "Immunization Certificate" card, I had about 18 encounters with that ray gun and remember being cut a couple of times myself, but I refused to pass out.

Psychological, I.Q., personality, and occupational profiling testing followed. Tests, tests, and more tests consumed the balance of the day. I think they wanted to make sure you were smart enough to point your rifle in the correct direction and were malleable enough to become whatever they needed. We were told the next day we would be moved from the reception area to our basic training barracks and be assigned a permanent drill instructor.

Later that evening, after the test results had been reviewed, a list of names was posted for those who had to stay for more detailed testing. My name was on the list. I thought I must have failed one and had to retake it; tests were always my nemesis. When I was in high school and college, all of my counselors said "I didn't really apply myself." When I graduated high school, I believe I was ranked 557th out of 730 people. Although I attended 4 different colleges and universities, after almost 4 years I barely had enough credits to qualify for an Associate's (two-year) Degree; even that I never applied for.

I wasn't dumb. I just enjoyed life and all the extracurricular activities much more than studying. It turned out the Army simply didn't care about my lack of scholastic achievement; they were only interested in my test results. My third day in the army, I and about 40 other recruits were presented with more refined and task-oriented testing. The fourth day, there were only 15 of us. The fifth and final day it was just me and one other. I wasn't sure if I should be flattered or scared. Like I said, testing was not my thing.

An interview was scheduled for early the next morning with the recruitment officer. He offered me the chance to attend various logistic, engineering, computer, and administrative schools that would take 42 to 78 weeks to complete. At first it sounded pretty good to me. What better way to spend my two-year draftee active service obligation? But that daydream was a bust. I was told I would have to change my status to RA and commit to 4 years of active duty. Then I was urged to apply to OCS (Officers Candidate School). I probably made a big mistake but declined all the offers. I had only been in the Army about a week and had seen enough to convince me it was not a career choice I would willingly make. The lieutenant diligently tried to persuade me to reconsider, but I stood firm.

Afterward I was assigned to a basic training barracks and moved into my more permanent home for the duration with another new group of trainees. The barracks were a monument to concrete – the wall blocks, floors, ceilings and stairways were all constructed of this impervious, durable substance. Everything but the floor and stairways was painted white and a more sterile container could not be found. The Army green double bunks, with their wire grid supports and 4" thick mattresses rolled into a spiral, spanned our room which accommodated about four squads (60 trainees). Coffee tins half filled with water served as ash trays, better known as butt cans, hung on each of the 6 posts. The latrine was pretty basic but at least had dividers and doors to afford some privacy.

Our training sergeant introduced himself as drill sergeant Doug Meier and, without further ado, promptly proceeded to educate us on the proper way to make a military bed. Our mentor unrolled the mattress, neatly placed the bottom and top sheets with square corners, fluffed the pillow and smoothed the case, and added the army green blanket – again with the obligatory square corners. He took a quarter from his pocket, thumbed it into the air, and it bounced smartly when it landed on the assembly. He actually smiled (a rare occurrence) and gave us 5 minutes or the time it took for him to smoke a cigarette (whichever was fastest) to duplicate his accomplishment.

We all knew the consequence of failure and did the best we could. Needless to say, half failed the coin test along with me. After the obligatory 20 pushups, we had another go at it; this after our bedding had been flung to the floor. I was lucky and escaped the next round of pushups, but 10 guys had to go through the gauntlet again. Only one failed this time, poor private Joseph Mellon; and two more attempts ended with the same result. The last time he escaped with only being yelled at and called a "dud." Private Mellon sadly was somewhat limited. He was the only one of our class who was later recycled and had to take basic training again, and he should never have been there in the first place. Once again the ever popular phrase "failure is not an option" had been reinforced.

The very next morning at 5:30 sharp, three drill sergeants plus our now smile-less Sergeant Meier, all blowing annoying chrome whistles clenched in their teeth, ran through our barracks yelling "rise and shine" and "wakey, wakey, drop your snakey" at the top of their lungs. It proved to be an effective method of waking the troops, not to mention scaring the "bejesus" out of us. We stood at attention at the foot of our bunks dressed only in our skivvies. A more bewildered motley crew would be hard to find.

One foolish lad was naked and, as you would guess, this was a very big mistake. The ridicule of his manhood and intelligence was merciless and, of course, pushups followed. I wouldn't be surprised if he never slept nude again. Skivvies were the required sleepwear and after all that, nobody ever violated that rule.

After the rude awakening, we had 30 minutes for the 3 Ss (shit, shower, and shave) followed by another exquisite breakfast. After all that, we marched to another supply depot and were issued khaki uniforms, a dress green jacket, dress shirt and tie, hard-brimmed hat and folding dress cap, a back pack, web belt with suspenders and a canteen, helmet liner, field jacket, and poncho. While we still wore the dress green jacket, shirt, tie, and hard-brimmed hat, we all had our pictures taken for the basic training yearbook.

Later we stored our gear and then were introduced to the wonderful recreational world of PT (Physical Training). Jumping jacks, three different kinds of pushups, alternately touching our toes, sit ups, and running in place were the favorites. As we progressed, multiples of combined exercises dominated the routine. This was usually followed by jogging four laps on a quarter mile track which eventually grew into a two-mile challenge.

One memory will always be with me. Training Sergeant James Ridgemore looked to be in his early thirties, was 5'6", and maybe 170 pounds; he was in pretty good shape except for the well-rounded bulge of a beer belly. He would accompany us on our afternoon runs on that oval track spurring us on with infuriating comments. After morning PT, a couple of hours of close-order drill, maybe taking on the obstacle course or (one of my personal favorites) a forced march, and the two-mile run that followed sometimes seemed like 10. One day, Private John Clover was struggling on the track after the day's activities. Sergeant Ridgemore was on him like white on rice yelling in his ear that he was a dud and a disgrace to his uniform. Private Clover stopped and stared straight into the sergeant's eyes and challenged him to a run the next morning at 6:00, and whoever stopped first lost. The Sergeant stopped, smiled, and politely accepted the offer.

Of course our whole barracks was at the track the next morning to see that spunky little sergeant get his just rewards. Private Clover quickly outdistanced the sergeant and even lapped him after the first

4 go arounds; but Sergeant Ridgemore never changed his methodi-
cal pace and after 12 laps passed the failing Private. Our hopeful
hero collapsed after 18 laps. The sergeant stopped after running 20
and wasn't even breathing very hard. Another valuable lesson: Never,
ever judge a book by its cover. The sergeant thanked the private for
the race, shook his hand, and never said another word about it.

Our first bivouac followed shortly thereafter. We had to carry
our M14's and a bandolier with 10 magazines loaded with blanks,
a pup tent, air mattress, blanket, a change of clothes, field jacket,
and a poncho – about 40 pounds of gear. Our forced march started
up a mountain named Misery. As we approached the top, we were
ambushed by an assortment of NCOs with machine guns and M14s
blazing, firing blanks (we hoped); then we were informed we had all
just been killed. Our attackers had a great time laughing at us as we
continued to struggle up the mountain until we reached the summit
(or so we thought). Once at the top, we came to the foot of a steeper
sloped mountain rightfully called Agony; so named because it could
not be seen until reaching the so-called summit of Misery.

After the massacre and our disappointing progress, the drill sergeant increased the pace to a slow trot. Then he started to sing
cadence songs that got everyone's attention. "I know a girl that lives
on a hill, she won't do it but her sister will," and "I don't know but
I've been told, Eskimo pussy is mighty cold". There were a half
dozen or so other little ditties but they have all been lost to the passage of time. To set the pace after each verse he counted up in cadence from one to eight in time with each step. We were all drained
but the songs both improved our mood and hastened the end of our
journey.

On top of Agony, we established a campsite for a night's stay, set
up a perimeter, and fully expected to be attacked again. On top of
that mountain it was very cold that night and, without gloves, my
hands quickly became numb. We were told smoking was not allowed but when I was on guard duty at 3:30 AM, I really didn't care.

Unfortunately my *Zippo*© ran out of fuel when I tried to use it; but being a resourceful youth, I had brought lighter fluid with me. It was so cold I didn't know when the lighter was full and that fluid now dripped from my too-cold hands. When I tried to light my cigarette, my hands exploded into two torches. It took a while to put the fire out. I used to have very hairy hands, but since that moment, never again. I was very lucky everybody else was asleep, or I would have been subject to an Article 15 procedure at the very least. The Army kind of frowned on disobeying direct orders or even the slightest dereliction of guard-duty protocol; and my hands were red for weeks.

The next evening we returned to our barracks and I skipped dinner; I was completely drained and only needed to sleep. About 3:00 A.M. I was rudely awakened by an unknown but extremely rude drill sergeant – how unusual. This time it was different. It was only me, and he said in stern whispered tones that I had a board meeting with the Colonel at 6:00 that morning. When I asked what the hell a board meeting was, I was promptly told to shut up and to be there on time in pressed fatigues and spit-polished boots. All the clothes I had were dirty and my laundry had not been returned. So I spot-cleaned my clothes the best I could, pressed them with a borrowed iron until they were dry, cleaned and spit polished my boots, and dutifully but blurry eyed sat in the Colonel's office at 6:00. Of course nobody showed up until around 7:30. The Colonel didn't arrive until 9:00 and briskly walked right by me like I wasn't there. A little while later I was told to go in.

This was my first experience with the big brass, so I quickly came to attention and snapped my best salute. The colonel said "at ease" and asked me to take a seat. He looked me in the eye and said "Son, I don't understand you;" he wasn't alone. He told me my tests were outstanding and I had to rethink about making the Army my career. Then came a tirade about how the Army needed people like me and how it was a privilege and an honor to be an officer. I knew it was coming when he asked "Why don't you sign up for OCS"? I thanked him for his interest in me but still declined, saying I wasn't interested in a military career. He smiled, thanked me for my time, and I was dismissed. I knew I still had a lot to learn but also knew there was something about a military smile that was starting to scare the crap out of me.

The rest of that day was more of the same – PT, close-order drill, and a forced march. Then we were exposed to something new, enduring the effects of tear gas. We walked into a smoke filled room with our gas masks on to prove their effectiveness, then had to remove the mask and say our name, rank, and service number before exiting. Most of us hit the wall before finding the door and choked our way out of that honey pot. We ended the day with a mile and a half run in the rain.

Surprise, surprise, come 3:00 AM, as Yogi Berra is known to have said, "It was déjà vu all over again." Once again I was unceremoniously invited to a board meeting and had to scramble to prepare for it; the same questions and the same answer. This scenario was repeated two more times before I relented and asked my only question "Should I decide at a later date to drop out of the OCS program, what is the procedure"? The answer was short and simple: Write a letter of resignation. Whether it was true or not, I really didn't know or care and I signed up on the spot. My school choices were combat engineering (one choice had to be combat related), data processing equipment operator, and communication center specialist as my three school preferences. That night I actually slept without bother until morning – what a luxury.

A few days later I was ordered to the Colonel's again, only this time I spoke to a Captain. He said he had reviewed my OCS choices and wanted me to think about another. The new option was EOD (Explosive Ordnance Disposal). His misread my shocked expression as a question and proceeded to define EOD as simply the art of disarming or detonating explosive devices such as bombs, booby traps, mines, unexploded grenades, etc. Playing with firecrackers was one thing, but this was a whole new ballgame. I regained my composure and politely declined to accept the offer. After I was finally dismissed, all I could think of was how much I hated all those Army vocational tests I had taken.

One day while it was raining, our drill sergeant held a class in our barracks about the wonders of the M14 rifle. This seemed pretty stupid to me since I thought the weapon of choice in Vietnam was the M16; however, the M16 was not as accurate (but at least it did look cool). We learned how to break down a M14, the nomenclature for each part, how to reassemble it, and finally the proper cleaning procedure. Unfortunately Private Bamfeld (better known as "toothless Bob") found the exercise a little uninspiring and was sitting on the floor legs folded and his head sagging, sound asleep, and snoring lightly. Sergeant Meier never stopped talking as he picked up the nearest butt can and poured the slimy brown contents on Bob's nodding head. Bob jumped to his feet huffing and puffing and immediately knew he had screwed up. He then proceeded to do 20 pushups without being told to do so. Yet another valuable lesson – pay attention!

We were at the firing range a day later working on our proficiency with the M14 rifle. I was asked to demonstrate the durability of the M60 machine gun. They connected three belts of 100 rounds each to the weapon and I got into position with large yellow earplugs in place. I fired bursts of five-to-ten rounds each nonstop until all the ammo was spent. Unfortunately, I didn't notice that my ear plugs had fallen out. To this day I have severe tinnitus, and ever since have not enjoyed a single moment of blissful silence.

Sometime later we had to qualify for marksmanship with the M14 rifle, the only thing I had actually excelled at and expected to rank as an expert. As each target popped up I knocked it down only missing one at 300 yards. I noticed some awkward pauses in the timing of the pop-up targets and asked the spotter if something was wrong. He said "Well, you haven't shot any of the close targets to your right." Concentrating on the long-distance silhouettes, I had completely missed all the easy shots to my right, and, although I didn't miss another target, I still didn't rank as an expert. I contemplated requesting another opportunity but then thought better of it; as much as I actually enjoyed shooting, being a sniper was another a career choice I didn't want to pursue.

About six weeks into basic training, after first passing a proficiency test, we had earned a one-day pass to Louisville. We dressed in our khakis, survived a thorough inspection, and boarded the bus. Since I was 22, considered an old man, and much more importantly was able to buy "the hard stuff," I suddenly had a lot of newfound friends. I stuck to beer myself but bought a couple of bottles for my soon-to-be-gone buddies. A couple of real friends and I wandered the streets and stopped to have a few beers, took in a burlesque show, and afterward were approached by a prostitute. I don't know if was our Christian upbringing, the mashed potatoes, the Army syphilis film graphically portraying the wages of sin, or "the miles" on that gal – but without exception we all declined the offer.

Three other privates we knew ran up to us to show off their brilliantly colored, brand new tattoos, all exactly the same, brightly glorifying the American flag crowned by a bald eagle. They got a great deal, three for the price of one. They regretted that decision a couple of weeks later. The tattoos all became infected and each knew the resulting scars would ruin the artistry. Without a drill sergeant in sight they had learned yet another valuable lesson: "Caveat emptor." Or as an Oak Park High classmate had once observed, "It's not a deal if it's not a deal."

We were tired and although could have stayed the night, we decided it would be better to catch the last bus back to the base and save some money. The next morning was Sunday and so we were able to sleep until around 8:00. About 10:30, Private Jimmy Dix staggered in, fists clenched and ready for battle. He proudly stood there, his 5'4" frame and maybe 130 pounds swaying slowly in not-so-tight circles. He loudly declared in slurred speech, prompted by the infamous courage in a bottle, that he was ready to fight the biggest man there. I guess my 6'2" was good enough for him; so he bent over and fearlessly charged me swinging both arms like a whirligig. I put my hand on his head to keep those flaying arms at bay and started to laugh. He didn't see the humor and put his head down like a bull. With newfound strength he forced me to walk backwards the full length of the barracks, my hand still on his head. My back found the wall and my head bounced off the cement blocks as I came to an abrupt stop. When I released my grip, he stepped back, smiled, and punched me in the stomach. Now I was furious and seeing red, I used every ounce of my 160 pounds and gave him a quick jab to the head which knocked him off his feet. He stood up, tears streaming, holding his left eye and demanded to know why I hit him. I told him I didn't just hit him, I hit him back. With that, he returned to his bunk and soon passed out.

That evening he came up to me and apologized but still didn't understand why he had a black eye. When I told him what had happened, as did the others, nothing more was said and that was that. When we graduated two weeks later, he was still sporting the shiner. I never hit another soldier, but the thought did occur to me (several times actually).

The rest of my basic training experiences are all kind of a blur, but I do remember being exposed to a multitude of military disciplines and being educated in the finer arts of:

Dismounted drill (never did see any horses)
Manual of arms
Close-order drill
Guard duty
KP (yes, I know how to clean a grease trap with a teaspoon)
Hand-to-hand combat

First aid
Camouflage
Tactical training
Hand grenades
Marksmanship

Other than those way-too-influential reception area tests, I completed basic training without excelling in anything; sort of status quo concerning all my educational endeavors. My basic training classmates were scattered to various forts across the country to their AIT (Advanced Individual Training) assignments and, sadly, most were off to infantry schools. A couple of us were assigned to Fort Leonard Wood, Missouri for training as combat engineers, which is sort of like an infantryman seated on a bulldozer; and naturally, it had been one of my OCS choices.

Back in the civilized world, the issue of the draft was being challenged more and more every day. About the same time I was drafted, a young boxer was starting to make a lot of news due to his strong objections to the draft. Although named Cassius Clay at his birth on January 14, 1942, he had changed his name in 1964 to Cassius X, and soon after became known as Muhammad Ali. His name change remained a point of contention for many years and, depending on the reporter, the media waffled and sometimes called him Cassius or and other times used Muhammad. A prizefighter of unequaled ability, his arrogance and undeniable superiority coupled with his ever present boasted verbal distain for each combatant soon divided his followers into two groups who either loved or hated him; and he pretty much stayed the course throughout his boxing career. At first he became a member of the Nation of Islam and later in life moved on to Sunni Islam; because of his religious beliefs he was an ardent opponent of the war in Vietnam and hated the very concept.

On April 28, 1967, he refused induction into the army and as a result was stripped of his heavyweight title. Later on June 27th he was sentenced to five years in prison and fined $10,000. He appealed his conviction for years and was never imprisoned. While still continuing his appeals, he was finally allowed to return to the ring again for the first time on October 26, 1970, and he won that fight in three rounds. His conviction was decisively overturned by the Supreme Court in June of 1971. Although he was never in the Army, later it was my opinion he was an excellent example of RHIP (Rank Has Its Privilege). He remained a passionate anti-war protestor and a little later became a respected benefactor and mentor to those in need. In 2005 he was awarded the Presidential Medal of Freedom.

At the time I really didn't know anything at all about Mr. Ali. All I knew for sure was I had to board that bus to Missouri (or Misery as I later came to know it). I looked around one more time and sincerely hoped never to see the inside of a barracks at Fort Knox ever again. So far, that's worked out just fine.

3

AIT
Advanced Individual Training

FORT LEONARD WOOD, MO.
LEADERSHIP PREPARATION COURSE

July to August 1967

The bus drove out of Fort Knox and headed north to Louisville, then out of Kentucky and west through the lower quadrant of Illinois. We connected with Route 66 in St. Louis, still moving west on a direct path to Fort Leonard Wood. Once in Missouri there were advertising signs everywhere, most painted on the roofs and sides of aging barns. The Mule Trading Post, Meramec Caverns, Burma Shave, Daniel Boone's Home, and Onyx Caverns advertisements were the most abundant.

I had seen all those signs before. Every year my dad took our family on the very same route to visit his parents in Kansas. He had grown up just outside the small town of Columbus, Kansas, the county seat for Cherokee County. When World War II started, he and three of his cousins went to Chicago looking for jobs but then decided to join the Navy and hoped to stay together. Three of them looked forward to joining the Navy; although one seriously wanted to enlist in the Army, he relented. They all applied to the Navy, but only one passed the physical – and of course it was the Army man. So the other three (which included my dad) had no other choice except to join the Army; I don't believe any of them stayed together. You can always trust the military to shake things up a bit.

The towns rolled by until we came to the small town of Waynesville, just outside the main gates of Fort Leonard Wood. The town had more jewelry stores and pawn shops than I had ever seen in one place. Guess a lot of people felt the urge to buy engagement rings, perhaps so they would have something to come home to.

The 10-hour bus ride to the Fort had been pretty much uneventful and our only major accomplishment had been not to lose anyone at the rest stops. We pulled through the gates and went directly to one of the AIT companies. These barracks were much different – no more sterile cement bastions. These two-story structures had wood siding painted a beige-cream color, framed with brown trim. Every building was topped with a green shingled roof and each and every one of them had seen much better days.

The Fort had been activated in 1940 and trained 300,000 people for World War II until it was closed in 1946. It lay dormant until 1950 when it was re-activated shortly after our troops started fighting in Korea. In 1956 it became a permanent installation and its primary function was training combat engineers.

We disembarked the bus and, after a short welcoming speech, were assigned bunks in the second barracks. I was about half-way through unpacking and storing my gear when I was approached by a sergeant who told me to pack everything up again. Now what? When I inquired why he told me I had been selected for training at LPC (Leadership Preparation Course). The squad leader, an acting corporal, said to brace myself and wished me luck. I numbly packed the gear and was quickly transported with several others to another training barracks. I wasn't exactly elated and was more than a bit skeptical; but when we arrived, at least the building looked new and was absolutely immaculate inside.

After another welcoming speech by First Lieutenant Abernathy, we soon found out we were going to be schooled as platoon and squad leaders during a two-week condensed combat engineering training session. It was supposed to be just like 2 weeks of OCS. I could hardly wait for the fun to begin. There were about 80 trainees standing there and our super sharp Drill Sergeant Mason took 40 of us to the second floor and assigned bunks. We were told to store our gear, make the bunks, and wait for his return.

We dutifully unpacked and filled the wall and foot lockers. He returned with a thin Madonna-like smile, and by now I really hated military smiles. I had the first top bunk on the left so he naturally went for it first. Although my bunk passed the coin toss, nothing else I had done was acceptable. The clothes I'd hung in my wall locker were unceremoniously dumped on my bunk and the floor was soon strewn with the contents of my foot locker.

Apparently I had made grievous errors in proper wall and foot locker usage. He proceeded to hang the shirts and fatigue tops evenly spaced with sleeves lined up like good little soldiers, all in a row. My dress uniform suffered the same strict regimen, and then the footwear was strategically aligned underneath on the bottom deck. The footlocker had everything neatly folded and placed in the lower compartment all done very quickly. However, the top tray took a lot of time. First a towel was placed in the bottom and when folded looked like it had been glued in place. Then the contents of my Dopp kit were placed in equally spaced straight rows in a very specific sequence. It looked like a picture when he was done. Even the dirty clothes bag had to hang neatly at the end of the top bunk end frame exactly 8" from the left side suspended 12" from a specific type of knot.

He had everyone on our floor walk by and review his handiwork then told us the following morning there would be a very thorough inspection. After everyone had seen the prototype standard, he again emptied my wall and foot locker, explaining he didn't want me to have an unfair advantage. We were reminded that the shoes and boots were to shine like patent leather and that the brass belt buckles must be polished brighter than new. He also explained the demerit system only allowed for a total of 24 demerits, one for each infraction. After 24, you were kicked out of the program. A couple of guys thought that maybe that wasn't such a bad idea. I just knew I was going to love it there.

Sergeant Mason then advised us on the specifics of our house-keeping and cleaning duties. All floors were to be mopped clean and waxed daily, every horizontal surface was to be damp dusted, and the windows were to sparkle. The latrine had to be spotless, literally. The sinks and toilets needed to shine, as did the plumbing pipes, and all of the hardware had to be shined with Brasso©, including the shower heads and floor drains. The shower stall walls had to be pristine. I was shocked when I saw there were no dividers separating the toilets and thought how barbaric and crude, not to mention humbling and embarrassing. All part of the master plan.

In order to get everything done, we all got up at 4:30 AM, finished the three S's by 5:15, then proceeded to clean and polish everything like whirling dervishes. Just in case, we saved one toilet and sink to do last to allow for any emergencies. During this time we also had to make sure our individual locker and footwear presentations were up to par. Most of us acquired a second set of toiletries so that we could leave one unscathed for display purposes only.

At 7:00 AM sharp we had our first inspection and knew it didn't bode well that the sergeant was wearing white gloves. We were dumbfounded when he found a smudge of dust on the top framing of one doorway and another on the trim over a window – 2 demerits for everyone. Amazingly, everything else passed inspection in spite of all the nasty remarks; or maybe he was just being easy on us that first day.

That morning's training consisted of erecting two sections of a panel bridge. The components were pre-welded metal frames, beams, and decking that assembled with hardened nuts and bolts; sort of like a giant *Erector Set©*. It was all straight forward and easy to comprehend and, although the metal assemblies were very heavy, the work went quickly. In the afternoon we were introduced to the art of assembling a timber bridge. Wood beams and planks had been cut to size and pre-drilled but nothing else had been prefabricated. This was a lot more like work but we successfully completed one section. Not one gap had been spanned, but we had grasped the fundamentals. Still, a written test followed to make sure we knew the correct procedures and component nomenclature. We had all survived that first day.

That evening we decided to get a jump on the morning housekeeping. We polished all the metal in the latrine and cleaned half of the sinks, toilets, and showers. The following morning's inspection revealed some of the pipe fittings had a little residue from the Brasso© and a film had dulled the shine – 2 more demerits for everyone.

After we left for training, two sergeants scoured our barracks and I was scored 4 more demerits when they found four cotton balls in one of the pockets of my fatigue pants – not easy to find since the pants were in my dirty clothes bag. I had only been in LPC for two days and now had a total of 8 demerits; it looked like I wouldn't last the week let alone two, and could probably "kiss OCS goodbye" as well.

In the days that followed, we were consequently exposed to the proper use of pneumatic tools, road and runway construction using PAP (Pierced Armor Plate) matting, building bunkers, landmine arming and placement, and building hazard barriers consisting of barbed wire strands and concertina razor wire coils. We were also schooled in the proficiencies of leadership on how to teach, motivate, and properly control our charges. We were tested on everything and things looked to be moving along nicely – even the demerits had slowed to a trickle.

Unfortunately, I got into the bad habit of squatting on my boot heels during the outdoor hands-on training sessions. This resulted in black shoe polish stains on the seat of my fatigue pants which added more demerits to my tally. I was christened with the demeaning nickname of "gook" (a slur word for the Vietnamese peasants who often sat in the same manner). Even though I stopped the squatting, the name stuck, and I earned even more demerits because the shoe polish stains simply refused to come out in the wash.

Near the end of LPC, I was told someone had stopped by to see me. I changed into my khakis and went up to the visitor center and saw my parents, brothers, and sister. They were returning from their annual vacation to Kansas and decided to stop by and see me. I was given a 6-hour pass and we went to a nice little diner in Waynesville. We had a great visit, they told me how good the fishing had been and about everyone they had seen, and I told them some of my adventures to date. They seemed very concerned for me and I told them not to worry.

It was all very surreal to me. One minute I was enduring the trials and tribulations of leadership training and 20 minutes later I'm having a family chat. When we returned from lunch, we said our goodbyes and I assured them I would be coming home for a week after graduating AIT. Seeing them all was great, but it threw me off my game for a couple of days.

Despite all odds, I eventually graduated from the leadership course on July 19th with only 23 demerits. Amazing… one more and I would have been kicked out. A number of my fellow trainees had also just scraped by – how unusual – as a matter of fact, no one had failed the course.

AIT
ADVANCED INDIVIDUAL TRAINING
COMPANY C, THIRD BATTALION, SECOND BRIGADE

August to October 1967

I was transferred to a permanent AIT company, my new home away from home, with the rank of acting corporal. I actually thought the rank was underserved, but I was really more concerned about the responsibilities of overseeing a squad. It was a little disconcerting to be telling others what to do when maybe I wasn't exactly so sure myself. I was assigned a large squad of 17 men who had been sent there from various Basic Training schools. Well, actually only 16 had showed up. One had already gone AWOL (Absent Without Leave) and had never arrived to join in the fun.

Our barracks like all the others had been in use intermittently since World War II and was now really showing its age. Other than paint, these buildings had not benefited from proper maintenance and, although condemned several times, were still deemed serviceable. Not surprisingly one of my squad members fell through the floor the first night, resulting in a 3" gash in his leg. Platoon Sergeant Spitzer had been on the first floor and ran up the stairs, demanding to know what all the 'corrosion' was about. I guessed he meant "commotion" and I pointed to the private's leg. After we bound the wound with gauze, the sergeant helped the private down the stairs and summoned the medics. I had wondered why there were a dozen plywood patches scattered around our floor, and poor Private Bachner and his 16 stitches had found the answer. The remedy was another patch nicely matching all the other trip hazards.

After all the excitement, we were still storing our gear when a corporal asked to see Private Reynolds; his destiny had changed and he was off to LPC. I wished him good luck, gave him a few tips, and he was gone in a couple of minutes, poor bastard. The next morning's roll call revealed once again I was short yet another squad member, another AWOL. Sergeant Spitzer called me out of formation, pulled me aside, and with his face only six inches from mine screamed "Two AWOLs in less than 24 hours, two! I've never seen that before, so what the hell did you do to cause this disruption (desertion?). I told him the first never showed up to begin with and the other I hadn't even talked to. He didn't care and sternly warned me to "straighten up and fly straight." I had as hard a time grasping his logic as I did understanding his slaughter of the English language.

This little interruption was followed by a class introducing the trainees to some of the wonders of Combat Engineering. Close-order drill, a little marching, and P.T. completed the first day. That evening I called a squad meeting and told my men that, although I was new to the Army myself, I would do everything in my power to help them out and if they had any pressing concerns, they could confidentially talk to me at any time. A short while later, one of the youngest in my squad told me his father was dying and he had to go home; he was the heir apparent and was needed to help sort things out. I discussed this with our CO (Commanding Officer), First Lieutenant Jameson, and got him a 4-day hardship pass.

The next morning, two more of my squad approached me for a little chat. They heatedly explained in no uncertain terms how much they hated the Army and wanted out. Their families had pressured them to uphold the family traditions and each had signed up for three years. I told them I honestly didn't think there was much chance of them getting out of their commitment but would check it out and get back to them. When I explained the situation, the company commander's face glared at me, slowly glowing more and more red. "Those two duds have been a pain in the ass ever since they joined the Army and I will do absolutely nothing to help those two misfits!" He explained they were both the sons of Generals and as such had demanded unearned respect and privilege. Each had a handful of Article 15 judgments for disobeying orders, dereliction of duty, and for being disrespectful to an officer; they were lucky not to have already faced a court-martial. He added, "If those two fools want out, just tell them to keep acting like assholes and they'll get out, right after serving 3 or 4 years in Leavenworth."

I usually hated being the bearer of bad news, but not so much this time. I didn't sugarcoat anything and simply told the two prima donnas the consequences of their actions. I suggested the best course of action was to do as they were told, graduate from AIT, and pressure their families to get a decent assignment. Their reaction was short and to the point. They yelled "This is bullshit" in unison and stomped off. A few days later, both earned another Article 15 for dropping out of a forced march in the rain and proceeding to tell the sergeant that had urged them on to "F" himself. Predictably, shortly thereafter, two more of my squad went AWOL.

Early that evening I was called into to see the CO. Before I could come to attention and salute, he was all over me and pushing four fingers at my face. He was yelling "Four, four, four" and apparently was too upset to think of anything else to say. I was dumbfounded. He knew exactly what had happened, so why the shocked, angry act? What he knew didn't seem to matter. All he was concerned about was all the deserters in our company were from the same squad – mine. Apparently he had already suffered similar abuse and now it was my turn. This went on for a full half an hour and only ended when he was too exhausted and hoarse to continue. His parting threat to me was "and this had better never, ever happen again!" As I walked back to my barracks, I could hear that draftee from the reception depot in Fort Knox humming "You're In The Army Now" and couldn't help but smile.

I had never been a particularly enthusiastic recruit and my only pleasant thought after all that static was I only had to endure 21 more months of active duty. Then company First Sergeant Mueller also called me in, and I thought "Oh great, here we go again." He too was really pissed off, but not at me. His office was next to the Company Commander's, and he had heard the relentless tirade. He asked to me meet him again at 8:30 that evening to discuss this further.

I didn't exactly understand what was going on, but hesitantly returned to the Sergeant's office right on time. He said we couldn't talk there but he knew of a place and asked I follow him. He had parked his car between two empty buildings about a block away. At first it was so dark I could barely see. Then was very surprised to find it was a pristine 1957 Chevy Bel Air. I think he smiled a little when he asked me to get into the trunk (yet another military smile). Although more than a little uncertain and not smiling myself, I climbed in and he shut the lid. He drove off the base and after maybe 20 minutes, he opened the trunk somewhere in the country on an empty dirt road. I got out and sat in the front seat wondering if I was being set up. I didn't want to be the 5th AWOL or MIA.

He drove another ten minutes to a small crossroad's town that had one lonely bar. It was Tuesday and, except for the bartender, the place was empty. The Sarge ordered two rum and Cokes and the barkeep nodded when he added to put it on his tab. If this was a setup, then at least I was going out sort of in style.

In no uncertain terms, he called our CO a pussy and son of a bitch; I was pretty sure I had found a new friend. It turned out he had been a "full-bird" Colonel in World War II and Korea and afterward had been subject to R.I.F. (Reduction In Force). There were simply too many officers. Over time, he had been reduced in rank to a Captain then once again to a Master Sergeant. He was just treading water because in a year or so he would retire with a Colonel's pay. I wasn't sure who disliked the military more, but knew I was already a contender.

We each had half a dozen drinks before we left. He told me to hang in there. I said I would do the best I could during my short military career. He had read my 201 file and knew a lot more of what the Army thought of me than I did. He advised I stay in the OCS program until I was assigned a start date and, if I resigned at that point, I would probably have much less than a year to go. The trip back was a reversal of the original journey, and I returned to the barracks more than a little tipsy around 11:00. To date, that had been my best day in the Army. The Sarge and I repeated that excursion a number of times and he eventually added a couple of other recruits. After graduating AIT, whenever things got a little tough, I always remembered the kindness and generosity of the Sarge.

As acting NCOs with cut (printed) orders, we had heard a rumor that we could go to the NCO club. Being adventurous youths, a couple of us decided to test the waters, and with orders in hand marched into the club like we owned the place. After reading our orders, the bartender brought the drinks to our table. The place was empty when we arrived but was quickly filling up. Everyone saw our temporary stripes sewn on black velvet sleeves that were pinned to our dress khaki sleeves and this really got the place talking. Angry stares and comments about our lack of time in grade prompted the bartender to say he had made a mistake and we had to leave. We were smart enough to know some of our rights but knew enough that it was time to go. We made a hasty retreat and, although we had proved the point, we never did that again.

Half of our company consisted of a National Guard contingent from Atlanta, Georgia, proud of their heritage and some still fighting the Civil War. They were a cocky bunch and never missed an opportunity to let you know they were all going home after this little picnic. The National Guard service number prefix was NG, but we soon re-defined that to mean Nothing Good. Still, someone had connections and they were often excluded from the finer things in life like KP and guard duty.

It was just too much for me when the NG troops were selected for a special introduction on the proper use of the new M16 rifle while my men learned how to assemble a floating bridge. My entire squad was probably headed for Vietnam where I thought the M16 was used pretty much exclusively. The M14 was used for training purposes only because of the scarcity of M16's available in the States. So my men had the M14 while these righteous bastards got trained on the M16. This wasn't a Boy Scout Jamboree, this was life and death, and I was livid. I marched in and complained to our CO about the injustice and insanity of training stay-at-home troops in preference to those headed overseas. He looked up at me, smiled, and all he said was "Don't worry about it. Your boys will get trained overseas." I couldn't help but think that was the dumbest thing I'd ever heard him say or anyone else say, and that he was a sorry excuse of a training-unit Commanding Officer.

Because I was an acting NCO, part of my duties were to act as CQ (Charge of Quarters) for a 4-hour shift between the hours of 7:00 PM and 7:00 AM several times a week. It was no big deal except for the lack of sleep and was actually pretty boring since usually nothing happened. After the M14 vs. M16 meeting, I had struggled a couple of days with the stupidity of the Army and felt like I had been caught up in some long-running, obnoxious nightmare. One night while on CQ, I typed a short resignation from the OCS program, signed and sealed it in an envelope, then stuffed it in my pocket and contemplated its delivery date.

The next couple of weeks flew by and were pretty easy going, except for one little problem. One of my men had received the infamous "Dear John" letter and was very upset. His girlfriend was pregnant with his child but had decided to marry another man so that the child would have a father. Before I had a chance to speak to the CO, the trooper took matters into his own hands and was off and running. Oh my God, I was doomed – another AWOL.

The anger the CO displayed this time was much more restrained, perhaps because his speech was slightly slurred and tainted with a hint of whiskey. He calmly stated I was going to lose my stripes and be subject to an Article 15 or a court-martial, whichever he could make stick. I was dismissed without another word. That never happened and the only reason I came up with is that the Sarge had pulled a few strings and intervened on my behalf. I kept my stripes and the matter never resurfaced; thankfully, I had finally bagged my limit of AWOLs.

I was still scheduled for CQ and a couple of evenings later found a roster that listed all the company trainee names. Preceding each name was a meaningful colored dot. Red meant you were headed to Vietnam, Blue was for Germany, and Green indicated a stateside assignment. At least 80% had red dots and included every man in my squad except me; it was really depressing and I was disgusted. The day before, I received a notice my OCS start date had been delayed until April and I knew it would probably be delayed again. It was painful to think that after I completed 3 months of OCS hell, I would have to sign up for another two years. All that pushed me over the edge and I took my letter of resignation out of my pocket and left it on the First Lieutenant's desk. The next day the CO called me in and said I was making a big mistake; but I was determined and told him that I had made up my mind. I was surprised by how reluctant he was to accept my resignation.

A couple of days later while on CQ, I looked at the company roster again. Next to my name the blue dot had been crossed out and replaced with a red dot. Even though I'm sure everyone had been right and my resignation was undoubtedly a huge mistake, but that still is a decision I never regretted.

After all that, there were no more "soap opera" traumas and I finally graduated from AIT. Following a brief graduation ceremony, I said goodbye to my men and wished them all well. I looked for the Sarge but never caught up with him. I was given a 10-day pass and travel vouchers and told to report to Fort Lewis, Washington on October 5th. That afternoon, I hopped a bus to St. Louis to catch a plane to Chicago. I was no longer the same person and, whether better or worse for the experience, I had lived a lot of life in the past 5 months.

As a side note, I recently checked on the internet and found that none of the names of those twelve surviving members of my squad had found its way to the Viet Nam Memorial wall in Washington D.C., and I was so relieved. All I can say is hallelujah!

4

Welcome Home & Goodbye World

October 1967

The bus ride to St. Louis took just over 4 hours after we made a couple of stops, and I finally arrived at Lambert Field around noon. The next flight to Chicago was at 2:30; so having a couple of hours to kill, I grabbed a bite to eat and called home to let them know when my flight arrived. The time flew by and as the DC7 pulled away from the gate, I was happy to be on the last leg of my journey, to home, my reality, and sanctuary.

I had a window seat and watched as the piston engines pushed the propellers at blurring speed, lifting us effortlessly off the runway in no time. It was my first flight ever, and it was a cloudless, sunny day. I enjoyed the view of the farmland below as it rolled by as if on a huge conveyor belt. It was a relatively smooth flight, but for me it gradually became extremely painful. After maybe 20 minutes both ears hurt so much I thought they were bleeding. I asked the stewardess what to do and she suggested holding my nose and blowing to equalize the pressure. Repeated tries were to no avail so I suffered the duration of the trip. The only cause I could think of was that Basic Training M60 machine gun demonstration which was now complicated with a lack of proper air pressure in the plane's cabin. It took three days for the pain to subside to a tolerable level and I could sleep the night through.

As I remember, my whole family met me at the gate and never stopped smiling. I did complain about my ears but, other than that, said everything was fine. As we walked out of the airport I got a few disgusted looks from the long-haired, hippy types. I really didn't care about whatever was bothering them and was just so glad to be home again, for a while anyway. It was rush hour and the ride home seemed to take forever.

I literally ran upstairs when we finally arrived home and changed into my civvies, then stowed my Army gear on the little porch off my bedroom. That 6' X 9' porch and the stairs leading down to the back-yard held very fond memories for me. It seemed like only yesterday I had used them as my clandestine threshold to late-night adventures. I foolishly thought that portal was my secret, that is until my re-sourceful and somewhat sarcastic siblings decided to booby trap the porch door with a complete set of 8 "*Melody Bells©*," which had been inspired by the children's TV show "Ding Dong School©." Each of the different colored plastic shrouded metal bells had a distinctive pitch and there wasn't one I didn't find irritating. When I came home and opened the porch door one night at 2:30 AM, the silence was shattered when the bells hit the floor resounding in an unharmoni-ous ding-a-ling that woke the dead and almost gave me "the big one." Our house erupted in laughter that lasted a full five minutes, and that definitely was not cool. The next day nobody said anything, but laughter followed me everywhere. To this day it one of my family's favorite stories.

Our house was huge even though the lot was only 22 feet wide. It may have started as a four square bungalow; but with the addi-tion of two large rooms in the back, two bay windows (one on the front and one on the side), and three more porches attached to the rear of the house, it grew into a friendly monster. The main floor had three porches, a large foyer, small kitchen, nice-sized living and dining rooms, two bonus rooms, and a full bath on the first floor.

Upstairs we had four bedrooms, another full bath, and my favorite little porch. It's still standing and I hope it does so forever.

It was great being home. Each day was a holiday and every meal was a gourmet treat. I was a little surprised how much I enjoyed spending time with the family and realized I had missed them all. Still, although I was smiling, I felt a little out of sorts and sometimes really needed to be alone.

I also visited with relatives, friends, neighbors, and went out several times with a couple of buddies from high school. My friend Jerry was drafted a short time later and ended up at the DMZ in South Korea, and I think he saw as much or more action as I did. Things were very active at the North and South Korean border but it rarely made the news. Our country was hypnotized and diligently watched the nightly news to witness the progress in Vietnam like it was a scripted movie serial.

My brother Roy was the youngest and seemed like the most likely to succeed. He had an inquisitive nature, was mechanically inclined and goal oriented, and always was my biggest fan. Roy's tenacity would be rewarded with a master's degree from Northwestern and he became a senior manager for a large airline company.

My sister June was the third child and about 6 years my junior. She always was and still is the impetus that holds us all together and naturally is the family matriarch and historian. She became a grade school teacher and works extensively with special needs students.

My younger brother Keith was born 3 years after me, and I've been told I never talked very much until he was born. Sibling rivalry best describes our early years. We both felt the family bond but seldom agreed on anything. He married very early, shortly after I arrived overseas. He was always a hard worker and became shop foreman for a medium-sized foundry.

My mother, like most moms, was a saint. She had been an only child and I know her upbringing was peppered with too much stress.

She spent a lot of her youth with her uncle and his house became our home. She was a stay-at-home mom, and did her best to rein us all in, and must of done a good job because we all became contributing members of society. Still, we were quite a handful roaming the neighborhood and could often be found on someone else's garage roof, climbing an especially challenging tree, digging holes, experimenting with the wonders of fire, or hiding and exploring wherever an open door beckoned.

My Dad was a reluctant semi-absentee father. He worked as the freezer manager at a large dairy distribution center. His shift started at 2:30 AM, he rarely got home much before 1:00 PM, and was usually asleep when we got home from school. He got up around 10:00 so he could spend some time with mom. The freezers he worked in were kept at -25° or more, and later this prompted his early retirement; after which he enjoyed another 25 years with our mother. They made sure we each got a good education and, although never rich, no one in our family ever felt disadvantaged. We had all the accoutrements of the day including a black & white TV, Hi-Fi stereo, 2 refrigerators, a washing machine, and enough toys, bikes, and sleds for a family twice our size. Dad was a hard worker and a great provider.

Mom and dad were obviously very worried about Vietnam. I tried my best to still their concerns but was not very successful. The days flew by and all too soon I was saying my goodbyes and couldn't help but see the pain in their eyes. Still, it was time to pack up and let the adventure begin.

OFF TO THE NAM

The flight to Ft. Lewis, Washington departed O'Hare Airport at 10:30 AM and, after stopping in Denver and Los Angeles, the plane finally rolled to a stop at the Seattle–Tacoma International Airport almost 10 hours later. A military shuttle dropped me off at the Fort Lewis reception area around 7:30 that evening. I was assigned a barracks and told I might be there for a while. It seems that due to the increases in troop strength in Vietnam, the in-bound transferees were coming at a faster pace than the planes could accommodate. To fill the time we had to put up with PT and Close Order Drill on a daily basis, not to mention the occasional joys of KP.

The United States Army Personnel Center at Ft. Lewis had been established in March of 1966. The purpose was to relieve the stress put on the Oakland, California Center due to our increased presence in Vietnam. Even with two facilities, the Army was having a lot of trouble handling the logistics of such enormous numbers. When I arrived, Ft. Lewis was handling the movement of up to 50,000 military personnel per month to and from that "Pearl of the Orient." When the Washington State Personnel Center closed six years later, it had processed a total of more than two million embarking and returning troops.

After spending a glorious week sampling the amenities of Ft. Lewis, I was finally assigned a flight and told to gear up. We boarded a Flying Tigers Airline jet that seemed gigantic, then were crammed into too-close-together 4-across seats – that's 4 located on either side of the aisle. The late afternoon takeoff was very smooth and the only thing I was happy about was my ears weren't hurting too much. We landed in Anchorage, Alaska and spent an hour and a half on the ground due to "routine maintenance," still in our seats. We took off for Hawaii and way too many hours later eventually actually landed in Tokyo, Japan. Guess the pilots felt like setting a record and skipped the Aloha State. We were at last allowed to get off the plane and stretch our legs. I could barely walk. Thanks to some more routine maintenance we ended up spending six hours there before leaving. The next flight was to Guam, and after a short stop, we were off to Vietnam.

The last fight was very stressful. The uncertainty of what awaited each of us dominated our thoughts, and most of us were oblivious to the passage of time. I couldn't tell you if it was a two- or five-hour flight but knew my anticipation and concerns were legion, and they grew larger by the minute.

IN COUNTRY

We landed at the Cam Ranh Bay Air Force Base the morning of October 12, 1967. The place was gigantic and vibrating with Jeeps, deuce and a half (2-1/2 ton) trucks, airplanes and helicopters of every description, and troops from many countries. Vietnamese women were wearing the traditional "Ao Dai" white silk pant suit like dresses topped with the conical wide brimmed "Non La" straw hats. A large assortment of U.S. soldiers, marines, sailors, and pilots were included, all dancing the "Dance Fandango," and everyone appeared to be swaying in the heat along with everything else. It may have been organized chaos, but was still chaos all the same.

I stood on the threshold of Indochina and then slowly descended the pick-up truck stairway. Everything I saw and sensed was surreal. It was like entering a totally new dimension where the normal laws of reality and civilization no longer applied. We were unceremoniously herded to the reception area; once again no coffee or donuts, just glasses of water reminiscent of a swimming pool.

We were given a quick list of the rules of the road concerning Vietnamese etiquette. A stern warning was emphasized concerning ducking for cover and worrying about the consequences later. Whether it was the popping sound of a rifle being fired, the thumping of a mortar impact, or the whooshing of a rocket, hitting the deck as quickly as possible right where you stood was the key to survival. Don't try running to a bunker or any other structure, every step you take could be your last. You could be 20 feet from a mortar explosion and most likely survive if you were hugging the ground; standing or running 40 feet away would most definitely ruin or end your day.

After the mandatory lectures, we lugged our duffle bags to the supply building and traded our stateside fatigues and boots for the more appropriate jungle wear which included a sorry excuse for a baseball cap. I never understood why I had to bring all that stuff from Ft. Leonard Wood across the U.S. to Chicago and then half way around the world only to have it confiscated. But then, as usual, I had a lot of trouble understanding the army SOP (standard operating procedure). They confiscated all our greenback paper money and any coins we had in our pockets and exchanged them for military scrip; it looked like *Monopoly©* money to me, and I'd never seen paper money for five, ten, twenty-five, and fifty cents before. Next, our destination orders were distributed and I was unceremoniously assigned to the 588th Engineer Battalion at Tay Ninh. We had to report in the morning for a flight to our units and were given the rest of the day off.

The next morning I boarded a Lockheed C130 Hercules cargo plane through the rear drop-down ramp and chose a seat on the fold-down bench on the port side. I was joined by about 40 others. Some were inbound like myself and others were either returning from R&R or being transported to another unit. To complete the manifest, eight pallet loads of equipment were strapped to the center tie downs so the cargo bay was full. The plane rose easily but noisily into the sky and the shaky ride rivaled an E-ticket on a Riverview (Amusement Park) roller coaster. Maybe half an hour later we landed. A staff sergeant yelled out the name of the stop "Bien Hoa" (sounds like 'ben-wah). A couple of troopers deplaned and we lost three of the pallet. Since it didn't sound like the town on my orders (and it could be I wasn't paying attention), I remained seated.

The next stop followed about 20 minutes later when we landed at Tan Son Nhut Airbase which was just outside Saigon. Once again I didn't recognize the name of the airbase; so this time I asked a sergeant when I would be getting off. He looked at my orders and laughed. I should have gotten off at the first stop. He told me to get off now unless I wanted to visit the DMZ (demilitarized zone) separating North from South Vietnam because that was the next stop. Only later did I realize how very lucky I was. In short order I was on the ground discussing my plight with the duty sergeant and was told to go to the hanger office for new travel orders.

I had only missed my exit by one stop; but, instead of sending me back, they simply cut new orders – now that's army efficiency at its finest. It seems my new destiny was the 1ˢᵗ Engineer Battalion attached to the 1ˢᵗ Infantry Division, famously known as the Big Red One. I boarded a deuce-and-half with fold-down benches lining each side. I was given a helmet and flak jacket to wear and then a sergeant jumped on board and sat on the tailgate. He told us our destination was Di An (sounds like "Zee-On"); although only 6 miles by air, the road was 19 miles long and trip would take about an hour. Then, as if an afterthought, he grinned and warned us to hit the deck if we heard any "popping" noises (no one else was grinning). Damned military smiles!

We exited the well-protected north gate of Tan Son Nhut Airbase and found ourselves bouncing down a semi-paved road with potholes the size of cemetery plots, how inappropriate! Since there was a lot of local traffic I concluded being shot at was not imminent and then relaxed to get my first glimpses of the countryside. Flooded rice paddies, rubber tree plantations, and dozens of small villages passed by one after the other. Other than the military Jeeps and trucks, the roadway traffic included a myriad of two- and three-wheel scooters, Lambro/scooter buses, an assortment of failing French trucks and cars, water buffalo with carts, bicyclist, and Pedicabs. Both sides of the gravel shoulders were crowded with masses of people headed in both directions. Almost all of the civilians, and only God knew how many V.C., were dressed in free-flowing black silk pajamas topped with the ever-present pointed straw hats. The loose-fitting tops compensated for the heat and pants with way oversized legs accommodated the need to relieve oneself whenever and wherever necessary (something I reluctantly witnessed what seemed to be about a hundred times that day).

The material choices for some of the humble village abodes were of particular interest to me. Most of the huts had bamboo framing with grass and leaf wall panels and roofs; others obviously were constructed of recycled pallets and assorted rusty corrugated steel panels. However, a select few were much more creative, not to mention colorful. Each exterior wall was shielded in panels made from aluminum beer cans. The can tops and bottoms had been removed, the cylinders were slit and flattened into rectangular panes, and the edges were then folded and crimped to others until a wall of sheeting had been produced. Allowing for creative license, these beer-can hootches had one exterior wall that boasted "Budweiser," the adjacent wall proudly screamed "Schlitz," while the other was obsessed with "Old Style." The roofs where constructed with the beer names facing inside so the shiny sides could reflect the heat. I knew that somewhere, brewery marketing executives were probably happy with all the free advertising.

Due to the overwhelming pulsating sea of traffic, our short 19-mile journey took over two hours. Time wasn't an issue for us weary travelers; we were just happy there hadn't been any popping sounds. As we entered the heavily armed south gate of Di An, a billboard-sized sign greeted us which looked odd because it was only four feet off the ground. It proudly proclaimed the 1st Division motto: "No Mission Too Difficult, No Sacrifice Too Great." Funny, I came up with about a dozen exceptions in ten seconds flat.

After a brief stop at the gate, we proceeded to the induction center, then exited the truck and left our helmets and flak jackets under the benches. This is where we were to spend the night before being transported to our respective units. After a lackluster visit to the mess hall, we were issued more gear including my very own flak jacket, poncho, helmet, canteen, web belt, and a M14 accompanied by a cloth bandolier of 10 magazines with 20 rounds each. Guess I was about to become a real soldier; but, since we were playing for keeps now, where the hell was my M16?

We were given the rest of the afternoon and evening off. We spent the rest of the day BS'ing. Then at 10:00 PM sharp, it was lights out, and I was getting ready for some sack time. I had no idea when the next time would be that I was going to sleep on a real mattress. My head hadn't found the pillow when an air raid siren went off shattering the still of the night. A sergeant ran into our barracks and told us there was a red alert and we needed to saddle up. What the hell was a red alert? I hadn't even placed the camouflage cover on my helmet but grabbed both anyway, got dressed, and grabbed the flak jacket, poncho, M14 and the ammo. We were rushed to the perimeter and stationed in irregular lines between the sandbag-shrouded machine gun bunkers. As told, we lay down in a prone position on our ponchos and stared at the brush- and grass-lined outer wire silhouetted by billions of stars.

Apparently a guard had seen movement and military intelligence had confirmed the presence of the NVA and VC (North Vietnamese Army and Viet Cong). I inserted a magazine into my rifle. But being cautious, I did not put a round into the chamber. I never saw or heard anything that long moonless night but did enjoy the impressive celestial display, and was quite struck by the contrast and irony of the moment.

Luckily, our readiness and due diligence was all for nothing and, as the sun slowly rose and the stars faded, we were told to stand down. Nothing had really happened, except for the emphatic emphasis that unknown perils were an integral component of the Vietnam experience.

5

The Big Red One

October 1967

That morning there were only about 30 of us in the reception area and everyone to the man had once again received new destination orders (apparently the need for personnel changed minute to minute), that is, all but three of us who were told to report to Lieutenant Colonel Mann, the Commanding Officer, who oversaw the clerical functions for the entire division.

As we sat outside the Colonel's office and I pondered my fate, I couldn't help but notice how nice the facility looked. It was clean, everybody was cordial, ceiling fans cooled the place, and there was no hint of being in a combat zone. Adjusting to this duty post would be a piece of cake, and I wanted it so bad I could taste it.

After a brief wait I was invited inside and greeted by a tall, slender, well-groomed man with gray hair sharply crafted into a flat-top crew cut who appeared to be about 20 years my senior. His well-tanned face was in stark contrast to his faded jungle fatigues that had so much starch they actually glistened in the sunlight, and I wouldn't have been surprised if they shattered when he sat down. When I walked in, he extended his hand before I could salute. After a firm handshake, he sat down, put his boots on the desk, and asked me to take a seat.

A number of questions followed. Had I ever worked in an office before, did I know how to type, and how many hours of college accounting had I taken? There was no hint of intimidation or skepticism, no judgment of my credibility, just simple questions that I honestly answered. Color me very confused. I had been more than a little apprehensive of which fire base would be my new home, and here I was being politely interviewed for a desk job in what appeared to be nirvana.

I already knew that Di An was the headquarters base camp for the division and that it was protected by formidable perimeter defenses. In addition there were dozens of chopper squadrons at the ready, not to mention artillery batteries, and anywhere from 500 to well over 1,000+ infantrymen. The most important fact for me was that the base had never suffered a serious attack. It wasn't bulletproof; but, being the Divisional Headquarters, it was much better situated than any of the other three Big Red One base camps.

The Colonel told me that fully one half of the office staff would be completing their tour of duty and would be rotating back to the states in the next 12-to-16 weeks. Many had come over on the same ship about one year before and now they were going home. Some might extend their tour because they would be promoted to next highest rank (as was the norm), but very few were expected to take the incentive. After a short chat he stood up, shook my hand again, and said a job was mine if I wanted it. I may not have been the sharpest knife in the drawer but without any delay gratefully accepted the offer. Up to this point it was the easiest decision I had made during my brief military career. Although a 60-day trial period had to be successfully navigated or it was out to the boonies with me, I felt pretty confident. My first letter home from Di An probably made my family feel a little better about my permanent duty station, and my new post did wonders for my moral.

We three were all offered jobs and had agreed to stay. Then we returned to the reception area and were processed into the division and given a quick tour of the Admin Company area. Even more supplies were distributed and I hauled everything back to my newfound home away from home. Then I was given a crash course in the necessary Admin Company combat SOP. I even got to shoot my M14 and emptied a couple of magazines into a target-less berm of dirt. This pretty much was full the extent of my intense in-country jungle training.

Afterward I was assigned a bunk with a foot locker in the rear corner, closest to the perimeter, in hootch number thirteen (really?). The structure was about 20' X 60' and had no windows, but the walls consisted of overlapping boards attached to the framing at a sharp 15° downward slope and were backed by screens instead of solid panels. This design provided great circulation, the interior was a little brighter during the day, and it was dry when it rained. The overhead open trusses supported the corrugated metal roof and three large ceiling fans, and it was home to an incredible number of spiders and other such critters. The floor was constructed of well-worn raw concrete. There was a simple rubber strap that closed the screen door, and a windowless solid plywood door acted as a storm door, these were located at both ends of the barracks. The building wasn't exactly picturesque but it did offer great ventilation, stopped most of the mosquitoes, and provided adequate shelter. Ten bunks lined both sides of the building and each was adorned with a mosquito net tent. Other than that, it was exactly the same as every other barracks I had been in. The rear door was adjacent to my bunk; if it was open and you stood in the doorway, it offered a stunning panoramic view of the perimeter bunkers, shower, and "the pisser."

The shower building was constructed just like the hootches but had 10 shower heads on either side of the interior. Two large cylinder-shaped tanks perched high on stilt-like framing provided the water which was warmed by M67 gas-fired immersion heaters. That's all very interesting, but the water tanks were only partially filled once daily at 6:00 AM which fed the showers for maybe ten-to-fifteen minutes of continuous use. The immersion heaters never had a chance to work their magic and, if you weren't in line before the tanks were filled, you didn't get to take a shower. Unfortunately, the men on guard duty were dismissed at 7:00 AM – "xin loi." I never enjoyed a hot shower until many months later when I was on R&R.

It was still the rainy season and, a couple of weeks later, I got so tired of missing my morning shower, I decided to take one in the rain as the water cascaded off a corner of the hootch's roof. After a quick splash in the rain, I used my bar of soap to liberally lather up but soon found there was one little problem. Rain water is freezing cold! Even after a half dozen attempts to rinse off, I was less than half successful. I had to stop because I had turned blue and my teeth were chattering. I never chose that remedy again. I set my alarm clock to go off a half hour earlier, and soon after changed it again to an hour earlier to avoid the crowd. Although up to this point I had always enjoyed sleeping in whenever possible, I have been a morning person ever since.

The "pisser" was a free-standing outside convenience surrounded on three sides by a four-foot-high corrugated steel fence; the urinal itself consisted of a 55-gallon drum without a top or bottom. This tube was filled with rocks and lime and topped with a screened cap. It worked well enough until one fateful day just as someone approached the necessity; it suddenly blew up, drenched him with its vile contents, and the screen cover flew into the air like a wayward UFO. Luckily he dodged most of the rocks and had escaped serious injury other than to his ego; but with no water in the shower, we had to use our canteens to help rinse him off. Never found out if the "pisser" exploded because it had been booby-trapped or resulted from a chemical reaction with the lime, urine, etc. Regardless, most of us never used the damned thing again since the surrounding open area worked just fine...

The soil was mostly clay and not very absorbent; this fact not only dictated the construction of the urinal but also of the latrine. The "crapper" was a "four banger" without dividers (what else is new); the walls and floor were the same as the hootch's, and it was topped with a slanted corrugated metal roof. Surprisingly there was no pit, just 55-gallon drums cut in half placed beneath each "throne" as receptacles. Every morning, rain or shine, a remorseful crew (most of who were in the infantry and better known as "honey dippers"), had the nasty chore of removing the outhouse drums, dousing them in gasoline, and setting each on fire. This was the army's solution for sanitation and it worked quite well considering the circumstances. But as we trudged off to the mess hall each morning for breakfast, it looked like the entire base camp was recovering from an attack with dozens of pillars of black aromatic smoke spiraling skyward. Let me assure you this is not an appetizing way to start the day.

My first day with the Big Red One had been a little stressful to say the least. After I was assigned a bunk and had unpacked everything, I walked around the hootch and introduced myself to the others. Most were friendly, except for some of the short timers who were more than a little distant. Four of the guys were playing poker; payday often opened the door for a little gambling recreation. They asked me to sit in and I thought why not; it was as good a way as any to get to know some of the guys. I could not win a hand and never held anything worth betting on. After losing twenty bucks to the ante in only fifteen minutes, I had had enough and stopped playing, more than a little suspicious of my bad luck. I had learned yet another valuable lesson and never lost any money that way again. And that was what I consider to be my first welcome to my new home in "the Nam."

Each morning started with everyone standing in platoon formations in front of the hootches for a roll call and announcements. Once each week we were handed a (M-11), a pink horse-sized pill, which was supposed to fight malaria, and were instructed to take it then and there. Since none of us knew anyone in our base camp that had malaria, we were not anywhere near a swamp, and the inescapable side effect was always an unpleasant sudden urge to visit the "crapper," virtually nobody took the pill. After we were dismissed, hundreds of pink pills littered the ground in neat little rows until we stomped them into the dust or the mud, whichever was available.

During the dry season, the ground we walked on was covered with at least a permanent three-inch-thick level of dust that got into everything. It was so bad that about six months after I arrived, the engineers eventually built sidewalks leading everywhere constructed from empty ammunition crates. Even then, there was always a persistent blanket of dirt on everything until the rainy season put an end to it. Everywhere you went, you smelled, tasted, and felt the grittiness of the coarse dust. It got into the food, the pockets of your clothing, and all the office equipment; if it was a windy day, nothing was safe, even the inside of your skivvies and boots were not immune.

The mess hall menu was pretty much the same every day and made its state-side counterparts look like fine dining establishments. The breakfast menu was pretty much the same as in the states, except that the bread and biscuits turned into soggy dough and fell apart if you looked at them, the milk and juiced tasted a little more odd, and canned apricots graced every meal. And for the record, then as now, I still hated canned apricots. Sadly they were a mainstay served at every meal, and sometimes even found their way into the dessert, including the chocolate cake and every type of pudding. Lunch offered sandwiches sometimes with sinewy meat unknown to mankind, served on bread which compressed to a gummy disc when you picked it up. Dinner had more choices and offered a variety of pasta combinations, chicken, turkey, or ham; and soft white piles resembling mashed potatoes that were always served with gravy that poured like molasses.

One time, lamb made its way to the menu and I decided to try it because I'd never had it before. This proved to be my first and last time. It must have been only partially thawed and it was burned to black charcoal on the outside and was raw and cold on the inside. I now know lamb gets stronger tasting with each passing day and have concluded this one was probably "older than dirt." Having been on KP too many times I also knew the cooks did their very best with what they had to work with. Logistics often delayed shipments and, even after the supplies finally arrived, there were usually shortages. This always tested the cook's creativity.

The Admin Company consisted of 8 large office buildings and a scattering of smaller structures. Each was constructed very similarly to our barrack hootches except there were continuous unobstructed screened panels from 3' off the floor to the roof line; these were our windows. The corrugated metal roof overhung the sides by about four feet which served as very effective awnings shielding against the sun and the rain. The finance office was a large U-shaped building with one leg solely devoted to processing troops in and out of country. Only the non-commissioned people were serviced in our offices. Another office complex across the courtyard was devoted solely to the Division's higher ranking NCOs and officers.

The 1ˢᵗ Admin Company and its leadership were unique in many ways. An average Army company usually consists of 80 to 225 people; our company had well over 600 people. A normal company is commanded by a Captain (which is what we had). However, our company also consisted of two Lieutenant Colonels, several Majors, and additional Captains with lots more time in grade, all of whom outranked the company Commander. The Admin Company Captain was in charge of the day-to-day functions including supervising perimeter security and orchestrating the guard duty roster, the mess hall, maintaining the grounds and buildings, administering company discipline as necessary, and was the conduit for all Divisional military directives. Since the Captain was outranked by so many others, the chain of command was a little tricky at best; so detailed guidelines were in place which accurately delineated each officer's responsibilities. I wouldn't say the company Captain's command was all that awkward and unappreciated; but, then again, maybe that's why we went through six or seven of them while I was in country.

Besides Finance, the 1st Admin Company breakdown consist-
ed of Personnel Services (201 files), the Judge Advocates Office
(SJA), Adjutant General (AG), Inspector General (IG), Awards and
Decorations, the Information Office for propaganda (IO), Special
Services (for R&R and special leave of absence), the Replacement
(Repo) Depot, a host of small specialty groups, and was also home
to the division chaplain and his staff. A high-ranking contingency of
the Headquarters and Headquarters Company staff and 1st Division
Band were also stationed at Di An, but rumor had it the HHC would
soon be moving out to another base camp.

Like birds of a feather, most people tended to socialize with those
in their own office section. In addition to working with these people,
you also bunked with them since the hootches were all loosely set up
by departments. I thought this was a little crazy since a single mortar
or rocket could take out a whole department. Once again I marveled
at the military mindset and sense of practicality – or lack thereof.

The 1st Admin Company originally departed the continental
United States on September 30, 1965 and traveled with the rest of
the task force aboard the USNS Barrett. They landed on October
19th, close to two years before me. When they arrived at Di An,
the base camp was still under construction. The combat troops
were deployed as needed and the balance of 1st Admin Company
construction was completed by the Admin Company clerical staff
under the direction of the 1st Engineer Battalion. They helped
build the offices, bunkers, showers, our company's solitary tower, latrines, mess hall and all of the hootches. During the day,
they poured cement and pounded nails. At night, they not only
completed the necessary division's paperwork and payroll tasks
but also provided the guards to arm the perimeter bunkers and
the gates and performed perimeter sweeps. I don't know when
the original crew slept and never met anyone who was involved
with the initial construction; they had been replaced by another

shipload of people. It was no wonder only a few elected to extend their stay and enjoy the party.

I was a newbie and didn't have a clue of how to prepare a payroll voucher – or anything else for that matter. So without fanfare or ceremony, I became the office clerk for the finance department. Even after completing a 24-hour detailed course on the finance department functions, my first responsibilities were limited to distributing all the incoming paperwork for anything concerning payroll changes including allotments, insurance, rank, reassignment, assorted fines, advances, and, sadly, KIA (killed in action) notices, which was later changed to KHA (killed, hostile action). Once everything was sorted and prioritized, the paperwork was given to the 25 or so payroll clerks. I acted as the messenger between finance and the other company offices. I was told my duties would also include driving a Jeep for some of the brass, but that never came about. To run errands, I did have a nice red bicycle for a while, but it was soon stolen and never replaced – truthfully, I never really missed it.

The most gratifying part of my job at first was also being in charge of mail call. Every day I went to the company commander's office around 11:00 and picked up a huge canvas bag of mail. Several months later, as Christmas approached, this soon grew to two then three bags; and I swear some weighed as much or more than me. All those very important letters and parcels were everyone's conduit to reality, including mine. I witnessed every emotion known to mankind as I called out the names. Some got 6 or 7 letters almost every day and were bored, others got mail once or twice a week and were thrilled, and a few rarely got anything and seemed resigned to their fate, but still showed up daily just in case. Anyone receiving a box from home immediately became everybody's best friend, and even the hint of candy or cookies could start a stampede.

Unfortunately, some of the news from home was painful. The death of a relative or friend, or any other family tragedy, generated all the expected emotions but was frustrated even more by the literal and figurative distances that separated them from their homes. For me, the worst news I delivered was the notorious "Dear John" letter; it usually had a devastating impact and I know I handed out my fair share. About a week before Thanksgiving I delivered one I'll never forget, although over time the name has faded, the consequences are engraved in granite. It was from his childhood sweetheart who apparently was a gullible fool. Her newfound, draft-dodging coward of a boyfriend had convinced her that her payroll clerk fiancé was killing babies, and that she'd be much better off going to Canada with him.

The poor man quietly returned to his desk but soon lost every sense of right and wrong. He grabbed his rifle and bandolier of ammo, ran to his hootch, climbed onto a top bunk, and proceeded to put a round through the roof every couple of minutes. His barracks emptied immediately and all that approached were warned to stay away. He shouted through the closed doors that he was going to kill himself, then kept on ventilating the roof for over an hour. After unsuccessfully trying to negotiate a cease fire, the company commander decided he was too much of a risk and orchestrated a plan to have a sniper take him down. Someone threw open the door and, when the trooper turned and pointed his M14 in that direction, the sharpshooter shot that poor wretched soul in the shoulder. He dropped limply to the cement floor then struggled for a short time. They later discovered his carotid artery had been pierced by shrapnel from his rifle butt and he had bled out in just a couple of minutes. As far as I know, he was the first casualty in our Admin Company and I dreaded every mail call from that day forward.

Soon after that senseless tragedy, my responsibilities slowly began to change. The senior finance clerks were closer to going home and busy making their preparations; so every time someone had guard duty, KP or went on R&R, I filled in to help get the payroll out. I was soon taught all the necessary payroll procedures. Once trained, I realized that any competent high school freshman could more than likely handle the chore. I was doing payroll about 50% of the time and was still responsible for the paperwork distribution plus all the other miscellaneous chores. Soon it was simply too much for any one person to handle. I discussed my dilemma with the duty sergeant, and a couple of days later they pulled another combat engineer from the troops in processing from the states, how appropriate. He was well educated but just like me needed to be taught everything. The first responsibility I gave Tim was mail call. In short order my newfound protégé allowed me to work payroll about 80% of the time. I never considered him my assistant; he was most assuredly my equal and very much appreciated.

I helped pay the medics, engineers, the newly formed LRRP (Long Range Reconnaissance Patrol), and eventually the MI (military intelligence); and, yes, my first thought was the term "military intelligence" was an oxymoron. But all kidding aside, both the LRRP and MI troops had some very dangerous assignments; they were always getting additional pay for TDY (Temporary Duty), TDA (Temporary Duty Away), and TDT (Temporary Duty Travel) as well as other payroll adjustments for miscellaneous expenses. Since everybody in country got the $65.00 per month Hazardous Duty Pay adjustments, those troopers must have had some very interesting adventures. I later found out they were the ones from our division who often found themselves in North Vietnam, Laos, or Cambodia, and wherever else their clandestine services where required.

The office hours were constantly changing depending on the workload and number of available personnel. Sometimes a third of the people were away from our office. The normal work hours were 8:00 to 4:30 and, if needed you might have to come back at 6:00 and work anywhere from one-to-four additional hours. The simple fact is the payroll absolutely had to get out on time to help keep up the morale. We normally worked seven days a week but usually got whatever time was needed to run errands, see the medics, etc. Sundays were the only exception. If you attended church, you got the morning off, and (as noted before) most said they did this "religiously."

Tradition dictated that thirty days before anyone departed, those on their way home could carry a little 12" long carved wooden cane topped with a dragon's head. These were appropriately enough called short-timer sticks. Whenever those happy few felt the urge, they could rap you lightly on the head and remind you how "short" they were and how long you still had to endure. If you were a recent arrival, you were also called a "snake" (among a host of other derogatory terms). It soon became apparent that there were a lot of reptiles in our department. I tried to come up with an appropriate acronym for snake but failed, so I simply accepted the nomenclature and taps on the noggin as rites of passage.

About once a month they had an office party which featured a water buffalo steak barbeque, tubs of cold but odd-tasting beer, and an assortment of snacks. It was a great way to get to know everyone; but, as time progressed, some of the short timers had become so obnoxious eventually they were the only ones in attendance. Once you earned the title of short timer, it seemed your whole persona changed. Although happy on the surface, many became nervous, touchy, argumentative, and paranoid. After waiting so long for your ride home, there was always the nagging fear something would happen to mess things up. On rare occasions something did happen to delay the process; but, for most, it was simply a long, bumpy ride back to the "World."

We were all in the same boat, working insane hours, living at best in Spartan conditions, and suffering through long days and the rigors of guard duty, KP, and whatever else needed to be done. Although it was a piece of cake compared to what the people in the field had to endure, everybody I knew could tell you exactly how many days and hours were left until their DEROS (Date Eligible to Return from Overseas) including me – only 339 days and 6 hours to go, wow!

6

DI An Base Camp

October & November 1967

When I first arrived in the 1st Infantry Division and had received all my gear, I found a small vertical oval unit crest pin that had been included. The one-inch-tall oval pin had a thin red frame on the top and thin blue frame on the bottom with the word "Victory," and in the center there was a small angel with extended arms in a bright brass finish. The pin was supposed to be attached to the baseball hat we all wore, placed in the center of the front panel. It was the unit crest for both the 1st Admin Company and the Headquarters and Headquarters Company. I never found out the significance of the angel, and all the nicknames I heard were mostly a challenge to her morality. The impact of this little adornment was that I was frequently saluted by many of those I approached whenever I was outside our company area. In the sunlight, the brass center was a brilliant gold blur, just like a Second Lieutenant's gold bar. At first I tried to explain I was not an officer but soon gave up and simply returned the salute. It was kind of fun actually, who needs OCS.

It took about two weeks for me to get the first letters from home, after that the flood gates opened and it seemed like it was a rare day that I didn't get something in the mail. At first I diligently wrote home every couple of days and always had lots to say. But as the days dragged on, I soon ran out of pleasant stories and fairy tales to pass on. My situation really wasn't that bad but then it certainly wasn't all fun and games, either. Although all was well at Di An, there were so many bad things happening all around us that I couldn't write home about. There was no way I was going to burden my family with depressing statistics; they were scared enough already. Later, after I had been in country for only a couple of months, I had to be told to write home more frequently. Still, I found it impossible to keep up with the lies and make up happy little stories all the time, so I kept putting off writing the next letter, sometimes for a week or so.

Feeling more than just a little guilty about my lack of communication, a couple of weeks before Christmas I took advantage of a very lucky opportunity to phone home. I had tried twice before but they could never make a connection, but it was worth another try. It was an effort that was orchestrated by a volunteer group of amateur ham radio operators who patched a wireless radio call into a collect phone call. I knew the timing was poor, but I called anyway when the opportunity presented itself. Unfortunately the phone call reached home at 1:30 AM and they had to call twice to get an answer. There was only one rotary dial phone in our house downstairs in the living room; it took a little time to wake up, throw on a robe, and make it down the stairs.

I talked to mom and then to my sister and youngest brother; dad was already on his commute to work and I guessed Keith probably wasn't home yet. The call was a bit awkward because you had to say "over" every time you stopped talking. We chatted for about ten minutes before losing the connection. It was great to talk to everyone, but afterward I felt so removed and out of focus. Although I was given the opportunity to call right back again, I didn't know what else to say and so declined the offer.

After all that I decided to take a walk to the post PX (Post Exchange) and get some cigarettes. As I remember, the price had just gone up and now a carton cost $1.65, but I had just been paid so that wasn't a problem. The PX was a short walk past Bob Hope

Field. When I arrived I gave the clerk my ration card and got a carton of Kools. I had a persistent cough and the menthol was a little easier on the throat.

I was just about to leave when I saw something that stopped me in my tracks. It was a Teac reel-to-reel tape recorder housed in a walnut box, with the necessary shiny metal faced Sony amplifier sitting next to it, and knew I just had to have them. The PX was usually poorly stocked and electronics literally "flew off the shelves." I would have bought them on the spot but first needed to save $350 to buy the pair. To complete the ensemble, two speakers were also needed which added $100 to the cost. Not sure if I could ever save that much the money, but knew I had to try. This savings goal would take some time; so this perceived necessity would be "on the back burner" for a while.

I had forgotten to pick up my laundry and I so went straight to the "Kansas Laundry" to get my things. My dad really liked the laundry's name, but to me it was just another ironic footnote. When I looked at my things, I couldn't help but notice that every time my fatigues were laundered, they came back just a little more reddish brown colored than before -- presumably from being washed in the muddy Saigon River. The smell was getting more and more unpleasant; but just like everything else in that country, you got used to it eventually, whether you wanted to or not.

In addition to the laundry and Army PX, there were a number of other stores in the L-shaped shopping complex mostly operated by Vietnamese entrepreneurs. There was the popular Di An 5¢ & 10¢ store which was similar to a "Woolworth's," but the quality wasn't any way near as good. Still, I must have bought a dozen Zippo® lighters from them while I was in country; for some unknown reason, I kept losing them. Each had been engraved with the Big Red One logo, my name, rank, and company name and the face side had a map of Vietnam locating the 1st Division's base camps. Only one lighter survived that I know of, and it's the one I sent home to my dad. I also went to that store to have my photos and slides developed and probably unwittingly let the enemy know everything they ever wanted to about Di An.

My favorite place was the barbershop that offered a really "big bang for the buck." Your hair was always washed before being cut, you got a professional haircut, then your face was wrapped in a steamed towel, and a close shave with a straight razor followed. The only problem I ever had was once when I had them trim my moustache, and it almost vanished leaving only a pencil line remnant; I never did that again. After the shave, a pleasant looking young lady came out, put her two hands together as if to pray, and used the palm edges to softly beat your neck, back, and arms. This was a Vietnamese style massage that only lasted a couple of minutes, unless you were willing to add a little tip. While this was all going on, someone was spit polishing your boots and another manicured and polished your fingernails. If I remember correctly, the cost of this extravagance was 300 piasters (less than $3.00); but being a generous soul I always added a 50p tip. Much later, near the end of my stay, we were all surprised when one of our barbers was found shot to death on the outer perimeter wire of the Korean compound. I cringed at the thought of that straight razor held in his hands at my throat, but somehow I still miss that old barbershop all the same.

There was also a Kwiki Freeze that offered frozen treats but had trouble attracting customers and usually wasn't open; the best thing about the unusual-tasting ice cream was that it was cold. Bradford Tailors provided custom suits and clothing, could make any necessary alterations or repairs to your uniform, and would sew on new insignia. Several other souvenir and miscellaneous shops completed the retail complex. It was nice to have a variety of stores, but it was far from being a shopper's paradise. Still, it was the best base camp collection of shops I saw while in country.

Although the rainy season was supposedly over, it started to rain lightly again so I quickly jogged back to my hootch. I hung the clean shirts, pants, and fatigues on a couple of nails and stored everything else in the foot locker. I sat down and lit a cigarette, then proceeded to assess how to best arrange my personal area. When I arrived in country all the beds were level with the floor, but recently we were allowed to convert them to bunk beds -- virtually doubling the available floor space. I now had the top bunk and the space closest to the rear door was all mine which allowed for at least a hint of privacy.

Depending on the company commander and our current alert status, our bunks were periodically changed from single to bunk beds, then back again. The thought being it was always better to keep your head down rather than to double stack the bunks. But when double stacked, the result was much more open floor space and a little more privacy, and most preferred it that way. Regardless of the height of the bed, I always thought it was remarkable that so many men could live is such close quarters, witness every quirk and body function known to mankind, and have to deal with a litany of sometimes very strange personalities, all without going nuts. After I returned home, I savored the private sanctuary and solitude of my own bedroom, it was magnificent. Now I have had no trouble sharing my bedroom with my wife, and don't mind being alone; but having to share a room with anyone else would surely be the end for one of us.

That luxurious 6' X 7' area seemed huge to me at the time. To fill the space, I had bought a folding aluminum chair and a cheap throw rug and had bartered a carton of cigarettes for a funky 2' wide by 3' high bookcase with the face covered by printed yellow plastic fringe strips. That completed the accommodations of my little "slice of heaven" for the moment. It was rumored we were going to get wall lockers; but, until then, the nails in the wall framing would have to suffice. I enjoyed every minute whenever when I found the time to sit down, have a cigarette, and revel in my new serene refuge. And although infrequent, I really enjoyed those brief respites in my sanctuary, all alone.

After contemplating my new upscale living arrangements, I returned to the office. The work was starting to pile up again so I asked Tim to distribute the promotion roster and associated paperwork, and then had him help me type the payroll vouchers. Most of the vouchers were very simple; all we had to do was list the gross pay, add the hazardous duty and any other additional pay factors, then compute the deductions such as the amount being sent home, monies applied (to savings bonds, alimony or child support), and the cost for life insurance. Almost everybody had the life insurance; $1 bought $5,000 and $2 got you $10,000. Each man we paid had a file incorporating the documents concerning changes in rank, allotments, bond purchases, travel pay, insurance, etc. After you typed the pay voucher, a copy was added to their file and the other three copies were sent to the disbursement office.

Tim and I stopped working around 5:30 and, after a short break, we met at the mess hall for dinner. We each took the opportunity to find out a little about the other. After I gave him the *Cliff's Notes*© version of my experiences; I found out that Tim and I had a couple of things in common. He had gone to college, and, for whatever reason, had dropped out of school after two and a half years; naturally, he was promptly drafted. Tim had been married about a year before being drafted and, although only 20, he had a 2-month-old daughter.

Once drafted he had gone to Ft. Dix for basic training and afterward had been sent to Ft. Leonard Wood for combat engineering school. After AIT he had a hardship leave due to a death in the family. When he returned, he spent the next five months in Missouri before being sent overseas. He was assigned to the 1st Infantry Division Engineers and was as shocked as I had been when he was pulled out of the line and had that little chat with our Lieutenant Colonel. Of course, he was very concerned about his family – especially with everything going on all around us. I tried to reassure him we were actually in a pretty safe place considering everything and that he and his family would be fine. He probably didn't believe me and I had a little trouble with that BS myself. After an hour break, we returned to the office and worked until 7:30. All of the vouchers were now typed and filed and we both had high hopes that the next couple of days might be a little easier.

The following day when I returned to the office, we all went to a meeting room. It seems the army was taking a stab at modernizing and we were the first unbelievably lucky overseas "guinea pigs." Computers were coming and they were boasted to be the salvation of mankind, or at least for the finance department anyway. All too soon, six shiny new 40' long semi-truck trailers sat ganged together side by side adjacent to the finance offices. Each trailer had a huge air conditioner strapped to the top which ran 24/7 and, when coupled with the noise from the necessary generators, a constant din and vibration were the result. We provided massive piles of paperwork that had to be keypunched onto rectangular punch cards, which in turn would be transcribed into computer-generated payroll vouchers. I thought that the "handwriting was on the wall" and we were all doomed to become obsolete.

The computers were supposed to improve production time and reduce the manpower needed for the payroll each month; but the finance group had added six key punchers, twelve computer programmers and maintenance personnel, and two officers to oversee everything. And perhaps preordained, just before payday, a generator had failed and a computer overheated. The resulting fire destroyed two of the trailers along with most of those lovely multicolored punch cards. As usual, we didn't know if this was due to equipment failure or sabotage, and actually we really didn't care too much; our jobs were now more secure.

There was a downside to this salvation. Since it was the end of the month we had to stay in the office until all the payroll vouchers were manually typed and distributed. This little endeavor took about 36 hours, but at least there was no delay in getting the payroll out. I can't tell you how thrilled we were. So now we had 20 additional people in Finance and millions of dollars of new equipment, but the end result was the payroll took longer to produce and we still ended up typing all the vouchers by hand. I've seen this same scenario played out many times since; it seems progress can be a painful, slow process. In time, the computers were able to generate preprinted pay vouchers, but they were always plagued with errors of every type. After being audited by the finance specialist, many of the computer vouchers had to be manually retyped. Ultimately, in the end our work force was never reduced by a single man. For the record, my experience with computers has always been a mixed blessing and remained the bane of my existence for the next 45+ years.

Of course, since we had been temporarily exempted from guard duty, KP, and the other company chores, now we had to catch up; no rest for the weary. First I had 24-hour guard duty and KP the day after, which meant I had to work late the next couple of days to catch up. It seemed like we were always rushing to handle one crisis or another, and frankly that was OK; it helped the time pass more quickly and there was little time for boredom or depression. Probably all part of the master plan. Now I could relate to all those lucky enough to have been in the first wave that set up the administration company two years prior.

When we had free time there weren't too many recreational options available; so you were left to your own imagination for the most part. There was a swimming pool of sorts but it wasn't always open, and let's just say proper maintenance wasn't part of the program. The EM (enlisted men's) club was just four of blocks away, but I only went there a couple of times. All they served was "near beer" which was normally not cold enough and tasted like it was three months past the expiration date. And I got real tired of the drunken few who were either looking for a fight or boldly demonstrated all the various means that one could use to eliminate whatever when overserved.

When the work day was finally over, some played catch with a softball, practiced taking shots with a basketball using a hoop without a net, or tossed a football around. But by far the most popular thing to do was throw a *Frisbee*®. At any given moment there could be a dozen or so discs gliding gracefully through the air in search of their designated targets. Others jogged, did sets of exercises, or jumped rope in an attempt to get a little workout. Most of us just sat outside behind the hootches in our folding aluminum framed woven web chairs and chaise lounges every evening, enjoying the view, catching some rays, and watching the antics of those with more energy than sense running around in the heat.

After dark you only had a couple of hours before lights out; so, if we were not working late, that's when we wrote our letters and caught up on reading the various books, magazines, and newspapers that circulated in our hootch. I had been gifted a subscription to the Chicago Tribune which proved to be quite popular although they were typically anywhere from two-to-four weeks late.

Some had TVs that were almost useless due to the lack of programing and bad reception, so almost everybody I knew soon sent their new TV sets home in short order. I had a small radio, but the reception was so bad that only two stations came in clear enough to be tolerated. One was the AFVN (Armed Forces Vietnam Network) which featured an assortment of male and female DJ's that played popular music including rock & roll, country western, classical and even comedy routines; but the army reenlistment commercials were a bit tedious and fell on deaf ears.

The other radio station featured both American and Vietnamese music and was hosted by several of our English-speaking neighbors from the North. My favorite was the one who had been christened "Hanoi Hannah," but she was also referred to as the Dragon Lady. Her real name was Trinh Thi Ngo, but she sometimes used the alias

Thu Huong (who knew). Daily she would read an updated list of American casualties, note those recently imprisoned, and gave detailed reports on our troop movements. Her propaganda centered on questioning why were we throwing our lives away (which only a few of the more paranoid short-timers took seriously). Her tirades and information were very one sided; but, when true, the impact was more than a little chilling. AFVN tried to discredit her facts but often failed. Being an administrative company, we could usually confirm if she right or wrong; it was a little depressing how many times she was actually correct.

We had another respite and, if the mosquitos weren't biting, most took advantage of it whenever we could. About twice a week, a sheet was hung on the outside of a hootch and a movie was projected onto the wavering screen. Most times we saw TV shows: "The Wild, Wild West," "Bonanza," "Gunsmoke," and sometimes a mundane movie mystery or a feature-length cartoon were shown. A few comedies were added to complete the set but were the least favorite unless they were movies that included Bob Hope. Nothing too stimulating was shown in fear of exciting all those restrained rampant hormones. When I left Vietnam, I had seen and almost memorized every episode of "The Wild, Wild West." Ah, we were all living the life.

Accounts of gruesome events and appalling statistics were part of each day. You couldn't let them get to you or your life would be miserable. There were a few "sad sacks" but, for the most part, we didn't dwell on the negatives and concentrated on the good things. Perhaps we were in denial, but that was a lot better than suffering with self-pity and/or a dismal outlook. Whenever the news wasn't so good, I often fantasized about going on my upcoming in country R&R anticipating the hot showers, round eyed girls (I hoped), maybe a little Crown Royal with a nice cigar, and had high hopes for real food and a comfortable bed. Right now I didn't know when, and it was still all just a "pipe dream," but what a great dream it was.

Returning from one of my treks to the PX, I took a short cut through an open field behind the Bob Hope stage and couldn't help but hear the Korean attachment yelling. They were doing one of their daily callisthenic routines on the opposite end of the base camp. Every day they had three one-hour-long exercise sessions: one at 6:00 AM, one at 1:00 PM, and the other at 7:00 PM. Most of them spoke very little English and, although they were a cordial group, they pretty much kept to themselves. The Korean compound occupied about a quarter of the Di An base camp; unfortunately, I never had the opportunity to visit it. They were a tough bunch and to showcase their skills put on a monthly taekwondo exhibition. They performed a number of mock fights and miraculously appeared to defy gravity and glide through the air as if in slow motion. One guy would break five 100-pound blocks of stacked ice in half using only one forearm. Another man would jump and break 6 terracotta roofing tiles (held in the air by three volunteers) with his feet, all in one leap. Still another guy snapped a stack of six 1" X 6" boards in half using only his head. They were tremendous athletes and very tough soldiers.

Each South Korean soldier had a two-year tour in Vietnam that was part of a 6-year mandatory active military commitment. Their government used Vietnam as a training ground to train and maintain a well-seasoned and experienced fighting force just in case the North Koreans got too jumpy again. In addition to all the PT and athletic displays, they went out and set up ambushes almost every night. The Koreans never brought back a prisoner but supposedly always had detailed information about VC troop strength and movements.

We also had nightly patrols and occasionally would capture a dozen or more prisoners, but it seemed like they only rarely got any useful intelligence. Although the U.S. troops were more than capable of gleaning whatever covert information was needed, they were usually held back by the mandates of the Geneva Convention, and the enemy knew it; so when captured, they didn't talk or simply lied when they did. Presumably we had to always project a positive image of America. I often wondered just who we were impressing and who we were helping with our restraint. Although seriously never a war monger, I know it is an unfortunate truth that, in war, being humane is not necessarily an effective asset.

It is significant to note that the NVA and VC means of doing business were the extreme antithesis of the U.S. doctrines and was something they practiced daily without restraint. I firmly believe that good ol' Ho Chi Minh took quite a few notes from the Japanese WWII guidebook on how to retrieve intelligence, dispatch those not needed, and terrorize and demoralize both the civilian population and the enemy. The VC and NVA were skilled and quite inventive when it came to torture and executions, often leaving horrifying remnants of their helpless victims as a sickening signpost meant to generate fear and disgust.

To reinforce the VC troop strength, the Ho Chi Minh forces employed a harsh strategy that was both simple and effective. They would go into a village in the middle of the night and wake everybody up and have them stand in a circle. When the village elders were identified, two or three were coldly and summarily executed with a single pistol shot to the temple. The VC then asked for volunteers; anyone who refused their invitation suffered the same fate. The VC would then take as many men and women as needed but usually left the younger children behind. These new recruits soon became porters, were used as fodder in frontal attacks, and dug the many transportation and storage tunnels that honeycombed the countryside.

The VC and NVA were a cruel and heartless, and not surprisingly, witnessing the consequences of their grotesque tactics, would easily spawn our reprisals. This is not offered as an excuse for any atrocities because there is none; rather, I ask you to consider the perspective of all those in harm's way, trying their best to do the right thing, but sometimes blinded by rage. Unless you've experienced it, it is almost impossible to comprehend how a human being can be so merciless, and that the undeniable need for revenge can result in Armageddon. A cast of countless tyrants throughout history have wreaked genocide on whole populations – not the least of which were the Romans, the Mongols, the Crusaders, the Japanese, the Germans, the Russians, definitely the North Vietnamese, and yes, you can add the United States to that list.

Although for all intents and purposes I was now a legitimate payroll clerk, MOS (Military Occupation Specialty) 73C20, I still remained the office clerk and a PFC. I knew I had to be promoted to Specialist 4th Class (Spec 4) before I could be a legitimate part of the payroll team. I had almost made it past the 60-day trial so I felt that a promotion would follow but had no indication as to when.

It was now the end of November, and the Big Red One had seen a lot of action. Although our base camp remained relatively calm, things outside our perimeter where quite a different story. I had only been in country for seven weeks and the 1st Infantry Division had been involved in eight major battles. None was more than 90 miles from where I hung my helmet and there were 768 enemy reported dead. I never knew any of the BRO casualty totals but am sure they were significant.

I have tried to keep this narrative as objective and respectful as possible but find it difficult not to interject my repulsiveness for the horrors of war. Any reasonable human being knows that war is hell. By now you would think the human race would have figured out how to avoid this endless, stupid, pervasive insanity. Although war has always been entwined in the fabric of our lives, don't blame the combat soldier for all the pain and loss. It is the leaders not in harm's way that are responsible for the travesty, and they deserve all the credit, and are liable for all the pain.

It is important to remember that it is the duty of every American citizen to honor the sacrifices of those chosen few who gave up everything for his or her freedoms; and with charity, love, and compassion, help those who come home distraught still the memories that may forever conjure up demons.

7

Before All The Uproar

December 1967

As Christmas neared in mid-December of 1967, Bob Hope was scheduled to put on a show for the 1st Division at "Bob Hope Field" on our base camp. Everyone wanted to see his much-applauded USO Christmas Special. To me he represented America at its finest and his unique style of humor made everyone feel better about themselves. As he twirled his golf club and made fun of just about everything and everybody, his faithful audience laughed, applauded, and cheered almost non-stop. He always had an entourage of talented movie stars, popular entertainers, and a bevy of pretty girls.

That year actress Raquel Welch basically stole the show as she joked with Bob and pranced around the stage, and even danced with a couple of enlisted men. Suzanne Pleshette, Barbara McNair, and Elaine Dunn where also there, all famous actresses and singers. Miss Universe, Madeline Hartog Bell, joked with Bob Hope and proved to be very popular. Bill Crosby (son of Bing?) sang a couple of songs accompanied by legendary Les Brown and "His Band of Renown." An actor named Earl Wilson did a couple of comic skits and sang a comedy routine with Bob. As he always did, Bob Hope and his troop made a point to visit the area hospitals to cheer up the place. Anybody injured but still mobile enjoyed front row seats at the show.

Yes, it was quite a spectacular show – sure wish I had seen it. The guard duty roster was tripled for that night, and almost everyone with a lower rank and "new to the hood" was on the duty list; like me for instance. That night we could hear the cheering of the crowd and some of the music, but all the words sung and spoken on the stage were lost to the exhilaration of the audience. Since I thought I never had even a remote chance of seeing it I wasn't too disappointed, but I sure would have loved to be there. Thankfully, I wouldn't be there for the show the following year; but knew I would enjoy watching it, reclining in a comfortable chair, maybe have a beer in hand, without any barbed wire in sight.

A few days after the show red alerts slowly became more frequent, but Di An remained relatively quiet compared to the other Big Red One base camps. There had only been two mortar attacks in the last week. Lucky for us they had been directed at the engineers and Koreans (my guess is the 1st Admin Company was a pretty low priority target). Every time there was an attack of some sort or even just a sniper firing, we always reacted the same way – kill the lights if they were on and fortify the perimeter. It occurred to me that half a dozen snipers could substantially tie up all the resources of our base camp.

Our camp's perimeter security was due in a large part to the diligent and frequent displays of our air defenses. Daily I witnessed a cadre of the air support available to our troops. Although the technological sophistication pales in comparison to today's capabilities, ours then were eons beyond what the VC and NVA could muster in South Vietnam. Helicopters and airplanes of every description and purpose peppered the bright blue skies, hid among the clouds, and stalked the night. There were so many aircraft flying overhead at any given moment that, even when choppers flew so low you could feel the prop wash, I only rarely noticed.

Almost all of the prop-driven airplanes took off from the runways at Tan Son Nhut Airforce base just outside Saigon. This included light observation planes, cargo planes, smaller bombers, and gunships. The fighter jets were usually station on aircraft carriers and the B52 Bombers were based in Thailand. All of the different types of choppers were based at Di An and they came in all shapes and sizes. The Huey (Bell HU1 Iroquois) was by far the helicopter of choice because of its multi-tasking utility, transport, and attack capabilities. The guppy-shaped Loach (Hughes OH-6 Cayuse) was used for observation and it's fighting ability. The Chinook (Boeing CH-7) transport helicopter was a real workhorse and could often be seen moving troops, artillery pieces, and small trucks.

The cobra (or Snake) attack chopper (Bell AH-1 HueyCobra) had two pilots who sat in tandem to each other and it was armed with rocket pods and machine driven mini-guns. It was a very narrow helicopter and was impossible to target if it was coming toward you; it was an awesome weapon. Occasionally I saw the old reliable Bell H13 Sioux helicopter, it's clear bubble cabin and open-truss tail assembly made it easy to spot. It had been used more during the Korea war to transport the wounded; but in Vietnam it was only used to shuttle VIPs on short excursions. There were many other varieties of helicopters used in Vietnam, but these were the ones I saw on a daily basis.

When I arrived in country and fatefully ended up stationed with the 1st Infantry Division, I was blissfully unaware of the Big Red One's starring role in the hostilities. The year I arrived had been very eventful and they had been entrenched in numerous "combat operations" and "major battles." These two terms are referenced in both volumes 1 and 2 of the book "1st Infantry Division in Vietnam," published by the U.S. Army, which dutifully chronicled each hostile encounter. I had a very difficult time trying to find accurate definitions of these two terms. Eventually I came up with these descriptions: (1) a combat operation is a joint operation conducted by U.S. forces usually in reaction to some hostile event; and (2) a major battle is a well-thought-out (and sometimes not) decisive strike with specific goals and is planned to inflict the most casualties and suffer the least losses. Whether these definitions are accurate or not, the resulting statistics leave no doubt we were at war.

In 1967 our division's infantry, cavalry, combat engineers, mechanized groups, scouts, artillery, medics, and a cast of thousands were involved in 10 combat operations and 16 major battles. This doesn't include the untold thousands of minor skirmishes, ambushes, mortar fire, booby traps, and sniper attacks that were added to the mix. The following list identifies the number of enemy killed in those all-too-frequent clashes with the 1st Infantry Division:

1967 COMBAT OPERATIONS

1.	Niagara Falls	(Jan. 5 – 7)	Body Count: 12
2.	Cedar Falls	(Jan. 8 – 26)	Body count: 389
3.	Tucson	(Feb. 14 – 21)	Body count: 13
4.	Junction City I & II	(Feb. 26 – Apr. 15)	Body count: 1,776
5.	Manhattan	(Apr. 23 – May 11)	Body count: 123
6.	Dallas	(May 17 – 25)	Body count: 19
7.	Billings	(Jun. 12 – 26)	Body count: 347
8.	Paul Bunyan I	(Jul. 19 – Aug. 13)	Body count: 0
9.	Paul Bunyan II	(Aug. 16 – Sep. 11)	Body count: 3
10.	Shenandoah II	(Sep. 29 – Nov. 19)	Body count: 957

1967 MAJOR BATTLES

1.	Prek Klok I	(Feb. 28)	Body count: 167
2.	Prek Klok II	(Mar. 10 – 11)	Body count: 197
3.	Af Gu	(Mar. 31 – Apr. 1)	Body count: 609
4.	Xom Bo I	(Jun. 14)	Body count: 60
5.	Xom Bo II	(Jun. 17)	Body count: 222
6.	Da Yeu	(Oct. 6)	Body count: 60
7.	Ong Thanh	(Oct. 17)	Body count: 163
8.	Srok Silamite 1	(Oct. 29)	Body count: 24
9.	Srok Silamite 2	(Oct. 30)	Body count: 83

10. Loc Ninh Air Strip	(Oct. 31)	Body count: 82
11. Srok Silamite 3	(Nov. 2)	Body count: 263
12. Bu Nho Rung	(Nov. 3)	Body count: 56
13. Srok Rung	(Nov. 7)	Body count: 66
14. Bu Dop	(Nov. 29 – 30)	Body count: 31
15. Hill 172	(Dec. 8)	Body count: 49
16. Xa Cat	(Dec. 10)	Body count: 143

These conflicts all occurred in 1967; the results for 1968 will follow in the last chapter of this book.

In 1967 these 26 Big Red One conflicts reportedly racked up a total body count of 5,914 enemy souls. On the opposite side of the coin, our losses were difficult to add up; but let it suffice to say we paid a heavy price to achieve this tally. These encounters were often joined with other divisions, and there were many other battles that didn't include the Big Red One. I don't know how many 1st Infantry Division troops were killed in 1967, but 11,058 Americans died that year. Virtually every square inch of South Vietnam was a potential battlefield.

The war in Vietnam was a combination of jungle and urban battlefields and there were no definitive lines delineating who was in charge of what. In past "conventional" wars there were usually well-defined boundaries and for the most part, you controlled one side of the line and the enemy the other. In Vietnam if you wanted to properly control an area, you needed to enclose it with barbed wire fences protected by a heavily armed and well-staffed perimeter; but anything outside that wire was literally "no-man's land." Even this enclosed area was not necessarily safe and you needed to be vigilant to keep it secure.

There was another problem to deal with, all too often it was impossible to identify the enemy. The NVA wore a uniform of sorts consisting of light beige or light olive green, loose-fitting, lightweight tops and pants, normally topped with a pith helmet. The NVA also wore civilian clothing when it suited their purpose. The

VC were not so encumbered and wore the everyday dress of black silk tops and pants worn by the peasant population.

When you couldn't recognize the enemy combatants, it was a hopeless pursuit to correctly define the enemy or the battle lines. Even after it appeared you had "won" a battle, it was very tough to distinguish who were the enemy combatants. If they weren't killed or wounded while caught in the act, you didn't know if the casualty was the enemy or a civilian. After a day or night of conflict, these clandestine warriors simply melted away and blended in with the local population, retreated to their tunnels, or meekly went back to work on one of our U.S. and ARVN base camps. The total number of civilian losses will never be known as a direct result of all this confusion; and it is also due to the incredible quantity and variety of active combat action locations.

At first, Washington had a lot of pressure to justify the incredible cost this "police action" had in lives lost and those wounded (not to mention the related costs of logistics, supplies, and equipment). They really needed to show some tangible results to prove we were winning the war. Since there were no territorial gains, some underpaid statistician or political hack apparently decided to use the quantity of enemy killed as a benchmark of our accomplishments. Soon the media dutifully reported the count every day as a measure of our success. So the term "body count" was touted daily in every newspaper and magazine and heard on the radio and TV stations all around the world. To me this term will always be an appropriate and poignant reminder of America's sad involvement in the Vietnam tragedy.

The body counts reported were always somewhat suspect. A lot of battles took place in or near villages, and it was impossible to tell how many of the dead were innocents. But to the generals and our leaders in Washington, the accuracy of the count was not the primary concern, just as long as the total enemy dead justified the actions taken and the totals were more than the losses we had incurred.

One popular theory speculated that the body counts were all exaggerated to falsely booster our perceived superiority. An even more horrific concept theorized that the emphasis for larger numbers was so great it encouraged the slaughter of civilians. I have no doubt that revenge and rage did add to the body count, but I firmly believe that most of the civilian deaths were the result of peripheral damage and confusion. The word "peripheral" is harmless enough by itself; but, when coupled with "damage," it denotes very tragic circumstances. Although it is difficult to fathom the ramifications of all the injustice, the undeniable demand for death to validate our success was a major impetus for the continuation and escalation for the Vietnam War (or any other conflict for that matter).

I then as now hate the term "friendly fire." Not only is it an oxymoron; it is the ultimate deadly result of fear, stupidity, error, and bad decision making. The action was either too spontaneous, reactionary, or the result of misinformation; and there was an ample supply of all those things in Vietnam. Wars have been ignited for many supposedly just reasons: to meet the growing need for land and resources, in order to "help" the world by spreading one's ideology as the sacrosanct remedy to everyone's problems, or in retaliation for past grievances. But I believe self-righteous indulgence and materialism are the most common motivations. Going off to battle apparently is a basic need branded into our persona, and I doubt this will ever change. Unfortunately, as noted before, war is usually orchestrated by those who never have to fight it.

Although my focus was only on Vietnam, the world was still spinning and a few other things were happening. On November 27th, President Johnson asks Henry Kissinger to become his National Security Adviser and he accepts. Two days later on the November 29th, 1967, Secretary of Defense Robert McNamara followed through with his earlier pledge and decided now would be a good time to resign. On December 1st, Jimi Hendrix releases his new album, *Axis:*

Bold as Love. On the 3rd, the first human-to-human heart transplant takes place in Cape Town, South Africa. Dr. Spock, the famous "Baby Doctor," and 584 other Vietnam War protesters, were all arrested on December 4th, 1967 in New York. On December 6th, the U.S. reports the Vietcong killed 252 civilians in the town of Dak Son. Gary Beban is awarded the Heisman Trophy on the 7th. Two more new albums were offered for sale: on the 8th, The Rolling Stones releases *Their Satanic Majesties Request*, and on the 9th, Cream also releases a cult favorite titled *Disraeli Gears*. On December 14th, Truman Capote's book *In Cold Blood* is released. On December 21st, the movie *The Graduate* opens to the public.

On the 23rd, President Johnson visits Cam Ranh Bay and with bluster announces how we are undoubtedly winning the war; he needed to speak a lot louder – somehow Ho Chi Minh never got the message. Each event was a milestone of some sort, most of which I didn't know about until much later; I only knew where I was – and where I wasn't.

Logically there is neither honorable rationale nor creditable logic that warrants armed conflict. To me, every war is simply a feud gone ballistic; you took or killed mine, so I'll take or kill yours. Regardless of the stimulus, the end results are never worthy of the costs. The pursuits of ideological victory, material gain, and retribution foolishly fuels the senseless and endless need to fight and destroy. Ultimately our humanity is forfeited to some ill perceived sense of justice – maybe for 10,000 days or so.

8

The Lunar Tet Offensive

January 1968

1967 came to an end and 1968 began, both loudly signaling pivotal and very troubled times. January started just like December ended with a series of unrelated events making the news each day. On the 14th, the Packers beat the Raiders 33 to 14 during Super Bowl II. On the 15th, a huge earthquake hits Sicily and 380 people perish. Aretha Franklin releases a new album labeled *Lady Soul* on the December 22nd; and Rowan & Martin's TV show *Laugh In* debuts on NBC. Also on the 22nd, the unmanned Apollo Mission 5 is launched and successfully tests the descent and assent capabilities of the Lunar Module. On the 28th, the U.S.S. Pueblo and her 83-man crew are captured by the North Koreans, and it will take 11 months before the crew is set free. Near the end of the month, North Vietnam's General Giap attacks the Marine base at Khe San with an estimated 20,000 NVA and VC.

As the end of the month approached, most of the old timers had the last of their parties and were off and running, back to the "World." A couple of them I would miss, but I felt it was about time for the new crew teams to pick up the slack and get going. The office took on a new vibe and to me it seemed much better than the old one. We were processing increasing numbers of people into the Division and I thought that they all looked so very young. You have to remember I had just celebrated another birthday and now was already an old man of 23 at that time.

Then it was January 30th and, no big surprise, once again I was on guard duty. I couldn't complain much, since hostilities for the last four weeks had been drastically reduced in our immediate area; the frequency of these little excursions to the perimeter had been reduced to every five days. I shared this bunker with two other "Admin Bad Men." Jim was sleeping because he had the third shift starting at 9:00, but more likely because he had partied a little too much the night before. Tim had the first shift starting at 7:00 and I had the 8:00 watch. Each staggered shift lasted two hours; the mandate was at all times two people were to remain awake while the other one slept. We only had one folding green canvas army cot and, since fire ants usually made sleeping on the ground impossible, it was pretty easy to follow the rules – although not always.

The 1st Admin Company was situated in a corner of the base camp so we had twice as many bunkers as those adjacent to us. At the time we had a total of eight bunkers plus a 40-foot-high tower that stood further back from the perimeter corner. I thought it would be nice to have tower duty just once, since the view was supposed to be spectacular and at night you'd see the lights of Saigon dancing in the distance.

Each bunker was basically the same. The 8' X 10' interior was dug about four feet into the ground and it had a wood floor. Heavy timber walls and ceiling added another four feet to the interior height. The structure was reinforced with concrete and then covered with many layers of sandbags so the walls and ceiling ranged anywhere from three-to-four-feet thick. The front of the bunker facing the perimeter was poured concrete and had two openings about four feet apart, one for each of the two machine guns. Each 18" wide port had a fixed obtuse angle left-to-right range of movement so the machine guns in our bunker and those in the adjacent bunkers had a permanent crossfire set up. The guns were aimed just ten inches off the ground, the premise being when shot in the leg the enemy would fall into the path of the bullets that followed, and lying on the ground offered no escape from the onslaught.

The back side of the bunker faced the hootches and had a slender stepped entry. A couple of feet behind this narrow portal a large wood timber bunker box sat filled to the top with sandbags; this protected the bunker entry from an attack from the rear. The folding cot was normally set up behind this box on the hootch side to afford a little privacy at night.

The walls inside the bunker were plastered with hand-drawn maps illustrating the numbered zones of fire that bunker position had. If attacked, each bunker would call the command post and pin-point the location of any hostile movement. With this info it was easy to coordinate our available fire power. On paper this sounded great; but with all the stress of being under fire, making a phone call was not an easy decision to make. The top of the bunker had a domed shape similar to that of an igloo and was designed to deflect any incoming fire. I never wanted to see this defensive refuge in action but, regardless, thought it and I were ready if ever needed.

Before we did anything else we had to secure the bunker. The first thing on the agenda was to check the placement and connections for the Claymore mines. The M18 Claymore mine was an army green curved plastic box about one and one half inch thick and five inches high by nine inches wide, and it had two pairs of folding scissor legs to be stabbed into the ground when placed. Its convex shape had "FACE TOWARD ENEMY" embossed on the business side, and you really didn't want to point that thing in the wrong direction.

Once the Claymore mine was aimed and set in place, a blasting cap was inserted into the top. Then wires were strung back to the safety zone. Just like in the field, these wires were buried to help hide the device. The blasting cap looked innocent enough; it was a metal tube about the size of the larger firecrackers I had used to terrorize the Kansas countryside when I was a kid. You had to be very careful. If you were holding the cap in your hand and it accidentally exploded, you could "kiss your fingers goodbye." The mines were already set up about 50 meters in front of the bunker position. The kill radius was supposed to be 50 meters in front and 20 meters behind the mine, but it could be deadly up to 250 meters in front and 100 meters behind. It was best to hug the ground as far away as you could before pressing the handheld clacker (detonator). The mine contained 700 ball bearings one quarter inch in diameter encased in a plastic wrapper and backed by C4 plastic explosive. When fired, it went off like a giant shotgun shell blasting a widening path of devastation and there was nowhere to hide.

Our perimeter defenses were a permanent installation; so the Claymores were already set in place and backed by sandbags. All we had to do is take a little stroll out to the perimeter and make sure the bad guys hadn't turned the mines around and that the wires had not been cut. This had happened years earlier to other units on our base camp, but it was a much more frequent problem for the grunts out in the boonies. The only risk during our inspection was that a sniper might consider you a target. Snipers had not been an issue for a long time so there was little concern, but I always wore my flak jacket and helmet whenever I was on guard duty, just in case.

It was rumored we had a resident sniper christened "Admin Charlie" who resided in a spider hole maybe 400 yards in front of the west side of our outer wire. Presumably, once daily, he dutifully pointed his rifle skyward and fired a couple of times before closing the lid to his residence. If it was true, no one wanted that reluctant sharp-shooter shot (he or she just might be replaced with a more dedicated soul) and so he was left alone. I never knew anyone who had seen him and since shots were always being fired all around us for target practice at nearby ranges, no one paid much attention to the occasional shots being fired; that is unless you found you were the target.

While close to the outer wire, we surveyed the minefield that separated our killing field from the outermost barbed wire fences and concertina coiled barbed wire installations – all nasty stuff. The mine field was about 35 meters across and was mostly made up of individual compression-type anti-personnel mines. As a result of the rainy season, our minefield on occasion had been transformed into a raging river, resulting in the mines being partially or fully exposed, some upside down and others lying on their sides. They were easy to spot, their plastic housing had a bright robin's egg blue color. The mines had the diameter of a medium sized can of beans but were only half as tall. The explosive charge and serrated metal loosely wound spring provided shrapnel which was meant to maim and not kill, this is because an injured fighter needed one or two people to help him; the enemy KIA were often simply left in place by their peers. It seems the VC did not have the same regard for retrieving the dead our country always strived for. We were told there were still enough mines in place to act as an effective deterrent, but I doubted it since I knew the mine field had already been scheduled to be replaced.

After our little tour, Tim and I entered the bunker and made sure everything was securely in place. We looked at the control panel and checked to make sure the plastic safety covers for the foo gas (AKA fougasse) cannon firing and Claymore Mine switches were in place. The foo gas cannon was a very effective deterrent which acted like napalm when detonated. It was made from two 55-gallon drums welded end to end and buried into the ground at maybe a 30° angle with a loosely fitted metal cap. It was filled with jelled gasoline or napalm (I never knew which was used) and had a stick of dynamite as the ignitor. It had an effective range of 150-250 meters and when fired made a deep roaring sound as it consumed all the air and transformed anyone in its path into crispy critters. The control panel was armed and ready to go. The EOD engineers made weekly checks and verified all the detonator wires were in working order, so it was never on our "to do" list.

Next we inspected the machine guns and made sure the 200-round belts were inserted into the guns' firing chambers and that the ammo boxes that held them were properly aligned. There were an additional 4 ammo boxes set in a storage shelf unit bringing the total machine gun ammo count up to 1,200 for both guns. The shelves also had grenades for the M79 launcher, a dozen frag grenades, a couple of smoke canisters, and half a dozen handheld flares. The M79 grenade launcher looked like a huge sawed-off shotgun with a 2" diameter barrel. When fired, it made a noise that sounded like a hollow "thump" and so was apply nicknamed the "thump-gun." It shot a 40 mm grenade round that armed itself after 3 revolutions and had the impact of a hand grenade. The advantage was it could be aimed and accurately placed much further away than its hand-thrown counterpart. In addition, each guard had a cloth bandolier of six 20-round magazines for our M14's. Never thought about it much then, but we had a hell of a lot of firepower at our fingertips.

After completing our audit and making sure everything was in order, Tim and I started taking pictures. Sunset was about half an hour away and made a great backdrop for the action shots we took of each other in various standing, sitting, and prone shooting poses. We still had the M14 rifles; so the pictures were reminiscent of many of the World War II and Korean War photos and movies I had seen. The slim crescent of a waxing moon did little to light up the night, but a huge spray of brilliant stars had followed the sun and blanketed the heavens with an intense glittering display; and we knew it was time to settle down. Even on such a clear night, the outer wire was a mosaic of shifting shadows and shapes. We sat on top of the bunker box protecting the bunker entry looking at Saigon and started to "BS" about everything and nothing – just another boring, sleepless night on the perimeter.

The time passed slowly and eventually Tim jumped off and sat on the bunker steps. Everything was so still you could almost hear your own heartbeat, and my eyelids started to get very heavy in search of a little tranquility. It was only 10:30, but I was beat; I had skipped my 9:00 nap and was now paying the price. I looked down from my perch atop the rear bunker box and saw Tim holding a small flashlight in his mouth and writing another letter home. The wind was still and a serene silence cloaked the night. I imagined myself in a hammock gently swinging myself to sleep, but then my due diligence intervened and spoke to me: "OK, Wake Up!" Then I looked up toward the Big and Little Dippers and wondered how far away they were and how we looked to them. Once again common sense came to the rescue: "Hey, Wake Up Stupid and Get Off Your Ass!"

I grudgingly got up and slowly walked around a bit; I had another hour and a half to go and needed to keep moving in order to stay awake. The Vietnamese Lunar Tet Celebration was starting at midnight and we had been told a cease-fire had been negotiated; it was supposed to be a break in the hostilities and a time of rest, just like it had been the previous year. It sounded pretty good to me and I thought a little peace and quiet would be good for everyone.

After a while I saw the sergeant of the guard approaching and warned Tim to join me up top. We had a cigarette with the sarge and he said it looked like the cease fire had already started and we could take it easy. That was great news and I couldn't help but start to think about my upcoming in-country R&R in Vung Tau due in about a week. I couldn't wait. The beach, the ocean, the girls, beer that didn't taste like it was tainted with vinegar, sleeping late, eating too much, hot showers 24/7, and maybe a cigar or two; it was going to be heaven.

Tim had hit the rack, Jim was off to the latrine, and my mind began to wander back to the days before the Army changed everything. I never knew how good I had it until it wasn't there anymore. Wasting time and self-indulgence were my majors in college. Even with all the vocational testing, I had no idea what I wanted to be. But I knew it wasn't law enforcement that the University of Illinois tests had indicated (knowing my anger issues I just might have added judge, jury, and executioner to my duties). So I chose accounting simply because I couldn't think of anything else. Reading, studying, and concentrating had always been very difficult for me. Knowing what I do now, I think maybe dyslexia had something to do with it – but that was no excuse then. Still, my choice of an accounting major was the reason I ended up at the Big Red One, very lucky. But then again, if I had kept my wits about me, I would have stayed in school and made something of myself and never would have been on guard duty that night. Fate, if it exists, is a fickle master.

Finally it was 12:00 AM and time for my nap. I smiled, told the guys to try and keep it down, and fell asleep as soon as my head found the cot. Maybe 40 minutes later, Tim roughly shook me awake and shouted I had to see something. I sat up and as my eyes found the light, I heard it before I saw it. Behind us, on the other side of the basecamp toward the chopper pads and Korean compound, mortars pounded the earth. There was a bright flash of light and a moment later you heard the explosion. I got up, looked at our perimeter, and couldn't see a thing. But in the distance, the lights of Saigon were no longer dancing – they were exploding. Mortars and rockets arced over the city and reminded me of the days when I held a Roman candle in my hand and shook it until all the different colored balls of fire were exhausted. It may have looked like a 4th of July celebration but actually was more akin to Sodom and Gomorrah.

A staccato of an AK47 firing immediately got our attention and, as mortars started to hit the perimeter 300 yards to our right, the 3 of us dove into the bunker. The pounding was intense, but we only heard the noise and felt the quake of the impacts. Luckily, none of the mortars were too close to us and so far no gunfire came our way. The attack was short lived but everybody hunkered down waiting for the next session to start. We took the safety off each of the two M60 machine guns, chambered the first rounds on the belts, and surveyed the perimeter but did not see any movement. We hung our bandoliers of M14 ammo on wall hooks and stored our rifles in the gun rack. I took the M79 grenade launcher and loaded it, made sure the safety was on, and then placed it back on top of the storage shelving unit.

There was an ARVN camp about a mile to our left and it sounded like they were in big trouble. We heard the distinctive sound of their 50-caliber machine gun being fired with abandon. It was mounted on a 360° track atop a 40-foot-high tower in the middle of their base camp. During WWII, the 50-caliber machine guns were used as anti-aircraft weapons. Apparently unskilled or unable, they could not keep the gun aimed at the VC. Slowly but surely the line of fire got higher and higher and the bullets headed our way. Every 5th round is a tracer designed so you can see and adjust the line of fire. We could see all right. As we looked out our machine gun ports, we saw the minefield brightly exploding here and there after being torn up by the 50-caliber rounds spewing their damage, then they slowly but loudly stomped our way. We hit and hugged the deck and I heard myself say a little prayer. You could hear the sandbags around us taking hits that shook the bunker. Then one solitary round blasted through the wall and disappeared into the other, about two feet above our heads, but it did not find a mark.

Surprisingly I really wasn't scared in the moment but instantly became very, very pissed off. I wasn't Audie Murphy, but I seriously wanted to let those little bastards know we were here and had some "teeth." For me, there was something about being shot at that transforms one's perceived sense of humanity into vengeful insanity. I was smart enough to stay put but capable of doing whatever was necessary that night to protect myself with complete abandon. That probably explains why I never held or owned a gun after I returned to the "World."

Soon it was fairly quiet again except for distant gunfire, the wail of our company sirens, and the loud speakers shouting "RED ALERT." Our line of defense filled in as the troops from the hootches quickly set up positions between the bunkers and two more people joined us at our bunker. Everyone was ready. Helmets, ponchos, flak jackets, and M14s were the dress code for that evening. The ARVN camp was still burning and all you could see of Saigon was an intense glow and a ball of smoke, periodically shattered by the glare of rocket trails, explosions, and constant streams of tracers swaying and snaking back and forth, upward and downward, everywhere.

A few infantry guys joined us on the perimeter and had starlight scopes mounted on their M16s. A starlight scope intensified the available star brightness and moonlight as it greatly enhanced and magnified both the range and clarity of view into a light green image; you could literally see in the dark. The only trouble was on that night there was too much light, making the devices useless; so they were soon detached and stored. Every 10 minutes or so, someone in a bunker or one the troops in between, set off handheld flares to light up the outer wire to see if anything was out there. Everybody strained intently to see as the flares burned brightly – hanging and swaying from their tiny parachutes, they did their job of lighting up the area for a minute or so; but nothing was there.

We were ready for and fully expected a frontal attack. Thank God, it never came. As dawn approached and for a good number of days afterward, there were constant streams of squadrons of five or six Bell UH-1 Iroquois choppers, better known as Hueys, flying sorties around our camp and out to every direction on the compass. Many headed straight for Saigon. Our company made three perimeter sweeps that day and, although they found evidence of movement, they saw nothing else. The tower was now staffed with half a dozen people all with binoculars glued to their faces, surveying everything in front of us.

As the sun rose, it became apparent our company compound had been very lucky. Other than the need to inspect and repair our minefield and replace sandbags on a couple of the bunkers, nothing had been destroyed. Still, the rumor mills were in full gear and you heard everything: it was all over for us, we lost the other 3 base camps, generals had been killed, the next attack would be much worse, and somewhat hopefully that we had been victorious. Very few believed any of that B.S. or any of the other nonsense gushing out by the minute.

Eye-burning smoke from the ARVN camp filled the air, Saigon had all but disappeared behind a dense haze, and the lingering smell of cordite and burnt wood assaulted the senses. Occasionally, a startling melody of gunshots were heard, some close, but mostly far away. Distant mortar strikes, napalm explosions, the Air Force jets and our Army Hueys, both launching rockets and firing machine guns, all pretty much rattled any hope for tranquility. It all seemed so surreal to me. I felt like an isolated observer safely removed from any harm but mentally recording everything, or maybe I was just in a state of shock.

For the present, we were safe. The attack left the 1st Admin Company mostly unscathed and we had no casualties. I'm not so sure how things worked out for everybody else on our base camp; mortars and bullets usually take their toll. Two of our basecamp gates had been attacked with RPGs (Rocket-Propelled Grenades), mortars, and machine guns; everything had been thrown at them, but they had stood strong and neither was breached. In addition to frequent heavily armed perimeter sweeps, choppers also swept our perimeter, and squads of U.S. and Korean troops launched both search-and-destroy and ambush missions to help determine and direct our next course of action. Our responses were all well thought out, quickly implemented, and thankfully proved to be very effective.

During the day, supplies were brought up and we filled and replaced the sandbags on our bunker, adding another layer to the top and the side facing the ARVN camp. More ammo was brought up and stored inside the bunker, and a lot more handheld flares were added to our supplies. The five of us stayed at the bunker until 6:00 that evening before being relieved. We were exhausted but not sleepy, and each of us was very thankful to still be alive. A couple of days later they started to dig two more bunkers to reinforce our perimeter.

The Tet Offensive of 1968 was the start and end of everything. Our Vietnamese and U.S. military clandestine resources had clearly seen something unusual was happening. The people in charge failed to believe there was any real potential for disaster, or maybe they were simply too stupid and/or arrogant to heed the warnings – who knows? I do know that in Saigon the previous evening there had been a party for about 200 officers in progress when the attack started (guess they weren't too concerned either). Simply said, I believe the whole intelligence community had too much conflicting information to make an accurate assessment. Or maybe it was just another example of "SNAFU" and "FUBAR" used in tandem to run (or ruin) the show.

The whole mess smelled and reminded me of the treachery the Japanese perpetrated on December 7th, 1941. While the Japanese representatives were in Washington D.C. involved in peace negotiations, their fighter planes were approaching Pearl Harbor. Guess it's true – history has an annoying habit of repeating itself. The devastation visited upon Pearl Harbor was much worse than Tet, and the only option for America back then was to immediately join the fight in WWII. Although the Tet Offensive was a different type of deceit, the act was a wakeup call to strengthen our defenses and for us to be more aggressive in our offense strategies

The U.S. had observed troop movements but simply thought it all was all in anticipation of the upcoming holiday. Nobody knew the enemy's strength, resolve, or how much danger there really was. For months the NVA had used the Ho Chi Minh trail to bring in huge quantities of arms, ammunition, and lots of troops, and apparently we had no idea of what or how much had been brought in. The Lunar Holiday had always been a time of peace and previously a ceasefire was observed by both sides in respect for the time-honored event. Before Tet, hostile engagements, particularly in the south, had been reduced to a trickle and seemed to indicate a time of rest for both sides. Ultimately we all believed the upcoming holiday observance would only be as peaceful as it had been before.

Au contraire.

9

Say It Ain't So-History

It may seem a little disjointed to insert this history now, but it is important understand what had happened to Vietnam up to this point in my story. Before continuing my personal chronicle and diatribe, I believe it's about time to review the annals of how America became involved in the Vietnam War before I got there – and, yes, it was very much a war.

I don't know about you, but I define war as a hostile conflict between two or more parties or countries with the intent of each to defeat the other. In Vietnam, the United States provided advisors and training regimens, weapons and ammunition, housing, equipment, supplies, transportation networks, air support, security protocols, and too many American lives – everything required to find and kill the enemy. I think General Patton said it best, to paraphrase: "The purpose of war is to find and kill the enemy son of a bitch before the enemy son of a bitch finds and kills you."

To refer to people shooting and killing each other by the then politically correct term of "police action" may be fine for the present day cities of Chicago, New York, Detroit and, unfortunately, so many others; but when literally hundreds of thousands of people are involved, politically correct phraseology simply doesn't cut it and without a doubt it is in fact insulting and demeaning.

OK, now that you know that I think the Vietnam Conflict was actually an American War, let's take a look at the Vietnam saga. I am by no stretch of the imagination any kind of historian or wannabee; the following is my interpretation of everything I've researched to date. It may be fraught with errors, and I sincerely apologize if in any way I offend or misinform anyone; but I think you'll get the general idea anyway.

VIETNAM & THE UNITED STATES

1940 to 1949

When WWII started, basically the Japanese kicked the French out and occupied Vietnam. Soon a seemingly simple gentleman returned, after a 30-year hiatus, to help set up and direct the resistance. His chosen name was Ho Chi Minh whose name translates to "he who enlightens." Although a devote Communist, he asked America for help and we quickly agreed (liking the Japanese the way we did back then). For several months, the U.S. provided training and weapons for Ho Chi Minh's Viet Ming resistance fighters (the same thing we continue to do for so many others even today). To inspire his followers and supporters, he even had an American officer (a Major) help him draft an influential speech using quotes from the American Declaration of Independence.

When WWII ended, British forces declared martial law in Saigon, then supplied arms to the recently released French troops. The French strived to regain control of Vietnam which they still considered a colony. This was not popular with the Vietnamese. Riots immediately broke out and each side committed horrific atrocities on the other. To help restore order, the British commander ordered some of the Japanese prisoners of war, whom they still had interned, to open fire on the Vietnamese. An American lieutenant colonel was accidently killed (who at the time was considered to be the first U.S. casualty in Vietnam) and soon after America withdrew all support.

1950 to 1959

Due to Communist widespread incursions throughout the whole country, in 1950 President Truman became the first president to involve the United States. He formally recognized South Vietnam and dispatched a group of military advisors. Shortly thereafter, China in turn formally recognized North Vietnam and agreed to provide assistance.

At the time the French were still trying to reclaim Vietnam as their colony and had captured Dien Bien Phu in 1953. In response, Ho Chi Minh sent 100,000 Viet Minh troops with almost as many additional support people to retake the area. The consequent siege ultimately trapped about 15,000 French troops. On May 7, 1954, the French surrendered after suffering many losses. As had been agreed, the next day on May 8th, the Geneva Peace Conference talks convened, and soon after an agreed-upon list of compromises were signed. The exit of the French begins. The agreement effectively divided the North and South countries of Vietnam with a Demilitarized Zone along the 17th parallel, just as in the Korean era along the 38th parallel (with similar ramifications).

In 1955, President Eisenhower offered economic aid to South Vietnam which began in January; by October, South Vietnam declared itself the Republic of Vietnam. A nationwide election had been proposed and was to be held in 1956 to unite the North and the South, but the South refused to participate and blocked the inevitable Communist victory, fearing Ho Chi Minh would be elected. A little later that Year, Ho Chi Minh went to Moscow and readily agreed to accept Soviet aid.

In December of 1955, North Vietnam Communists under the guise of land reforms, took many land owners to "people's tribunals." Thousands were executed or sent to labor camps. Meanwhile, in South Vietnam, President Diem rewarded Catholic supporters by giving them land seized from Buddhist peasants, but did not take anything from any of the large land owners. Peasants hoping for land reform were left in the dust and once again were most assuredly not happy.

In April of 1956, the last of the French troops left the country. In North Vietnam during November, peasants protesting for land reforms were squashed by Communist forces – resulting in about 6,000 dead and many displaced to unknown destinations.

In May of 1957, South Vietnam's president Ngo Dinh Diem visited President Eisenhower, and Ike proclaimed that Ngo was a "miracle man." Eisenhower promised to continue economic and military aid. About this time, the term "Viet Cong" became popular signifying a new Communist strategy, and it replaces the name of "Viet Minh."

A Communist insurgency of terror started in 1957; by year's end, over 400 South Vietnamese officials had either been executed or assassinated. In 1958 they made gains by establishing militia strongholds in the Mekong Delta.

In March of 1959 Ho Chi Minh proclaims a "People's War" to unite all of Vietnam, signaling the dawn of the "Second Indochina War." A couple of months later, construction of the Ho Chi Minh trail begins. Because of the catastrophes it fueled, it became a tragic "Trail of Tears" unparalleled by anything else in the sad history of Vietnam. The Ho Chi Minh trail eventually became a 1,400-mile-long passage spanning north to south along Vietnam's western border, and it journeyed through portions of Laos and Cambodia. In 1959, it took about six months to travel from North Vietnam to the south. By 1968, it took only six weeks, and in 1970 a pipeline for fuel was added. In retrospect, in a limited way, it truly rivaled President Eisenhower's United States cross-country super highway initiative as an effective transportation corridor.

About 4,000 troops originally from South Vietnam who had moved north returned as NVA and infiltrated the southern region via the trail. In July, two American advisers were killed and historically became the first official casualties of the Vietnam War.

1960

In 1960, North Vietnam imposed universal military conscription for a tour in the military with an unspecified length of service. In November there was a failed coup in the South against President Diem by his own disgruntled officers. Unbelievably, about 50,000 of the malcontents were eventually arrested, many innocents were tortured then executed, and Diem's popularity waned. Thousands fearing arrest escaped to the North and later, just like before, many returned as VC or NVA.

It is impossible to know how many South Vietnamese citizens eventually joined the Viet Cong. Some were forced into conscription under the threat of death, which the VC willingly exhibited way too many times. Others were angry with the ever-evolving leadership and politics of Saigon, whose mandates were prejudiced and very destructive to their way of life. And let's not forget about the impact of the war itself. Whether on purpose or resulting from "friendly fire," the consequences were always death and destruction. Even a superficial glance reveals that the South Vietnam government and its partners, including us, inflicted a lot of agony ultimately resulting in rage. I believe the combined allied forces of the South were more responsible for the escalation of the war than anything else. But then that's nothing unusual – all part of the "War Is Hell" rule book.

1961

January 1961 sees Premier Nikita Khrushchev offer his support for "wars of national liberation" and this emboldens North Vietnam. A little later John F. Kennedy is elected and says at his inauguration: "We shall pay any price, bear any burden, meet any hardship, support any friend, oppose any foe, to ensure the survival and success of liberty." He becomes the third president to provide support and by doing so inevitably escalates America's intrusion into South Vietnam. And so the line was most assuredly drawn in the sand, Democracy verses Communism. After the speech, President Eisenhower confidentially tells the newly elected superstar he believes the U.S. will soon have to supply fighting men to Vietnam.

In May, Vice President Johnson visits President Diem and assures help is on the way. President Kennedy then sends more advisors and helicopters to aid in the training of the ARVNs (Army of the Republic of Vietnam) and to improve the response time in combat situations – leading to more U.S. involvement in battle situations. The number of "advisors" sent will eventually total 16,000 people.

1962

In January of 1962, Kennedy was asked if any Americans were involved in the fighting and he simply responds "No." In August, he signs a Foreign Assistance Act, and a U.S. Special Forces base camp is quickly set up at Khe Sanh, near the border of North and South Vietnam, to monitor activity along the Ho Chi Minh trail.

1963

Buddhists riot in the south in August of 1963, protesting Diem's oppressive dynasty, and accuse Kennedy as being part of the problem. A number of Buddhist priests commit suicide in protest by pouring gasoline on themselves while seated and then igniting it. More and more become outraged every day and Diem imposes martial law controlled by his tyrannical brother Nhu, whose onslaught only fans the fire for action. In September Kennedy tells news reporter Walter Cronkite that President Diem is "out of touch" with his people; but then he warns that if America was to withdraw from South Vietnam, many other Asian countries would be at a real risk for a Communist takeover (this concern later becomes known as "The Domino Theory").

Predictably, another coup follows in November and Diem and Nhu flee but are soon caught and arrested by General Ming's rebel officers. While traveling back to Saigon, they are both assassinated, and this time the people of Saigon were not unhappy. Sadly, on November 22, President John F. Kennedy is also assassinated in Dallas, Texas. I believe that if he had lived, J.F.K would have started to reduce the numbers of Americans stationed in Vietnam. President Johnson is quickly sworn in and becomes the fourth president to oversee the Vietnam War. However, the new President did not think that a reduction in force was a good idea and soon campaigns for a more aggressive strategy of American involvement. He is the one who oversaw and promoted the incredible increase in American troops on the ground, placing hundreds of thousands of young men in harm's way.

In November of 1963, President Johnson simply states he will not "lose Vietnam." In January, General Khanh becomes the leader of South Vietnam. Later in March, the U.S. secretly backs bombing raids on the Ho Chi Minh trail. Then the American National Security Council recommends that the bombing of Hanoi needs to stop. Johnson holds off, but he does approve covert operations using South Vietnamese commandos.

Confused or disgusted yet? Wait – the history of Vietnam makes so many twists and turns it gets even crazier. Every country's history is convoluted, but few can match the perplexity of Vietnam. It's sort of like Chicago's weather; if you don't like it, don't worry; it'll probably change in a couple of minutes. And now, as Cole Porter prophetically wrote, we "Begin the Beguine."

1964

In July of 1964, General William C. Westmoreland becomes the American commandant in Vietnam. In August of 1964, three North Vietnamese patrol boats attack the American destroyer U.S.S. Maddox in the Gulf of Tonkin, firing machine guns and torpedoes. Almost everything missed and there were no casualties. In retaliation, the U.S. surprises the North Vietnamese and bombs oil refineries and seaports. Two of the American pilots were shot down, one died, and the other became one of the first guests at the infamous Hoa Lo prison better known as the "Hanoi Hilton." Almost everyone in the United States applauded President Johnson's decision to attack, and he was nominated as the candidate for President at the Democratic National Convention. While campaigning, he pledges not to send American boys to do what the Asian boys should be doing.

In October, the Soviet Leader Nikita Khrushchev is replaced by Leonid Brezhnev. A few days later, China tests its first atomic bomb and sends troops to the Vietnamese border, all in response to what becomes known as the Gulf of Tonkin escalation. On November 1st, the Viet Cong attack Bien Hoa airbase for the first time. It was only eighteen miles north of Saigon and five Americans were killed. On the 3rd, Lyndon B. Johnson is re-elected President with an overwhelming majority of the vote. There are now 23,000 American advisors in country.

How many coups were there in Saigon in that 1960's decade? I lost count with all the turmoil, so my best guess is a couple of dozen; but I really don't know for sure. Coalitions of military and political forces were constantly struggling to either take over or hold onto the leadership, but it was a continuous melee and the control of South Vietnam was often up for grabs. Hard to keep up, ain't it?

1965

President Johnson takes the oath of presidency on January 20th, 1965 and announces "We can never again stand aside, prideful in isolation." On the 27th, after another coup, General Khanh finally seizes full control of the South Vietnam government. On February 8th, the Viet Cong attack the U.S. camp at Pleiku killing eight Americans. We answer by bombing a North Vietnamese base camp by Dong Hoi. In Hanoi, the Soviet Prime Minister Kosygin agrees to provide surface-to-air missiles. Also in February, yet another Saigon coup removes General Khanh and replaces him with a new government led by Dr. Phan Huy Quat.

What a world!

February 22, 1965, General Westmoreland requests two battalions of Marine reinforcements to respond to the estimated 6,000 VC near Da Nang; the request is granted. An operation called Rolling Thunder starts in early March of 1965 (and lasted on and off until the end of 1968). Rolling Thunder was an orchestrated mission to bomb North Vietnam's transportation system, industrial targets, and air defenses to stop the flow of men and supplies to the South. Basically the plan was to inflict as many casualties as possible in an effort to demoralize the North. On March 8th, about 3,500 U.S. Marines land at China Beach and join the 23,000 advisors now in country. This was the first time since the Korean War that American battle-ready ground troops set foot on the Asian mainland. On March 29th the VC attacks the U.S. Embassy in Saigon.

April 1, 1965, the President calls up two more battalions of Marines, plus about 20,000 additional logistical personnel, and later announces troops in Vietnam are eligible for combat pay – sure sounds like war to me. In May, about 3,500 United States Army soldiers from the 173rd Airborne Brigade arrive. Rolling Thunder intensifies and wanes many times in an attempt to entice North Vietnam to join peace talks. This appeal never worked. And no surprise, all the North did was put off answering the invitation to negotiate a peaceful settlement whenever the bombing stopped, then hurried to repair the damage and relocate troops before the U.S. got frustrated and started "Rolling" again. This scenario was repeated an unknown number of times until the U.S. stopped the program late in 1968.

OK, I have to interject something here. Although I am not a war monger, I do believe that if you are in a war and you plan to win it, you need to be very dedicated and willing to fight it without restriction, even with bombs when necessary. Repeatedly, we demonstrated a lack of commitment in Vietnam, and this only strengthened the enemy's resolve. We paid for this shameful, stupid, ineffective bombing strategy with an unnecessarily high cost in American and Vietnamese lives.

In my opinion, the almighty media in all the many forms that were prevalent during the Vietnam era, owe the American people and every soldier on the planet a long overdue apology. I know they will never do it. I mean, who is going to say anything if they don't? Still, they do deserve some of the credit for all the losses suffered. The freedom of speech our Constitution guarantees does not exonerate nor condone the pompous media responses that encouraged, manipulated, and covertly threatened the politicians responsible for all those bad decisions which resulted in the death of so many. I wonder if this country's so-called political leaders, the always "knows what's best for the country" grandiose entertainment industry, and our ever-invasive media will ever get it through their self-righteous, know-it-all, thick skulls; you cannot legislate morality – period. You can teach it, reward it, define it, punish it, and confine it, but you will never be able to wave your magic wand and make it so.

War is a terrible thing, and I sincerely hope one day it will no longer be; but until that most unlikely day, we need to be prepared to defend ourselves and act as aggressively as necessary to sustain our American values and defend our Constitution. If you decide to go to war, then you must fight to win. If your only battle plan is to make everyone happy, do not go to war. Enough said. And now, on with the rest of the story.

On July 28, 1965, President Johnson promises to send 44 combat battalions to Vietnam increasing our presence to 125,000 men in country. To sustain the increased military support, the number of draft notices sent out is increased to around 35,000 a month, double the previous quantity.

The Big Red One arrived in Vietnam on July 12, 1965. On July 17th, the 1st Infantry Division's 2d Battalion, 18th Infantry, came under fire near Bien Hoa; this was their first hostile action since WWII. The following night they were mortared by the VC and suffered their first man killed in action. By fall of 1965 the United States has about 150,000 people in country; and about 250,000 NVA and VC are waiting for them.

In mid-November, the 1st Cavalry Battalion responds to an intelligence report that 200 NVA are in the Ia Drang Valley. First they had the artillery bombard the enemy positions for half an hour to clear the LZ. Then they send 450 Air Cav troopers by helicopter. Each chopper can only carry six soldiers and their gear on each trip, so many sorties are required. Getting everybody there is further complicated by the size of the landing area, LZ X-Ray; it can only accommodate about 6 choppers at a time. After less than half of the Air Cavalry had been dropped off, they capture a lone NVA soldier. He quickly tells them there are not 200 NVA in the area; there are three battalions (or about 1,600 of the enemy).

The balance of the U.S. troops arrived by nightfall under horrific conditions. By the next morning there are 85 U.S. dead and wounded. Two misguided attack aircraft drop napalm on the U.S. positions, killing and injuring four troopers. The fighting intensifies and the battle becomes a nightmare. The 1st Cav commander makes an urgent call for "Broken Arrow" which diverts all aircraft in the area to respond immediately and drop everything they have on the enemy. Two days later we win the biggest battle to date, but 234 U.S. are dead. It was later estimated that there were 3,000 dead NVA. Because of the better than 10:1 kill ratio, the term "body count" becomes the standard measure of our success. It was about then it was also decided the use of "search and destroy" missions was the best attack strategy to use going forward. My only question is, best for whom?

You may have noted that although we were supposed to be fighting an enemy force of an estimated 1,600 NVA troops we had somehow managed to kill 3,000. This is probably due to the fact that many more nearby enemy troops had been added to the fight. Still, the battlefield intelligence and statistics were often somewhat questionable and the accuracy of the resulting tallies was at times considered debatable.

1965 saw a steady increase in Vietnam War Protests, and burning one's draft card became a rite of passage for many potential draftees. So much so that in August, President Johnson signs a law punishing burning the card with a 5-year prison sentence and a $1,000 fine. It didn't work, and protesters burning cards were broadcast nightly on TV. Vietnam was the first televised war. Each and every day, newsreels depicted the aftermath of horrific acts with graphic details, all painting a very ugly picture. War is horrid, brutal, and terrifying, and you can't exactly blame people for not wanting to be drafted. Still, although I firmly believe you have the right to protest, I also believe you have an obligation to serve your country.

The end of 1965 sees our dead and wounded tallies growing daily, resulting from the increasing number of hostile encounters. In South Vietnam, it is estimated that at least 30,000 ARVN troops had deserted and that the Viet Cong control 50% of the countryside. On a brighter note, General Westmoreland is chosen as 1965's" Man of the Year" by Life Magazine.

1966

In January of 1966, there are 180,000 U.S. troops in Vietnam. In March, there is an attempt to repeal the Gulf of Tonkin Resolution, but it failed miserably. The battles continue and the U.S. finally bombs the city of Hanoi. Maybe it's better late than never, but I think it was way too late. By September, there are 300,000 U.S. troops in country. Also in September, French President Charles de Gaulle visits Cambodia and asks that the U.S. withdraw from Vietnam. In November, President Johnson visits Cam Ranh Bay to boost morale. Later it is estimated that 40% of the economic aid America sent to Vietnam was either stolen and/or could be found on the black market. 1966 ends with 389,000 troops in country, more than double the number there in January. The total killed in action now totals 5,008 or about 140 per month since January of 1964, four or five men, each and every day.

1967

In 1967, things were really beginning to ramp up. During WWII soldiers were in combat for an average of 10 days per year. In Vietnam the average infantryman was in the boonies in harm's way for as many as 240 times a year. Most Vietnam combat groups went out on patrol for 30-to-40 days at a time, rested maybe for a week, and then went out again. In February, Operation Junction City is launched and four weeks later there are 2,700 VC dead with 30 captured; our losses were 280 killed and 1,600 wounded. We were still maintaining that 10:1 kill ratio and seemingly winning every battle, but there was very little to celebrate.

On April 20th, U.S. bombers target the Haiphong harbor in North Vietnam for the first time; and notable for me on that day, I was inducted into the Army. Also in April, Senator (and Presidential hopeful) Richard Nixon visits Vietnam and complains that anti-war protests are "prolonging the war;" and General Westmorland agrees. That same month, Martin Luther King, Jr. says the war is undermining President Johnson's "Great Society" social reform programs. 200,000 anti-war protesters gather in New York and San Francisco. In April and into May, the Marine base near the northern border of South Vietnam at Khe Sanh becomes involved in heavy fighting. The NVA (North Vietnamese Army) lose 950 troops and 160 Americans died.

In early May, the United States is condemned during a mock war crimes tribunal in Stockholm orchestrated by a British philosopher. In New York, 70,000 march to support the war led by a Firehouse Captain. Fighting intensifies as North Vietnam launches a well-thought-out, year-long offensive strategy against the South. In July, General Westmoreland requests 200,000 more troops, but Johnson only approves 45,000. At the end of July, a punctured fuel tank on the USS Forestall in the Gulf of Tonkin catches on fire and 135 crewman die – the worst naval disaster since World War II. In August, California Governor Ronald Reagan says we should get out of Vietnam because too many targets are off limits (smart man). By the end of September, a total 6,900 Americans had died that year in Vietnam - more than in the previous five years combined.

In October of 1967, it is determined about 50% of Americans are against the Vietnam War and think we should pull out. I never got the message and so arrived at Cam Ranh Bay on the 12th. A little later that month, 55,000 protesters accost the Pentagon and in London the American embassy is also assaulted. In November, President Johnson strives for peace talks, but Hanoi is not interested. Later, General Westmoreland is quoted in Time Magazine as saying "I hope they try something because we are looking for a fight." (He all too soon gets his wish).

The NVA and VC were an elusive enemy and they preferred ambushes and surprise attacks rather than prolonged battles in the field. Whenever the battle got too hot for them their primary strategy was to melt away into local villages, hide in the enormous network of tunnel complexes, or to flee to Cambodia and Laos. When nearby villages were searched, the people either sympathized with the enemy or were too afraid of brutal reprisals to say anything; whichever, the end result is no one said anything. Not one time did a villager ever warn our soldiers of booby traps or ambushes. To this day I don't think anyone really knew who or what we were fighting for and, for those reasons, the relationship of the U.S. troops in the field and local villagers was strained at best. Nobody trusted anyone else and the potential for more catastrophes grew each day.

In November 1967, 6,000 NVA had been found in the Central Highlands near Dak To, and 6,500 U.S. soldiers were brought in. The battle direction eventually centers on taking hill number 875. Taking the hill was costly; ambushes, hand-to-hand combat, booby traps, and hellfire plagued our troops. Almost three weeks later we finally took the hill. The U.S. lost 376 people with another 1,441 wounded; sadly close to 30% of the KIA and wounded resulted from "friendly fire." The NVA and VC dead numbered around 800 and the rest had escaped, most to Cambodia and Laos. Some named hill 875 the first "Hamburger Hill," and it was a meat grinder of a fight; but later, another battle also earned that hard-won, dubious title. By the end of 1967, there were now 460,000 U.S. in country, and that year the U.S. had suffered losses of over 16,250 sons of our Nation, the enemy losses were an estimated 186,000 combatants, and the end still was nowhere in sight.

Protests at home and a scattering of battles and hostile events in South Vietnam continue to rage into the new year of 1968; President Johnson boldly states "...all challenges have been met. The enemy is not beaten, but he knows that he has met his master in the field." The bravado of Johnson and Westmoreland was encouraging to some, but not for all those U.S. young men serving our country; and all the bluster really didn't seem to bother Uncle Ho too much. This concludes the United States and Vietnam history lesson for now.

UNCLE HO

1890 to 1953

Now let's take a closer look at the architect of all the anarchy, Ho Chi Minh. As you know, his chosen name of Ho Chi Minh is roughly translated to mean "He Who Enlightens." That is all very poetic and inspiring, but he first chose the name Nguyen Ai Quoc (Nguyen the Patriot); although it is thought his real name was Nguyen Sinh Cung and, as far as I know, other options are also possible. To make things simple, he was lovingly christened "Uncle Ho" by his countrymen and not so lovingly by us. Presumably his primary purpose was to unify all of Vietnam, something that did not happen until long after his death and with questionable success.

He was born in 1890, the son of a civil servant for the Imperial Court. He became a student at the prestigious National Academy in Hue but left without graduating. He briefly worked as a teacher before traveling to Saigon to study navigation. In 1911, he found a job working in the kitchen of a French Steamer sailing between Saigon and Marseilles and he eventually moved to London in 1917 during WWI. In 1919, he traveled to France (where he took the name of Nguyen Ai Quoc). He worked humble jobs and became active in the Socialist movement. Also in 1919, he tried to give President Woodrow Wilson a proposal for Vietnam's independence at the Versailles Peace Conference, but he was unsuccessful.

He stayed in Paris still working at menial jobs until 1923, then traveled to Moscow to train insurgents at the headquarters for Communist International. He became active in the fifth congress and criticized the French Communist party for not opposing colonialism. In 1924, he traveled to Canton, China to train Vietnamese exiles in the art of revolution. In 1925, he organized the Communist Youth League. In 1926, uncle Ho wrote a book called "Duong Cach Menh" (*The Revolutionary Path*) which was used as a training manual. He quickly decided to go to the Soviet Union when Chiang Kai-shek kicked the Communists out of China. The next few years he visited Brussels, Paris, Thailand, and Hong Kong, always promoting Communist takeovers – especially of the French.

In 1930, rioting erupted in Vietnam due to the worldwide economic crisis. The French responded to the popularity of the newly formed Indochina Communist Party started by Ho from afar and arrested at least a 1,000 of his followers; many were given long prison sentences. In 1931, Ho Chi Minh was arrested in Hong Kong by the British and remained in jail until 1932. By 1932, the French had over 9,500 political prisoners in Vietnam. Upon his release, Uncle Ho returned to Moscow and stayed until 1938 to study and teach at the Lenin Institute. He returned to China and acted as an adviser during the Sino-Japanese War.

When WWII started, Germany and Russia agreed to a non-aggression pact and, without hesitation, the French in Vietnam banned the French Communist Party. Ho went to China in 1940 and then returned to Vietnam (after an absence of 30 years) and organized the Viet Minh. It is at this time he begins to actually use the name Ho Chi Minh. America briefly intervenes to provide supplies and training to help him fight the Japanese but quickly exits the scene. In 1942, Ho returned to China and was once again arrested and imprisoned for two years; guess no good deed goes unpunished. In 1944, Uncle Ho is allowed to return again to Vietnam. As leader of the Viet Minh in 1945, he declares independence from Japan (no surprise here). At the end of WWII, the French rush to regain control of their former colony and another Indochina conflict begins which continues until 1953 when they finally leave, unsuccessful in all their endeavors. Shortly thereafter, the U.S. sticks its nose in, thinking we can be the ones to resolve all the problems.

And once again, au contraire.

THE STORY OF VIETNAM

500,000 BC to 1941

Vietnam has been home to humanoids for eons, and examples of Homo erectus dating to 500,000 BC have been found in North Vietnam mountain caves. In 2900 BC, during the late Bronze Age, the Dong Son culture saw many advances in civilizations and the country prospered. Soon after, China targeted the county and its resources. Although China and many other invaders were victorious, in the end Vietnam always reclaimed its territory. A long succession of Vietnamese dynasties and foreign entities fought for, then won or lost control of the country repeatedly over many centuries.

There were peaceful times; but it is fair to say that Vietnam was in a state of mayhem many more times than not. Without a doubt most of the cultures of the world share a similar lineage. But in Vietnam, the struggle for power had been an ever-evolving, never-ending process and each conflict merely set the stage for the next confrontation.

The country name of Vietnam is considered by some to have been penned by a 16th century well-known doctor, poet, and educator named Nguyen Binh Kheim. He was a respected political clairvoyant whose prophecies have been compared to those of the world-famous Nostradamus. Most cities in Vietnam have named streets in his honor and, coincidently, 40% of the Vietnamese people have a first or last name of Nguyen.

Vietnamese exposure to Westerners started with the Romans in 166 AD, which led the way for more and more visitors. Marco Pole came there in 16th century, and Portuguese, French, Dutch, and many other traders followed. Then the missionaries arrived, and they stayed and set up delegations with sincere hopes to teach and convert the Vietnamese people. By 1700 many of the Vietnamese Mandarins became very concerned that Christianity was undermining their society, and in fact it was in direct conflict with the Confucian social order. For a time the prominence of the foreign missionaries was diminished; but, as the decades passed, Catholicism became more tolerated. Then, early in the 1800's, a French missionary encouraged a revolt to install a Catholic "Emperor." The consequence of this deceit was that countless Catholics, both Vietnamese and foreign born, were severely persecuted and trade with the West slowed to a trickle.

The French used the persecution of the Catholics as an excuse to invade Vietnam. And so it begins. Battles follow and, starting in 1859, the French took control of six Mekong Delta provinces. By 1882 the French captured Ha Noi in North Vietnam (and the French renamed the area Tonkin) and then took control of the entire country. In October of 1887, French Indochina was formed which included Burma, Thailand, Malaya, Laos, Cambodia, and Vietnam. The Vietnamese resisted and about one third of all Christians were murdered during the rebellion. Although the

French regained control, there was a strong desire by the citizens for Vietnamese independence.

Marxism is introduced in 1930 when three separate Communist parties united to form a coalition to install a Communist leader. Later that decade, the alliance was nearly completely wiped out by the French. In 1940, Japan invaded Vietnam and kept the Vichy French colonial administration in place as a puppet. In 1941, Ho Chi Minh arrives and formed the Viet Minh, then proceeded to stir things up a bit.

ENOUGH HISTORY ALREADY

At best I am a lousy historian, and that's probably on a good day. The above accounts are intended to set the stage for what happened in Vietnam. Please remember some of this history may be inaccurate and I'm sure it does not tell the complete story, but it is my understanding of what actually happened. To provide a complete history of Indochina requires a book 100 times the size of this one. If you are intrigued, I encourage you to do your own research. All I know for sure is that FUBAR doesn't even come close to describing what happened to everybody in "the Nam" during the 20th century.

10

"You're in the Army Now"

February 1968

OK, after the deceit and treachery of Tet, I think I'd finally pretty much had it all figured out: Vietnam was a combat zone and, although I wasn't in the battlefield, I had a ringside seat. I knew the people in the boonies had it so much worse than I would ever know, but I still believed being shot at and missed (even if only by the ARVNs) still counted for something.

At the time I had no idea how many battles started when the Tet Offensive began or how safe we were at Di An or not. We had heard that the 6,000 Marines stationed in Khe Sanh had been fighting for their lives since January 21st (against an estimated enemy total of 20,000), but that was about 400 air miles north of our location and had not posed a threat to us. Since Tet, Khe Sanh had seen even more intense fighting and was struggling to hold on. We bombed the crap out of the NVA and VC but they still put up a fierce attack that seemed would never end. The fight went on for months, and then Operation Pegasus added 20,000 U.S. troops and the siege came to an immediate end. A total of 275 marines were killed and another 2,550 were injured; it is estimated the NVA lost somewhere between 10,000 and 15,000 people. And then, just like everything else, not too much later we abandoned the base.

The ancestral capital of Vietnam at Hue was one of the cities hardest hit by the enemy after Tet. Hue was a historic city with significant ancient buildings and monuments. Because of this, the use of artillery and bombs was prohibited after the initial attack. The city had been poorly protected and was an easy target for the NVA and VC who promptly took over much of the city. A combined force of Marine, Army, and ARVN troops valiantly fought an estimated 10,000 enemy to retake the city, but they were severely hampered due to the heavy weapon restrictions. Eventually the ban was lifted and, after an intense battle, the city was finally liberated about a month later on February 24th when the Marines occupied the Imperial Palace in the heart of the citadel but at great cost. About 2,400 of the enemy had been killed; 450 ARVN and 220 U.S. were also killed in action. Besides the destruction of a beautiful city, the NVA had executed more than 2,800 civilians and government officials; their bodies were later found in mass graves. Hue was just about far away from us as Khe Sanh and, although it was horrible, once again it did not impact us.

During Tet there were over 100 cities scattered all over South Vietnam that were attacked including 36 of 44 provincial capitals, not to mention Saigon. A combined force in excess of 84,000 VC and NVA troops had attempted to destroy the government of South Vietnam and had hit all U.S. forces very hard hoping that the folks at home would demand our withdrawal. The attack on Saigon had been intense, but it was a complete failure. The embassy had been targeted and damaged but not breached, and every single VC gain in the city had been retaken. The fighting for and in Saigon soon ended and, although battles around the city and at Tan Son Nhut airport still raged off and on, Saigon had been saved in a matter of days.

Also during the Tet Offensive in Saigon, a South Vietnam police chief, General Nguyen Ngoc Loan, is caught on film by a NBC news cameraman and an AP still photographer executing a VC fighter with a single pistol shot to the temple. The photo and newsreel catch the exact moment of the pistol firing. You can see the grimace on the man's face and, when he falls, a small fountain of blood erupts from his temple. Of course it was on the front page of most American newspapers the next morning, and the newsreel was shown on NBC TV soon after. Nothing like a little live execution to brighten your day.

Everybody was enraged and appalled by the horror of it all. For the most part, no one really understood the whole scenario. The General claimed he had caught that poor little VC killing the wife, children, mother, and other people in the house of a close personal friend. Presumably, the VC had said something about them all deserving it and the General ended the discussion. The validity of this infamous extermination has always been questionable, but it seemed probable to many due to the frequent massacres and assassinations perpetrated by the Viet Cong. The execution was wrong; the murders were wrong; the whole damn war was wrong. The horrific torture and deaths committed by the VC were all too common and often resulted in retaliatory atrocities. I first saw the photo of the execution about six weeks later in one of my magazines, but up to that point I never knew anything about the story until then. Somehow the "Stars and Stripes" had missed the story.

I heard that on February 2nd President Johnson had said the Tet Offensive was a complete failure. Most of the VC in South Vietnam did not believe him or his perspective and the ambushes, battles, and assassinations continued. It is interesting and a sad footnote that also during this time, some anonymous officer was reported to have answered a news reporter's question with: "In order to save the town, we had to destroy it." Kind of says it all – don't it.

I was blissfully unaware of the intensity and frequency of how the Tet Offensive was progressing. Although those in our office might have been shocked and a little worried when we heard about what was going on outside our immediate world, if it didn't directly affect us, it was only bothersome and ultimately had little impact on our daily life. It may seem cold but, if you do not see or experience it you don't feel the impact.

In retrospect, I eventually concluded I had pussyfooted my way through my entire tour. Every day at the office was pretty much the same – I pushed paperwork around and made sure people were paid on time, handled payroll problems, and properly processed people in and out of country. I was literally working in a social club atmosphere, seated on a cushioned chair near a ceiling fan, had clean clothes, took regular rest breaks, ate comparatively well, and slept in a clean bed. Other than hearing horrifying rumors and losing a little sleep due to all the extended duties, I was completely isolated from the realities of combat and the American/Vietnam experience. It wasn't my decision to be in Vietnam, but I had plenty of choices of what I could do while I was there. To this day I am sometimes ashamed I didn't do more; but, in all honesty, I never once gave it a thought when I was in country. I always knew how lucky I was, but like a good little soldier still complained about almost everything anyway.

In the days following the start of Tet, everything changed in our company. We had guard duty every other day, and every second time it was for 24 hours. We had KP more frequently because no Vietnamese nationals were permitted on the base. Everybody covered for each other and with combined efforts and long hours in the office, we still got all the work done.

No supplies were coming in; so, in short order, at least one meal a day came out of a C-ration box. Actually the C-ration meals were pretty good, but there was always an oily aftertaste. Each box contained three cans: some kind of meat including Spam©, beef stew, ravioli or spaghetti in meat sauce, or the ever-popular mystery meat; a tin of vegetables, beans, or soup; and a can of dessert such as canned fruit (thank God no canned apricots); and a cupcake or muffin. A small flammable tab used to heat the cans was included along with a foil pouch containing eating utensils, salt and pepper, a P38 can opener, a *Hershey©* chocolate bar, and a paper napkin. The pouch also contained a small pack of four cigarettes, usually *Lucky Strikes©*,

Camels©, or *Chesterfields*©. Some came in a small green or white pack just like they had in in WWII but were probably left over from the Korean War. We always wondered how old these C-rations actually were and suspected the worst, but I never knew for sure.

The village of Thu Duc was the favorite "Den of Iniquity" for all those stationed at nearby Di An. It was a very small village only a couple of clicks away with more bars and other delights than all the water buffalo in our area. Every bar was staffed with a stable of very friendly girls and live bands loudly playing rock and roll music that shook the floorboards. Every type of beverage was available and, although perhaps most had been watered down just a bit, at least there were choices to be made. Dancing was encouraged and almost everyone had fun, but it was best to keep your hand on your wallet at all times.

Besides the bars, there were massage parlors (some of which actually gave massages). A couple of retail stores were added to the mix that offered a stunning array of useless trinkets, many inscribed FTA. Then there was the black market, a meandering alley of small booths selling an unbelievable variety of military food and equipment. Everything contained in a C-Ration box had been sorted and displayed, so there were six foot high stacks of cans of *Spam*©, mixed vegetables, spaghetti & meatballs, soups, cakes & muffins, and every other food item ever put in a can. Even the foil packages found in the C-Ration boxes had been opened and the contents offered separately for sale, like the condiments, the plastic knives & forks, and those cute little 4 packs of cigarettes. It was just like an open-air grocery store. And every can of food was wrapped in plain U.S. Army olive drab packaging with block print titles.

The clothing sold ranged from plain Army green or camouflage fatigues, jump suits, field jackets, socks & underwear, hats, and even included the Army's jungle boots. Local produce was there in abundance as well as American and Vietnamese civilian clothing. A large assortment of liquor was also offered; but, if you looked closely you could see that most of the seals had all been broken, and it was very expensive. Local remedies and creams and assorted cosmetics were also displayed. Other local products such as Vietnamese cigarettes and rice wine were available. Even rifles and pistols were being sold along with the ammunition; but these weapons were attached to small wood tables strapped onto the backs of scooters which were used to make a hasty retreat should the MPs made a visit. From what I could see, the MPs didn't find their way there very often.

The place was always open for business for anyone who had the means and transportation to get there. Before the Tet the place was usually pretty busy, but afterward everything changed. As soon as things cooled down a bit in mid-February, a Lieutenant jumped out of a jeep, landed on one of our little blue antipersonnel land mines, and lost his leg. That afternoon, without any warning, a small convoy of Rome plows arrived and leveled every building, including the black market and many of the villager's huts, until all that remained was an ugly pile of rubble. I later found out that unfortunate Lieutenant had been a Combat Engineer. The village of Thu Duc rebuilt itself but that "Red Light District" never returned.

So what does one do after all Americans in Vietnam are surprised by the Tet Offensive and every military facility and town is attacked, including each and every Company in the 1st Infantry Division? I don't know about you, but on February 6th I went on R&R to Vung Tau. When I think of it now, I shudder; it's impossible to believe that both the Army and I were that incredibly stupid to let this happen (well, at least me anyway). My only logical conclusion was the Army was more interested in keeping the troop morale high than in the safety of all those hopeful "vacationers," – and apparently I really didn't give a shit.

So, bright and early on Monday morning, our small convoy was on its way and exited the East Gate. This included jeeps armed with a M-60 and armored troop carriers (APC) both fore and aft, and three deuce and a half trucks accommodating about 55 grinning

"I really don't care, I gotta get out of here" troopers. As far as I could see, my fellow R&R escapees were a mix of people from my office, infantrymen, engineers, medics, and other insignia I didn't recognize. The trip to Vung Tau was about 60 miles by air which meant it was five-to-six hours by road. Everybody was smiling and telling jokes. The party had begun as soon as we were outside the gate. We had no problems during transport other than the endless series of potholes designed to rattle your bones and anything else that wasn't tied down. Also, it probably didn't hurt our security one little bit that a squadron of 5 Hueys kept an eye on our escape from reality – I always loved those guys.

When we arrived, we stored our weapons and flak jackets, were schooled in the proper rules of Vung Tau etiquette, and then quickly checked into the popular R&R hotel (barracks). We dumped our personal gear, changed into our civies, and then we all met at the nearest bar. We were all now "on the other side of the moon" and dumbstruck by the thrill of it all.

My buddies and I decided to grab a bite to eat first and then we'd go to the beach. Our gourmet meal consisted of hotdogs, fries, and a real beer (don't know how that happened). After that luxurious meal we changed into our bathing suits and headed straight for the ocean. I had never seen the ocean from shore before and was awed by the majesty of the rolling waves, the pristine sand, the blue sky, and the intense colors of everything; it was almost like being reborn and discovering the "World" again. That may sound a little overly dramatic, but that's exactly how I felt then and to this day still remember it.

We spread our newly acquired beach towels on the sand and sat down to survey and enjoy our new domain. Surprise, surprise – we were soon surrounded by a multitude of Vietnamese maidens, each lovelier than the next. All of a sudden going AWOL for a little while didn't sound so bad anymore, and we all decided to stay for another month or two. The girls were really friendly – we only had to buy them $4.00 drinks and they would stick around and be our friends forever. Except $4.00 was a lot for a small glass of weak "Saigon Tea," and they were very thirsty girls. One round was all we needed to feel the pain and all too soon we were on our own.

I decided to take a dip in the ocean and, although I tasted the salt and the water was pretty cold, I enjoyed every stroke I took. The saltwater buoyancy was a gift I thoroughly relished and I floated around for at least an hour or so. It was truly the nirvana I had hoped for and I appreciated every single minute. When I weakly returned from the sea, all of my friends wanted to return to town and check out the bars – all except Henry. He had locked eyes with a stunning little beauty clothed in an enticing leopard print bikini, and he certainly wasn't ready to go.

I agreed to stay with him while the others pursued other delights. His object of interest was very pretty and unsurprisingly also seemed to be very attracted to him. I encouraged him to talk to her and he went over and spoke to her for over half an hour. He smiled and returned to tell me he was going to spend the night with her in the town of Vung Tau, which was adjacent to our protected area. I reminded him that Tet had just happened, he was violating the rules of etiquette and every military mandate, and that, regardless of how things seemed, we were all still at war. He didn't care, and soon they left the beach hand in hand. I returned to town, found my buddies and later we all enjoyed a very nice and not-so-tender water buffalo steak; afterward we whiled the night away.

The next morning when I got up, Henry was still missing in action. After a quick breakfast, we all went to the beach and found our friend blissfully reclining in the sand oblivious to the world. He awoke about an hour later and told us his crazy story. He and his newfound love had gone to town and, after he gifted her $10.00 American (a very big deal, which she promptly gave to her mama-san, who was eating fishheads with chopsticks at the time). Then they found their way to her one-room hut. As soon as they got there, Miss Wonderful handed her girlfriend a padlock through the barred window. Then her friend proceeded to lock the metal door from the outside, concealing the fact they were both in the room. Then the object of his affections closed a heavy wood panel over the window, and placed a crossbar behind both the window and the metal door. Apparently both girls knew the VC were coming to town that night looking for stupid GI's.

That evening, after they got to know each a little bit, each fell asleep. Around 3:00 AM, shots and shouts were heard outside – scaring the crap out of Henry, the big dummy. Footsteps approached their door and someone kept rattling and banging on the door to see if it would give, then finally moved on. Amazingly, Henry found getting under a bed with only 4" clearance was no big deal. Regardless, although he was astounded by his stupidity, he was happy to have survived the ordeal. Early the next morning the loyal girlfriend returned and unlocked the door, and Henry sprinted to the beach which was the closest secured area. To this day I still think of him, his incredible luck, how we all survived terrible things, and I hope all is well with him and his and everyone else I knew back then.

Early the next morning I had a quick breakfast, headed to the beach alone, and once again enjoyed all the comforts of the rolling sea. I think I finally crawled ashore around ten that morning, then decided to take a little nap. Big mistake! I eventually woke up around 3:00 and thought I had been left in the oven too long. I was right – everything but my yellow swimsuit was a bright red and I was on fire. I jumped in the ocean to cool off then ran to town and took a quick shower – no relief. I bought suntan lotion – useless. I tried every remedy I could find – nothing worked. Eventually I could tolerate the pain and did my best to enjoy the remainder of my stay, wearing only my bathing suit regardless of the ridicule from all my so-called friends.

Although not happy about it, we eventually took the caravan back to our sordid reality and returned to Di An. The only thing that made anyone smile was little ol' me sitting there in my stunning yellow swimsuit, red as red can be. I couldn't tolerate clothing; so I only wore my helmet, swimsuit, and flip flops home – talk about dummies. The trip back to base was uneventful and mostly it was very quiet. Everybody was thinking what was waiting for us when we returned – not exactly a party atmosphere this trip. When we returned, I still couldn't bear to wear fatigues; so I was quickly summoned and justifiably awarded an Article 15 for damaging government property and being out of uniform. I can't find any now (maybe I accidentally burned them long ago); but I am sure somewhere out there, photos of me exist in my yellow swimsuit, wearing only a helmet and a bandolier of ammo, with flip-flops for boots, and carrying my trusty M14. What a sad, comedic sight I was. The next day I was back in my fatigues.

I returned to an office in disarray – not enough people and too much to do. Ah, still no rest for the wicked. Supplies were very hard to get and we had run out of ink ribbons for the typewriters (without them the pay vouchers or any other forms could not be typed), and the ribbons weren't likely to appear for another week. This was not exactly a crisis, that is, unless you expected to get paid, needed money before you went on R&R, or, even worse, would have to wait to get your final voucher and other paperwork so you could go home. The Army made sure we weren't bored and kept us all busy with guard duty, KP, company detail, policing the area, cleaning the office, and preparing for a general inspection – and this time by a real General. The supplies arrived a day earlier than expected; then we all pulled a 24-hour shift (again) and got the work done. Each voucher looked like it was vying for the coveted "most typo award." Messy looks aside, everybody got paid. We were rewarded with half a day off, then it was back to work again.

The general inspection followed a couple of days later. As instructed, each work area was clean, neat, and orderly. We had to remove all frivolous decorations, food and drinks, cartoons in bad taste, and, most importantly, hide pictures of any overexposed beauties. I did everything, except I forgot about the *Playboy©* calendar hung high on the wall over my four-drawer file cabinet. The General made his way through the office stopping to chat with people here and there. He was accompanied by a cadre of Colonels, Majors, and Captains, including the First Lieutenant in charge of our sector. When he got to my desk, the General walked up to my calendar and proceeded to look at each month like he'd never seen a woman before. The First Lieutenant stared daggers at me and I knew I would probably pay for this little breach of protocol. The General turned and thanked me for making his day, shook my hand and wished me well, and told me to never take that calendar down; I never heard another word about my oversight. A full-bird Colonel and a Captain also stopped by to review all the *Playboy© Bunnies*. No big surprise, the calendar disappeared a couple of days later.

News was still being made every day and it kept the media very busy. Richard M. Nixon declares his presidential candidacy on February 2nd. On February 18th, the U.S. State Department announces the highest one-week casualty total for the entire war before (and after) that date. During the previous week, 543 were killed and 2,547 were wounded. On February 27, 1968, broadcast on national TV, the much respected CBS reporter Walter Cronkite spoke these words after returning from a week-long trip to Vietnam: "To say that we are closer to victory today is to believe, in the face of the evidence, the optimists who have been wrong in the past. To suggest we are on the edge of defeat is to yield to unreasonable pessimism. To say that we are mired in stalemate seems to be the only realistic, yet unsatisfactory, conclusion… But it is increasingly clear to this reporter that the only rational way out then will be to negotiate, not as victors, but as an honorable people who lived up to their pledge to defend democracy, and did the best they could."

Just to keep things going, the very next day General Westmoreland then asks President Johnson for 206,000 additional soldiers. Fighting around Saigon and at Ton San Nhut airbase continued and 48 American soldiers had been killed. One week later, the *New York Times* breaks the news of Westmoreland's request for more troops and the White House promptly denies the story. By a very slim margin, President Johnson beats Senator Eugene McCarthy and wins the Democratic primary.

On February 29th, I was finally promoted to Specialist Fourth Class. I had more money to play with, a couple more chores (like office CQ) were added to my list, and I was now officially a Finance Specialist. My promotion was delayed because the Army only had a specific number of openings for each specialist grade; until an allocation opened up, you were stuck. Vietnam was the place to go if you wanted to be promoted; however, everyone else in the States and all other duty stations around the world were going nowhere. The Army started to cycle more of the available promotions to units outside Vietnam in an attempt to keep everybody happy. That really didn't do anything for our morale but it was done nonetheless. My Specialist Forth Class designation had been delayed about 6 weeks, but it was much better late than never.

At the end of February, I had now been in the Army for about ten months and in Vietnam a little over four months. So many events had occurred in that short time span outside the scope of Vietnam that it was impossible for me to keep up. A condensed ten-month list of the activity back in the real world follows:

- During that time, the U.S. had performed at least 7 nuclear bomb tests in Nevada, and the U.S.S.R. had responded with 8 tests of their own in Eastern Kazakh/Semipalinsk. Missions to the moon had become commonplace for both the U.S. and the U.S.S.R. Race riots continued daily all over the country and many were killed and injured. The U.S., Britain, and the U.S.S.R. ratified a treaty banning nuclear war in outer space (not exactly our biggest problem). The Israeli and Arab Six Day War takes place.
- The Beatles, Rolling Stones, Aretha Franklin, and Elvis Presley roll out hit after hit. The Movies: *Cool Hand Luke*,

The Graduate, *The Dirty Dozen*, *Valley of the Dolls*, and *Planet of the Apes* were all released during that time. The rock musical *Hair* premiers in New York. At *The Monkees'* concert in Forest Hills, New York, amazingly Jimi Hendrix is the opening act. *Mr. Roger's Neighborhood* premiers on PBS. President Johnson signs a bill supporting PBS.

- For the first time since 1948, the World Series did not include the Yankees, Giants, or the Dodgers. Mickey Mantle hits his 500th home run. In 1967, A. J. Foyt wins races at both the Indianapolis 500 and at Le Mans. Evil Knievel Jumps over 16 cars on his motorcycle. Former President Eisenhower (AKA "Ike") sinks a hole in one.

- The U.S. Senate confirms the first black Supreme Court Justice, Thurgood Marshall. Later the Supreme Court ends all laws against interracial marriages. President Johnson sets up a commission to study urban violence (today that still needs a little work). Sweden decides to switch from driving on the left to driving on the right; untold carnage follows. The first heart transplant takes place in South Africa. Many other noteworthy events happened every day, too numerous to mention here.

The end of 1967 and beginning of 1968 were important, crazy, and intense times; and I knew very little of what was really going on in the rest of the world. Although I received magazines and newspapers, they were usually so out of date I didn't pay much attention to them and, many were not read because leisure time was in short supply. On February 22nd I got a newspaper delivered that was dated December 29th, can't blame Tet for that; but because of Tet almost all the mail was still being delivered in a staggered, non-sequential succession. Maybe I was in denial or a little depressed; my only goal was to serve my time in purgatory and go home, not read about it. Still, it was nice to get something from the real world every once in a while just to keep me grounded. We all thought of Vietnam as being totally disconnected from reality – that's why we all referred to home as the "World," not the "States," not the "U.S.," and not "America."

Admittedly, I was absolutely insane to go to Vung Tau when I did, and I'm truly amazed about everything else that had happened to me without serious consequence. Maybe it is true: "God watches over fools." I was certainly young and dumb; but, even in that senseless scenario, I demonstrated more common sense than could be found in the White House at that time. To me it was like the people in charge were playing a giant game of Battleship©; but, instead of plastic ships, thousands of lives were at stake while all those self-righteous, egotistical bastards were guessing where to move next. Sadly, the games would continue for many more years.

11

Drugs & More Drugs!

1967 & 1968

About a month after I arrived in country, I developed an annoying cough. Slowly but surely it got worse and worse. Pretty soon I had a painful, hacking, productive cough. Every time I went to the medics, the doc would prescribe new antibiotics, cough syrup (with codeine), and a decongestant, afterward they sent me back to work. Sometimes I would be better for a couple of days, but mostly not; the cough always came back and worsened each time. Pretty soon I wasn't asking to go to the medics – I was being sent there every couple of days by my duty sergeant.

It got so bad that a couple of weeks before Tet, I was having terrible headaches and coughing so long and hard I couldn't hold down a meal. I was losing weight, had a tough time keeping focused, and work became more of a chore every day. I never took any time off and did my job the best I could, but I was feeling lousy most of the time. The doc eventually told me he had no more options of which medicine to use – guess I had tried everything they had. He finally said I probably had a virus and, while the decongestants offered some relief, the antibiotics were probably useless.

I stopped taking the antibiotics in hopes my body would develop its own immunity and resistance. Thankfully, by mid-March I finally began to feel better. Nature had run its course and I had survived the encounter. During this time I accumulated about 80 prescription bottles. I never threw the old ones out but kept them around "just in case." I never gave them a thought until the day when two MPs briskly approached my desk; and in short order I was under arrest and in handcuffs. There had been a surprise inspection of the hootches and they were looking for drugs. They came across my suspicious collection and thought they had found the company drug dealer. I was marched back to my hootch and confronted with the evidence.

I know I should have shown more decorum but couldn't resist saying "OK, Sherlock, did anybody look at the name and dates on the bottle labels?" A quick look proved my point, they were a little embarrassed, then we all shook hands and I went back to the office. The whole ordeal only took twenty minutes. For some reason I smiled; if nothing else, at least all those drugs had provided a little entertainment. As a side note, 14 years later I was rushed to the hospital with a collapsed lung. The event is called a "spontaneous tension Pneumothorax" which simply means the lung collapsed all by itself without any trauma. I was told I had a series of polyps due to an unknown cause on the surface of my right lung, and that they had ruptured for no apparent reason which caused the collapse. I've always considered the resulting 57 staples holding my right lung together my best Vietnam souvenir ever. Since I had seen it being sprayed around our basecamp, I originally thought that maybe Agent Orange had a little something to do with it, but now know I was wrong – the Army told me so.

Many recreational drugs were used in Vietnam. Pot (AKA: Ganga, weed, wacky tobaccy, grass, reefer, dope, Mary Jane, marijuana, etc. etc.) was by far the most popular and readily available. Opium was the only other drug I knew about. Using drugs was an offense worthy of a court-martial and could result in a sentence of internment in sunny Leavenworth, Kansas. All that said, where I was stationed there were a few people routinely busted; but it usually only resulted in an Article 15 for the first offense. This did make the offender much more cautious but really did nothing to reduce the drug use.

Don't get me wrong; among everyone I knew only a couple of people used weed on a regular basis. That's not to say you couldn't get a contact high on your way to the john, but almost everybody avoided it in fear of the consequences. I later found out if you bought a pack of Vietnamese cigarettes from a street vendor or on the black market, most contained marijuana, but all I knew was they tasted like crap. Still, I don't remember one person who hadn't tried it out of curiosity at least once – and yes, that included me.

One night I joined a guy from our hootch and went outside about midnight. We sat in our chaise lounges and had a cigarette. When I was about to go back in and hit the rack, he asked me to stay and share a joint with him. I had been a little curious about pot for a long time and so said OK. He pulled out a small plastic sandwich bag and rolled a joint. I saw some white powder on the marijuana and asked what it was. He said not to worry, it had only been laced with some "fairy dust." Later I found out the dust was actually opium – apparently there was no real limit to my stupidity. We shared one hand-rolled wacky cigarette and laid back to watch the stars. I'm not sure how long I reclined in that chaise and watched the stars go in tight little circles; but when I finally found my feet, he was gone and the sun was approaching the horizon. I thought it best to try and get a couple of hours of sleep before work and went back into the hootch. What the hell? Someone was sleeping in my bunk; in quick order I got him out of my bed and was asleep in no time. When I awoke a couple of hours later, I couldn't help but notice I was in the wrong hootch and everyone there was staring at me. I made my apologies and exited as quickly as possible. And that, ladies and gentlemen, terminated my experimental use of drugs.

I seriously felt a strong desire to wring the neck of my so-called buddy; but he was such a doper, I knew he simply didn't know any better, or care. When I asked about the pot he pulled out a cellophane bag about the size that would hold a one pound loaf of bread. The bag and its opium-enhanced contents had cost him all of $5.00; no wonder weed had become so popular. He thought I was too stuck up and pompous, and I was pretty sure he was too far gone, period; so we pretty much left each other alone after that. To my knowledge he was never busted; but I always wondered what happened when he returned to a less restrictive world.

As I remember, marijuana remained the mainstay of the Vietnam drug experience as long as I was in country. There were a couple of people I knew who thought the map of Vietnam resembled the shape of a hookah (and sometimes the whole country smelled like it too). They had plans to go into manufacturing similar water pipes when they got back home. Like I said, I don't condone it but I do understand it. For some it was recreational and fun. For others, it was therapeutic and made the place happier. And for many more, it was the only diversion they could find. I know, I know, I sound like a broken record when I say war is hell, but anyone who had experienced the torments of combat and casualties (or maybe just the fear of it) seriously looked for an escape.

Marijuana was not the only recreational diversion; I really believe alcohol trumped everything else. Then, as now, drinking was not only socially acceptable but was almost a mandate. Having a drink was the best way to relax with friends, forget your troubles, and enjoy a day's end (or any other time of day for that matter). And if someone happened to drink too much and make an ass of himself, that was just another great story to enjoy at the next get-together. Alcohol in all its various forms has been a boon and bust to mankind for eons, and that is most unlikely to end anytime soon.

If you were stuck on a base camp and were not an officer, getting anything other than 3.2 beer (5.0 or better was the norm) was a challenge. I had tried 3.2 "near beer" when I went to school in Kansas and didn't care for it at all. It would eventually do the trick after consuming copious quantities, but being bloated was not my idea of a good time. Di An base camp had a small EM club, but very few went there. We were in a combat zone and almost everyone was armed. If you had a gun, you were required to check your weapon at the EM club door and retrieve it when you left. When people are drinking and become a little intoxicated, maybe a little angry, and then handed a weapon – I mean, what could possibly go wrong? There were very few fights at the EM club because an MP was usually the bouncer. Still, there were the occasional punching matches and always lots of angry threats – enough to keep me out of the place.

You could always buy several different brands of beer at the PX, but they all pretty much tasted the same. The problem with the beer was it was sent over to Vietnam aboard a ship, unloaded, and stored in a yard under tarps for maybe a couple of months before being de-livered. Most beer has a shelf life of 3 months. The beer we got was at least that old and had been sitting in the sun for months. Let's just say that process didn't do anything to improve the aging process. If I remember right, a case of 24 cans cost about $2.50; and many times was available for only $1.00 per case (since it had become a little too ripe), and still it didn't sell.

The biggest problem with beer was getting it cold enough to tolerate. Eventually I inherited a small refrigerator, but it was al-most useless. With only part-time power available, it rarely ran long enough to cool anything down. There were several options avail-able: You could get some ice from the mess hall or go somewhere the beer was already cold. If the EM club was not an option and you had some time and permission, you could hop a truck and go off base to a bar in Thu Duc. The bars in Thu Duc were fun and the food wasn't too bad, but you really had to watch the bottled beers named "33" and another which was called "Tiger Beer."

You really didn't want to drink the beer if it had already been opened. One time when I went to the outhouse behind a bar, I saw a mama-san sitting on the ground, taking some half-empty bottles and combining them to fill another bottle. She was using a strainer and cheesecloth to filter out the cigarette butts or whatever other garbage had been put in the bottles, and then she pushed a bent bottle cap back onto the bottle. The bottle cap was always removed before serving to complete the deception, and the beer was served very cold to help hide the taste. I never drank another bottle of 33 (or any other kind of opened bottle of beer for the remainder of my stay in country) and always insisted on canned beer which I opened myself for the duration of my tour. As already noted, the Thu Duc bars and the entire town all suddenly disappeared after Tet. It had to be seen to be believed and doubt I will never forget that time and place.

As I remember, the U.S.O. club had a very nice bar; but it was really more an officer's club than anything else. It was a free-standing facility off base somewhere near Thu Duc. Once I had guard duty there and was assigned to protect the barbed-wire-enclosed motor pool area. Many of the Vietnamese youth liked to steal the trucks' tool kits which were easy to sell on the black market, and they were pretty good at it. I found a kid maybe 18 years old who had been snared while crawling underneath the barbed concertina wire. He just laid there and defiantly yelled at me. It did no good – I didn't understand a word. So I did my best to help make him understand me. I pointed my rifle at his head, chambered a round, and took the safety off. He shut up and just glared at me. A crowd of young kids had gathered outside the fence and were all screaming at me. I pointed my rifle straight up in the air and squeezed off a couple of rounds – he got the message. Although he was really caught up in the barbs, he tore himself loose and scrambled away, leaving bits and pieces of his clothes and himself dangling on the fencing. I watched them all run away, then squatted down and waited for sniper fire – but it never came.

A Lieutenant ran out and asked what the hell was going on. I told him and he sent someone else out to relieve me. When I went inside the U.S.O., a nice frosted mug of beer was waiting on the bar. He told me they had a lot of trouble with the kids stealing things and I was lucky to catch someone at it. I told him the kid had caught himself; but, nevertheless, I got another beer anyway. Best beers I ever had in country. I never understood why the U.S.O. was out in the middle of nowhere and really didn't think it was all that secure, either. After I left that day, it was just another place I never saw again.

It was very difficult for an enlisted man to get hard liquor. Only officers could buy it because, as everyone knows, RHIP. There were other options getting it on the black market, but that was very pricey. Some younger officers would buy it for their aides, but I never met one of those guys. The most likely means was to have someone who went to Saigon pick up a bottle or two for you. This too was costly, but a value compared to anything else.

Most people didn't drink very much either due to the quality, the availability, or the cost – but a few just had to have it and always found a way. There was a Native American Indian who worked in the motor pool. I hope you can believe me, this guy is neither a fictional character nor a stereotype, and he always found a way to get drunk. I never knew his real name because everyone simply called him "chief." One time around midnight, at a time when all the bunks were not doubled, I watched him stagger through our hootch. He fell on one bunk to his right, got up, and promptly fell on the one to his left. He did not miss a single bunk on his errant journey. He woke everyone up, and even with all the curses, he maintained his errant course until he exited the building. Once outside he fell flat on his face and passed out. I heard he was in a coma for a couple of days, spent a week in the hospital, and was very lucky to still be alive. Apparently he had already drunk an entire bottle of whiskey before he got to our hootch and then the better part of another as he passed through. I don't think his rank was ever anything higher than E1 (the lowest possible). Why he still had a job and was not in LBJ (Long Binh Jail) was beyond me. And the next time I saw him, no big surprise, he had another bottle of whiskey in his hand. C'est la vie.

Although I am a social drinker, I'm still fascinated at the number of times each day there is some mention of drinking on TV, in the movies, and in our literature. Drinking has been a part of our humanity for unknown millennia and will only end when we do. Whether it is a boon or curse to mankind, you will have to be the judge. There are a number of quotes concerning drinking, and here are two of my favorites: (1) from Ben Franklin: "In wine there is wisdom, in beer there is freedom, in water there is bacteria," and (2) from F. Scott Fitzgerald: "Here's to alcohol, the rose-colored glasses of life."

When it came to drugs of whatever type, our 1st Admin Company was simply a microcosm of every other locale on the planet – or any other time period, for that matter. Those who abused drugs and booze did so for a multitude of reasons that were far beyond the scope of their current environment, but being in Vietnam no doubt proved to be strong incentive to look for a diversion. Like I said earlier, I and most of people I knew did not use drugs other than to have an occasional drink; and, in that aspect, my life hasn't changed all that much. One more quote from Ben Franklin to ponder: "Be at war with your vices, at peace with your neighbors, and let every New Year find you a better man." Sure could have used that inspiration in the Nam.

12

Way Too Much Going On

March to May 1968

I was a member of a team with six finance specialists headed by a Staff Sergeant. Our finance section also had four other teams of five or more people each. The finance teams heads all reported to a First Lieutenant who was aided by a Warrant Officer Second Class. Although early on there had been some turnover, my team had remained pretty much intact for the majority of my stay. We each had a select group of companies to manage, which were reassigned as needed when the troop strengths began to increase. Our Staff Sergeant was always there to support us, was never one to overreact or become angry, and was genuinely a nice guy.

I still know the names of everyone; but, as I sit here and remember our time together, I realize I knew very little about any of their lives back in the "World." We were an industrious crew who worked together very well, and we all pitched in to help each other whenever needed; but none of us of spent our spare time together and, other than in the office, we didn't socialize very much at all. We spent so much time together that we needed to get away from each other after work – not too dissimilar to the need to sometimes be alone for a marriage to be successful.

There were a number of Vietnamese girls who worked as secretaries and gofers for some of the higher ranking officers in the finance area, and they routinely passed through our offices carrying messages and paperwork back and forth. They all wore a traditional Ao Dai dress, which was a long flowing gown in pastel colors with both sides slit from the waist down, revealing loose fitting full-length pants, and everything was made of silk. When they passed by your desk, even without a breeze, their lightly colored perfumed outfits floated on the wind, and these humble but always smiling young nymphs were a welcome distraction.

One of the guys on our team finally admitted he was in love with one of these girls, and I have to admit she was a beautiful young lady. Apparently she felt the same and had agreed to marry him. That was much easier said than done. I had heard it could take anywhere from 12 to 18 months to get the paperwork approved – sort of like the Army saying: "You better really think this over and make sure you know what you're doing." I don't know if the wedding bells ever rang for those two, but he did everything possible to get all the necessary paperwork approved and I know he extended his tour.

I would love to know if he was ever able to marry that girl and it would be great to talk to all the other guys and compare how the "World" had treated them once they had returned home. I've made a couple of attempts via the internet to locate some of them but have not been successful. Being a member of the American Legion, I gave that a try; but I had no luck there, either. One of the Legionnaires told me that mostly the only Vietnam Veterans who really stayed in touch after their tours were the ones who were involved in combat. Apparently those of us in the rear echelon just wanted to move on; and this also explains why I am only an inactive member of the Legion. I proudly support their cause, but I have so very little in common with the others. We each fought our battles in Vietnam, but on totally different levels, and our memories are of extremely diverse experiences. There is nothing else to say other than "qué será será." Maybe, if this book is ever published, it will reach out to some of my former team-mates.

I had to spend a couple of days a month either processing men coming into country or all those happy souls going home. The newbies were mostly in good spirits but had a million questions. Had I seen any action, how bad was it, what could they expect, and what were the odds? I told them that I really didn't have any answers for them because everybody's experiences were different. I did say to them they were in good hands, but to keep their heads down and do their jobs as best they could, emphasizing that there was no incentive pay for being a hero. Some of the first names were a little curious and apparently were the result of their parents not choosing a name for their birth certificates when they were born; Noname (No Name – this was my favorite) and Baby come to mind. Regardless of the names, they were all patriots and, although rarely spoken, I wished each and every one of them a safe journey.

When I asked the newly arrived about their life insurance choice, most went for the max of ten thousand for two bucks, several went for five for one buck, and only a few opted for nothing. Each of these men came from a variety of places and circumstances and, because of this, they had many contradictory views and priorities. Just like when I was drafted and on that bus to Fort Knox, Kentucky, some had joined with hopes of learning a trade or making a career. Many had been drafted and there were a good number of others who thought they had an obligation to fulfill in respect to honoring our country. That same dedication and patriotism seems to be lacking for too many of today's youth, much to their loss. We all need a sense of purpose if we are going to be able to help build a better world.

Many of the incoming had sad stories that ranged from being removed from their necessary supporting family roles, having their life's goals tragically interrupted, and simply making the wrong choice. I could seriously relate to the latter. Then one day we started to process National Guard Units in country. Wow, color me very confused again. The National Guard was exactly that – I thought they were to be held in reserve in the continental United States to uphold our country's security, aid when a disaster struck, provide militia to suppress violent situations, and do whatever was necessary to maintain the wellbeing of our country.

I was also surprised that all the National Guard troops we were processing into Vietnam had been sent over as complete units, regardless of the length of service obligation that remained for any individual trooper. I thought this was insane. I guessed the draftees weren't keeping up with the demand. Apparently this seemed to be the most expeditious way to fill the void, and apparently it wasn't the first time. I started to become a little worried about exactly what was happening all around me – just how bad off were we?

One of the National Guard I was processing in was literally crying and I asked why. He told me he only three weeks of active duty left until the end of his term. Twenty one days! His wife was pregnant with their third child who was due in a month and, since he was an Infantry Sergeant and a squad leader, he was afraid he would be one of the first to die in combat. I had heard a lot of stories, but this one got to me. I went over to the warrant officer overseeing the in-processing section. After our talk, he told me to get all the man's files and bring them to him. Then I was told to tell the NG to go to the mess hall and wait until summoned. When I came back with his files the WO added it to a short stack on his desk.

If I could remember the name of that WO I still would never reveal it. I think in total he kept a couple dozen true short timers from discovering the wonders of the Vietnam. That clandestine crew of twenty or so was split up and bounced from hootch to hootch until it was time from each to go home. Later I asked the WO if I hadn't talked to him would my NG have been assigned to the field. He said no, he had audited every NG file and did his best to correct the stupidity of whoever had choreographed that SNAFU. I remember this only too well because the next KIA payroll file I had to close out had been a member of that very same National Guard unit.

On March 31st, 1968, President Johnson announces in a speech the bombing of North Vietnam will soon come to an end; and surprises the country when he adds "I shall not seek, and I will not accept, the nomination of my party for another term as your president." The wheels are really starting to come off now, but the end is not yet in sight, and the carnage rages on. There seemed to be little hope for a peaceful resolution, and unfortunately this sad assessment proved to be correct for a long time to come.

The Reverend Martin Luther King, Jr. was assassinated on April 4, 1968 while standing on the walkway of the Lorraine Hotel outside his room in Memphis Tennessee. He was shot a 6:01 PM and was immediately rushed to St. Joseph's Hospital. After valiant efforts to save his life failed, he was pronounced dead at 7:05 PM. He had been shot by a racist, escaped convict named James Earl Ray.

MLK was a man of peace striving for racial equality, was involved in many peaceful protests across the country, and was often a victim of the heated and violent prejudices of the day. After his death, riots broke out across the nation, mostly due the frenzied rhetoric of extremists on both sides of the fence. At least 43 people were killed, over 2,500 were injured, and in excess of 12,000 people were arrested.

The riots were a sad epitaph to the efforts and legacy of a peaceful, loving man. The only result of all the rampage was to make the bumpy road to equality much more difficult. To me it always seemed senseless to mourn a loss or protest an unjust act by rioting, looting, killing, or attacking innocent victims. It is akin to trying to put out a fire using gasoline. In America you will always have every right to protest, but this doesn't include breaking the law and assaulting people and stealing their possessions. Those who do not respect the laws of our country need to be held accountable; otherwise anarchy and prejudice will be the unavoidable long-term consequence.

Personally I had never experienced or seen any racial violence when I was overseas; but after King's death, the racial divide became a very hard line. After he passed away, there were a couple of fights and one stabbing on our basecamp, but no one was seriously injured and things pretty much settled down in short order. The tension and distrust lingered for a long time but I never heard of anyone that had been shot – a rather amazing statistic considering everybody in the country was armed. Before his death I really didn't know very much about the Reverend, but after his assassination, I never forgot him.

Prejudice only generates hate and retaliation, and unfortunately this has always been the nature for all of the world's cultures. Because of this, I firmly believe that that word "prejudice" will never be abolished. We all deserve to live in peace, have no reason to fear for our families, and enjoy equal opportunities to be productive. For the sake of community, it is just as important that each of us makes sincere contributions to our family's well-being and share the same work ethics as everyone else. You cannot gift dignity.

Every person has a right to enjoy the same benefits and to share the same respect. Still, for this to really work, we must also embrace the same burdens and responsibilities. To successfully abolish prejudice, members of a society need to be both social and economic contributors. Unless these measures become a fact of life, there cannot be peace and racism will prevail. Equality cannot be legislated by politicians, or anyone else for that matter; it must be earned. Our multicultural society has spawned a mixed and diverse population with a dichotomy of religious beliefs, desires, needs, demands, fears, and hatred. To enjoy true harmony, some of these attributes need to align and others need to disappear. I don't have the solution and so far, apparently, neither does anyone else. I know it is a cause worth fighting for, but you really need to watch out for all those too frequent bumps in the road.

For the sake of my sanity, I made getting that reel to reel tape recorder a "must have" priority. I had high hopes it would allow me to escape into my own private world. It took six months; but as soon as I had saved enough, I went straight to the PX. They had just received a shipment and, lucky for me, there was one Akai M-9 still left. It was not my first choice, but it would do. As I pulled out the money, I couldn't help but smile, it was finally really going to be mine. I picked up a nice set of earphones, half dozen blank tapes, and a couple of prerecorded taped albums. Because I hated show tunes, my selection was limited to only two pre-recorded tapes and both were by artists unknown to me. One was by *Jimmy Walker and the All Stars®* on the *Motown®* label, this one quickly became my favorite. The other was titled *Enoch Light's Greatest Hits®* which was a collection of instrumental renditions that really didn't interest me at all – but it was better than nothing.

I quickly brought everything back to the hooch and stored my newfound bounty in my foot locker. I debated about whether to leave it in the hooch or bring it to the office. Even though it weighed about 42 pounds, I eventually decided to lug it back and forth every day. A couple of guys had similar tape recorders and stereo turntables so I was able to record and add a wide selection to my music library. Purchasing it and hauling it back and forth had proved to be one of my happiest decisions to date. A little exercise didn't hurt, either.

My new tape recorder was a wonder; it incorporated both an amplifier and speakers so it was a self-contained stereo player. The M-9 had a detachable cover that shielded the operating mechanisms and the case and cover was coated in a durable plasticized gray canvas. It spun two 7" diameter tape reels with ¼" wide tape long enough to provide one hour or more of playing time, depending on the speed. It had a four track stereo cross field bias system and a power output of 15 watts per channel. The face was adorned with speed controls and interchangeable capstans which when used in different combinations changed the speed from 1-7/8, to 3-3/4, to 7-1/2, to 15 IPS (inches per second). It sported two lighted VU (volume unit) meters so you could balance the volume for each stereo track. There were bass and treble adjustments and it had rectangular aluminum flaps that both protected and directed the 2" X 4" speakers located on either side of the cabinet.

The speakers were seldom used because 90% of the time I wore the padded earphones – with them on, the troubles in my part of the world seamlessly evaporated. Also there was a small odometer that tracked the number of revolutions so you could find the specific location of any song. I loved that machine. Much later in life, I gave it to my second wife's ex-father-in-law (that's another story) for use in his church. When he passed away, I declined to take it back, and that I do regret.

To conserve on power and to make sure we all got a good night's sleep so we would be "bright eyed and bushy tailed in the morning," the power was turned off at 10:00 PM every night. It was a pain in the butt because all the corded radios, TVs, and refrigerators also turned off. Most days there was never enough time when the power was on to chill anything in the fridge, making it almost worthless. Usually instead of selling one, it was given away or simply left in place. If there was a poker or any other kind of game in progress or you were reading a book or writing a letter, out came the lanterns and flashlights. On occasion the hootch was more brightly lit after it was "lights out." But when we were under a red or yellow alert, "Lights Out" meant lights out.

If you weren't sleepy, you could sit outside and "shoot the bull" with the others or do a little stargazing. Normally the offices were also locked up at 10:00 PM so there were no other recreational options. You got used to having no power. Because it was the norm, it was usually no big deal; but for me it made the thought of going back to the "World" all that much more appealing.

I was out of cigarettes and decided that morning to take the shortcut between Bob Hope Field and the perimeter and go to the PX. It was mid-morning and the sun was slowly rising in a bright cloudless sky. The dust was beginning to get thicker and a small puff of smoke marked each step. All of a sudden I heard an angry buzz fly way too close to my head. To my left a second later, I heard a muffled pop that sounded like it came from the perimeter. There had been no enemy activity in our area for quite a while and I couldn't believe someone just took a shot at me. Before I could hit the deck, another bullet plowed a furrow through the dust three feet in front of me. As quickly as gravity would allow, I was on the ground eating the sandy dust and tasting the sour grass. I quickly moved back toward the stockade fence that surrounded the Bob Hope Theater, gliding like I was on wheels. I heard another pop but didn't see the result. I felt naked and incredibly vulnerable. Since there hadn't been any red or yellow alerts, I was totally unarmed, without a helmet, no flak jacket, and was nothing more than a skinny target in a baseball cap.

I looked at the perimeter and the bunker guards were out of sight; they were presumably looking for my antagonist, I hoped. I stayed there for maybe ten more minutes and kept my head down. There had been no more shots fired and the guards were now outside and standing behind their bunkers, searching the perimeter through the sights on the rifles. I thought this was as good a time as any to get out the hell out of there. Running as fast as I could, I instinctively zigged back and forth, then stopped and started running again, hoping not to make an easy target of myself.

I arrived in the PX area out of breath but very thankful, and warned a couple of people to take the long way back to the office. No harm done, but I really hated being shot at, only I didn't exactly know what to do about it this time. Maybe the sniper was shooting at one of the guards and, because I was only a little more than 100 yards behind the bunkers, I had wandered into harm's way. But because the shots came way too close to hitting me, regardless of the circumstance, I took it very personally. The passing of each day was beginning to become more and more meaningful to me now; I just hoped they would start to move along little quicker, that's all.

In order to keep the Admin Company grounds groomed and clean, each day a soldier would supervise a crew of anywhere from 10 to as many as 15 Vietnamese women, some carrying infants. They expertly wielded their machetes and did their best to remove the weeds and pushed mowers to cut the grass. Some of them carried long cloth bags and picked up an assortment of litter that never seemed to go away.

Whenever I had that duty I enjoyed it. It was a very simple assignment and they needed very little supervision. Each knew exactly what to do and they did it. Almost all did a good job but they weren't exactly in a hurry. If permitted, they would try to take a break every fifteen minutes or so. If someone pushed them too hard, they became even slower and less productive; so I usually let them work at their own pace and I used gentle persuasion (a couple of cigarettes worked best) to keep things moving along. These local peasants were an easy-going and happy people. There was always a mama-san in charge of the others to translate my orders and to motivate them. Unfortunately, when she smiled, all you saw were black teeth. Many Vietnamese had poor oral hygiene and painful gums were the result. Most carried small round tins of a pink paste called Betel-Nut. That killed any oral pain, but it also blackened their teeth. When they smiled, it was not a pretty sight.

To me the mama-sans all appeared to be in their early sixties. One I got to know pretty well was slowly getting fatter and fatter, and I thought she was sick. That was not the case, and she actually gave birth to twins several months before I left the country. I never knew what to expect from the people of Vietnam, admittedly sometimes sad or worse, but my time in country never failed to be an entertaining and amazing journey.

Rumors were an intricate facet of almost every dialog. There was so much going on outside the boundaries of our company area there was always plenty of fodder to feed the gossip mills. Generally speaking, our daily routine was as predictable as the sun rising and setting. There was always something to do and boredom wasn't a factor; but being so isolated from the realities that literally surrounded us, we craved news of any sort that didn't involve paper-work and a typewriter. Legitimacy and accuracy were not all that significant. The most important thing was that the story was thought-provoking and offered an escape from our reality; and if it only proved true or possible for a short while, that was OK, too.

We were processing men in and out of country every day, handling payroll problems, and socializing with the other companies on our basecamp; so we had an abundance of willing and diverse resources. News from the home front was always in demand. The Stars and Stripes omitted many of the more intriguing political and special event details. The newspapers and magazines were so outdated they were almost insignificant; and the TV and radio news broadcasts were useless. We simply wanted to know what was really going on in the "World" we had left behind. What had L.B.J. said about the war? Did Vice President Agnew stick his foot in his mouth again? How many more troops did general Westmoreland ask for this time? How many protests had there been, and where? Was there any truth in the news that the peace talks would be resolved soon? The questions were endless and the rumors filled some of the gaps. Although in demand, most reports from home in all reality had very little effect on any of us.

What we really wanted to know was what the hell was happening in our neck of the woods. There were more than enough rumors concerning the local battles and ambushes, our strategies or lack thereof, and the likelihood we would be attacked anytime soon. If I had a five dollar bill for every time I heard we were going to be overrun that night, I would have been able to retire ten years sooner. As a matter of fact, most of the stories we heard were based on speculation, fear, or wishful thinking. Still, every once in a while, a rumor proved to be accurate and too many were evidenced by the number of KIA records we processed. Although such accuracy was pretty infrequent, each time a rumor proved to be true it was a heartrending reminder of where we were and what was happening. Still, nothing like a juicy rumor to help pass the time.

As I noted earlier, our minefield had been severely compromised due to the small rivers and sometimes rampaging rapids spawned by the torrential rains we had during the rainy season. It was now May and the rainy season had pretty much ended the flooding. Before the minefield could be replaced, we needed to remove or detonate all those little bright robin's egg blue plastic anti-personnel mines that had been unearthed. They were scattered everywhere on their sides, right and upside down, half buried at an angle, and many remained still buried as they were intended to be.

There was no way you could send an EOD technician to tackle that tangled mass of inhumane devices without him losing a body part or two. The only logical solution seemed to be to employ a Rome Plow mounted with a heavy-duty roller normally used to smooth the surface of asphalt roadways. The theory was that the weight of the roller would compress the mines and, regardless of their orientation, detonate each and every one without injury to anybody. The mines had a limited range of destruction; their primary purpose was to maim and not kill. The driver would be protected by both the bulk of the Rome Plow and the roller. It seemed nothing could go wrong.

I was on guard duty that day, sitting on the bunker box behind the perimeter bunker entry, and watched as the mines dutifully exploded one after the other. I was out of range of any shrapnel and was actually enjoying the show. The constant muffled explosions provided an irregular calypso beat, and that tattoo sporadically punctuated the procession. Then I saw a second lieutenant walking in the track impressions left by the Rome Plow, spray paint can in hand, marking any unexploded ordinance outside the width of the roller. He didn't see me, but I saluted him anyway; there is no way I would not have done that. They had traversed three quarters of our south perimeter proceeding at a cautious pace. Then maybe 75 yards to my right, I heard the muffled bang and saw the Lieutenant fall. One of the mines remained upright after the passage of the Rome Plow, and it exploded when the Second Lieutenant stepped on it. His scream stopped the plow. In a matter of minutes the medics were there and saved his life, but later I found out not his foot. Even now I can see his arms flying upward, paint can flying to the right, and him falling, crumbling as he fell.

It was one of the saddest things I had have ever witnessed. At that moment I hated everything – the Army, Vietnam, LBJ, all my bad decisions, and the senseless, inescapable insanity that had made me a bystander. Those feelings never really went away until my final day in country when I did my best to put all that misery behind me. Still, some of the memories will always linger.

13

Potpourri

June 1968

Robert (Bobby) F. Kennedy was assassinated on June 5, 1968 at 12:15 AM after winning the California Democratic Presidential Primary. He was shot at the Ambassador Hotel in Los Angeles by the Sirhan Sirhan and immediately taken to the Hospital of the Good Samaritan only a few blocks away. The surgery lasted for three hours and forty minutes, but he succumbed to his wounds about 26 hours later at 1:44 AM on June 6th. His brother John, the former President of the United States, had been also been killed by a political assassin named James Harvey Oswald years earlier on November 22, 1963. Sirhan, a Palestinian Arab with Jordanian citizenship, was a staunch anti-Zionist; and for whatever reasons, he had Bobby at the top of his hit list.

Had he lived, Bobby's political ambitions would have more than most likely been fulfilled. A sad footnote was, that only two months earlier, he had given a speech concerning the assassination of the Reverend Martin Luther King, Jr. His sermon praising King's accomplishments and mourning his loss is considered by many to be one of the greatest speeches in American History.

I was anything but political at the time but was seriously not a fan of most Democrats (Like L.B.J. for instance). Admittedly, I didn't know very much about the younger Kennedy, but I was truly shocked at what had happened. I began to think our country was falling apart at the seams, and somehow the demand for senseless slaughter had found its way from Vietnam back to the "World." His untimely death was mourned by many of those in country, but there were no violent outbreaks – except all those who had tied his death to Martin Luther King, Jr.'s assignation were now even more angry.

The planet continued to rotate on its axis, and there were still a couple of other things happening that did not involve Vietnam. On June 1st, Helen Keller dies at the age of 87. The Standard and Poor's index closes at above 100 points for the first time. The film *Rosemary's Baby* premiers on the 12th. Andy Warhol is shot and wounded by a struggling actress in New York City. On June 28th, President Johnson signs a bill adding a ten percent surcharge to income taxes (to help fund the war) and promises to reduce government spending (we should all be so lucky); he later admits it is impossible to provide both "guns and butter."

Since I was usually limited to the confines of our basecamp, most of the wildlife in Vietnam was unknown to me. Still, I did have a number encounters with a few of the local animals and way too many of the critters. Our admin company had a pet monkey that occasionally was used to clean up all the spiders in the rafters of our hootches. I had seen photos in a *National Geographic Magazine*© of all the colorful birds in our area, but I had only spotted one. When on guard duty at night, I had occasionally heard the infamous tokay gecko making its acclaimed mating call "FAA CUE"; I'll bet you can figure out what we all thought it was saying. His call seemed to be so very appropriate at the time. Only once in a great while did anyone ever see a snake, but when on guard duty, we always took a close look at the floor inside of our perimeter bunkers just in case one was looking for a new home. I had seen many water buffalo whenever outside our basecamp and they didn't seem to be happy beasts, but at least they were somewhat domesticated. There were a lot of dogs all over the place but they weren't very friendly; most were scavengers and, many had only three legs thanks to excursions through our minefields (kind of explains their demeanor).

Then there were the mice. Seldom seen but their handiwork was always easy to spot. Shortly after first setting up my desk and files, I found there was little problem with my choice for some of the filing locations. Simply said, I was a little too trusting. I had filed all the forms I would need on a daily basis in my desk drawers. When I returned a day later after 24 hour guard duty, I found every piece of paper I had filed in my desk had gone through a paper shredder; but there were no paper shredders in our office (or anywhere else in the world that I knew of) – that is, except for a couple of families of mice. They had transformed my orderly paperwork into chewed-up piles of confetti and constructed messy little nests complete with babies, poop, and pee. It was disgusting. I don't remember if I was more repulsed or pissed off, but the result was the same. I removed the affected drawers and took them outside and emptied them in an outside refuse container, leaving the contents to their own devices. I eventually found if I kept everything in the four-drawer file next to my desk the problem went away. No paper was ever stored in my desk drawers again. Every morning after that I started my day by opening and slamming the drawers shut several times. After a couple of days the squeaks and squeals stopped and those sorry little trespassers never returned, but I kept on slamming the drawers shut for a long time just to make sure. Horrid little creatures.

As far as insects were concerned, I saw more than my fair share. Flies were bothersome but only were there after food had been out for a period of time. Mosquitos were a constant threat but were mostly kept a bay thanks to the "bug juice" we were issued, the Army's insect repellant that was probably 100 percent DEET. I had seen a great variety of centipedes and my favorite was eight or more inches long with a Kelly green body and bright orange and red legs. Since some were poisonous, I tended to keep out of their way – that is, unless they were found in my hootch. I always kept a small broom hanging on the wall to dispatch any concerns. Spiders were everywhere, but I only rarely saw one that wasn't hanging around in the rafters of a building.

And then there were the fire ants – small, red, piss ants – and these insidious little beasts were the bane of my existence. They were very tiny and pretty much got into anything they wanted. Just to make things more interesting, they each had a stinger which could repeatedly inject a very potent venom; and, when you were stung it felt like your skin was on fire – thus the name.

My mother sent me my favorite treat for my birthday back in December, a German chocolate cake. It had been carefully wrapped in wax paper and then in foil, neatly placed inside a round metal tin that was sealed with ribbed fiber tape, and the whole assembly lastly wrapped up in thick Kraft paper. When it arrived I couldn't resist and just had to open it and take a taste for myself. Then I repacked it up in both the wax paper and foil wrap, resealed the tin with the fiber tape, loosely rewrapped the tin in the Kraft paper, and then set it the package on top of my file drawer cabinet. Before leaving the office later that afternoon, I decided to indulge myself and have a slice or two of my birthday cake. I picked up the package to place it on my desk but then had to drop it on the floor. My hands were ablaze and dozens of those vicious little thieves were swarming all over my hands. I had some lighter fluid in my desk and used it to wash my hands to get rid of the ants. I stared at the upside down package lying on the floor in disbelief as I saw a molten mass of those little bastards all over it. I spayed more lighter fluid on the package and eventually was able to turn it over and open the tin. Inside there were still more ants decimating my cake. So I sprayed even more lighter fluid all over the cake, carried the dripping remnants of my ruined present outside my office, and threw in a match. And that's pretty much how I celebrated my birthday that year.

In June, I had 24-hour guard duty and it had rained nonstop so nobody got any sleep. When I got back to my hootch around 5:30

PM, all I wanted to do was hit the rack. I stripped down and dried myself off as much as possible, had a cigarette, then jumped into my top bunk that was covered with the necessary mosquito netting. I laid down on my side and put my left arm under the pillow; it was only there for a couple of seconds before I discovered my mistake and found that a reception committee had awaited my return. I jumped out of bed rendering the mosquito netting and used a towel to remove the throng of those stinging sons of bitches from my arm. When I looked at my bunk I could see the ants had crawled down the strap that suspended the netting over my bunk. They had entered through a button-hole only used when the netting was placed inside a tent and had proceeded to make a nest under my pillow, little eggs and all.

I threw the bedding, pillow, and the netting into a large puddle outside next to the back door of the hootch. Then I removed the mattress, rolled it up, and stood it in the corner. Luckily my bunkmate had guard duty that night. After inspecting his bedding I decided to borrow his bunk for the evening. My arm was killing me but I was so tired I soon fell asleep. A little after 7:30 PM, I woke up and my arm was now swollen and throbbing with pain. I made my way to the medics and was given couple of shots of antihistamine and some thick white cream. The arm eventually felt better, but the swelling took about a week to disappear.

Suddenly I now had a new mission in life: kill every frigging fire ant I came across. The next encounter only took a couple more weeks to happen. It was raining outside; so we decided to lay about a dozen of our muddy ponchos on the tall grass between two hootches and left them there, hanging on the tall grass, to be hosed off by the monsoon. The next morning, after it had stopped raining, we went outside to retrieve the ponchos. We found each cape had been transformed into a canopy for colonies of fire ants fleeing their flooded homes. We removed the ponchos and hung them on nails outside the hootch, doused each pancake-sized mound of white eggs and many hundreds of irritated fire ants with lighter fluid, and proceeded to resolve the dilemma. The resulting sacrificial pillars of flame brought cheers to the onlookers. The fires slowly lowered until only the smoke remained; then it started to rain again which extinguished the remaining smoldering mess. Enough said about my ant phobia, and this also concludes the tales of my wildlife safaris in the Nam (never did see a tiger).

Every once in a great while I had to work the complaint desk. Well, really, it wasn't a desk at all, it was a simple box-shaped, open-faced counter hung on the wall bellow a rectangular screened window. There was a small hinged slot used to pass paperwork back and forth to the outside. A simple shelf placed below the window on the outside served as a writing surface for signing paperwork. Anybody with a question or special need approached the window and we did our best to help resolve the problem. The service counter was the responsibility of an older WO4 who had a rough-and-tough exterior; but in fact he was without a doubt one the easiest and nicest officers to work with.

Most patrons usually were looking for a cash advance needed for their R&R trips which were about to start. Having already spent their monthly pay allotments, they were broke for whatever reasons, and each was in desperate need for cash. Our normal cash advance for those with little-to-zero balances was $200. This worked for most but not for all. Some were still in debt from previous advances and others had too many debits affecting their pay, such as article 15 judgments, child support, alimony, et cetera. The bust-outs usually got $100 if they were polite; and if not, they went away empty handed.

There were also legitimate complaints about miscalculations, failures to add additional pay for promotions, and sometimes missed special-duty pay incentives. Most of the problems were due to paperwork mix-ups and delays. Regardless of the request or complaint, usually there were very few unhappy campers at the end of the day

– except for me. Now I had to go back to my desk and do my own work which had only increased as I had manned the window.

Every month the finance department would send finance specialist teams out on runs to all the other 1st Division base camps. They would handle any payroll issues, distribute statements, and pay the troopers their monthly allotment of military scrip. Each finance team consisted of a supervisor, two specialists, and two MPs to guard the cash, and then all would be taken on a chopper ride.

I always wanted to go on a payroll run. In due time, I was part of a team set to go to Lai Khe; it was about 25 miles North of Di An off of Highway 13, better known as "Thunder Road." Lai Khe was in the middle of a very active combat zone and it was a rare day or night that there wasn't some kind of attack. Still, I appreciated the chance for a break from the monotony of the office routine and was genuinely looking forward to this adventure because it would be my first ride in a Huey. We met at the office, packed all the necessary paperwork and stored the scrip in a footlocker then used a padlock to lock it up. We all jumped into a jeep and made our way to the chopper pad.

The Huey, a Bell UH-1 Iroquois helicopter, was a beast. It was 48-feet long and ours could accommodate up to 12 people including the two pilots. There were two M-60 machine guns, one on either side of the chopper, and each had ammo belt boxes with 200 rounds each. It had two rows of four-person folding bench seats each facing the other, and there were two bench seats along either side of the craft, one behind each of the machine guns. The blades were beginning to spin faster as we boarded the chopper and, even though the rotating blades were at about three feet over our heads, we all instinctively bent over as we boarded. Our office team consisted of my duty sergeant, another finance clerk and myself, plus two MPs. Three officers joined our troop; so we had a complement of eight people plus the two pilots. Both sliding side doors were pushed back and they were never closed. I was looking forward to the unobstructed views.

No one was sitting behind the machine guns so one of the pilots got out and asked if anyone knew how to fire them. Both of the MPs and I raised our hands. Since one MP had to stay with the foot locker, I moved over to the starboard side and buckled up behind the other M-60. The pilot came over and asked me if I knew how to chamber a round, unlock the safety, and fire the gun. I showed him and he patted me on the shoulder and hopped back into the pilot's seat. I placed the communication earphones on my head, fastened the seat belt, and made sure my flak jacket was properly closed. The guys in the cabin not by the doors were all sitting on their flak jackets, just in case – imagine that.

I was really looking forward to the trip and the lift-off didn't disappoint. As we rose skyward, the tail section lifted higher than the overhead rotors so the helicopter was slanted at a forward angle. We rushed onward and upward as if gliding up a hill and circled the chopper pads once to gain more height before heading to Lai Khe. I could see the entire base camp as the chopper slowly spun around and everything became smaller as we rose. Then I saw the ARVN camp, Thu Duc and all the other local villages, and the huge stretches of open terrain that surrounded our Di An basecamp. I also spotted another Huey to our port side that was joining our mission. Although it was still early, the sun was shining brightly and there were very few clouds in the sky. It was a beautiful day.

As we turned north I saw Thunder Road below, winding its way through the emerald green countryside. By the time we were heading straight for Lai Khe, we were about 2,500 or more feet above the ground. At first the view appeared to be a tranquil landscape with a scattering of rubber tree plantations, small villages, farms, and thousands of flooded rice paddies, each separated by small berms of earth. Not too far north of Di An, only rice paddies and stretches of dense triple-canopy jungle took over the entire view for as far as I could see.

The sun was still rising and the sunlight skimmed the surface of the flooded paddies reflecting the light in brilliant silver sheets that focused into wide beams piercing the shadows like searchlights. I couldn't help but notice how the sunshine spotlighted the thousands of pockmarked puddles, most maybe five feet across, that marred the surface of every pond and rice paddy; but some of them were huge and 50 or more feet across. I guessed all of these "puddles" were impact craters from mortar fire from firefights, plus beehive bombs and other gifts from the B-52s that graced the evening skies.

I had taken a small camera out of my shirt pocket and was trying to capture the unique reflective terrain below. Suddenly through my earphones came to life, one of the pilots was shouting "muzzle flashes at two o'clock from the starboard side." Shit, somebody was shooting at us and I had to do something. I chambered the first round into the M-60, took the safety off, grabbed the gun and was ready to fire, and scoured the area, but I didn't see a damn thing! The warning came again and, as the chopper turned into an evasive maneuver, I finally saw an irregular sequence of flashes that had been hidden by both the machine gun ammo belt and obscured by sun's reflections. The enemy fire was coming from the four-corners intersection of some rice paddies.

I had to loosen my seat belt and sort of half stand up. When I leaned over to see better, I aimed at the small clump of trees and squeezed off three or four short bursts. The vibrating chomp, chomp of the machine gun shook my arms and confirmed my action. The tracers gently snaked downward and told me I was a little short and right of the target. The flashes appeared again and seemed to intensify; so I tried to compensate for the speed of the chopper, and fired three long bursts of at least 60 rounds total. This time, as the tracers descended and wafted and waved, they appeared to slice through my designated target and smashed into the adjoining paddies. The surges of muzzle flashes stopped so I ceased firing, but watched the area intently until it was out of sight. The other chopper to our port side had turned away and climbed higher and was no longer in sight.

We returned to our course and continued on our way. Nothing more was or needed to be said. Did I kill someone; I'll never know, and, quite frankly, I never lost a minute's sleep thinking about it. All I could think was that he had done his job and I had done mine. It was pretty easy to be calloused and unaffected when we battled at a faraway distance. No one on our chopper had been injured. There had been no close confrontation, no confirming results, no bodies to count, and no nightmares. At least now I knew how I would react when duty called.

We arrived at Lai Khe without further incident, unloaded our cargo, and took care of everyone's payroll needs. There were no real problems and after lunch we boarded the Huey and headed for home (or whatever the hell it was). The return trip was uneventful and, still perched behind the M-60, I tried to enjoy the panoramic views of a country that had been entrenched in turmoil for eons and I knew the end was nowhere in sight. When we returned and disembarked, I saw a couple of bullet holes in the flap on the starboard side of the synchronized elevator wing just below the rear rotor on the chopper tail. I asked one of the pilots about it. He looked at me and said "I never noticed that before," winked, and walked away; and I was OK with that. It had been an exhilarating day, and, whether fortunate or not, that ended up being my one and only payroll run.

A couple of weeks later I was told the Finance Specialist on our team who normally handled the medics was on 24-hour guard duty, and that the medics had called and asked us to come over and see a couple of people who had a few questions. I volunteered to go. The medics were located on the other side of the base, but I decided to walk instead of waiting for a ride. It took about twenty minutes to get there and I had to sit and wait to see those men with complaints.

The place was buzzing with people shouting and running around like crazy. There had been an ambush with too many casualties, and they had their hands full. Maybe an hour later, things settled down, I met with a couple of the medics and discussed their payroll concerns, and everything was settled in short order without complaint.

Then we sat around and shot the bull for a while. I was curious, and it was obvious they really needed to decompress. The medics had saved everyone in that ambush except for the one who had been shot first, a sergeant who had been giving candy to the kids who swarmed around him in a small village not all that far away. A five-year-old girl with her hand inside a paper bag approached him, and when he bent over to hand her a *Hershey©* bar, she shot him in stomach with a 22-caliber pistol. At that point, snipers opened up on the rest of the troops and hit six others and a couple of the kids.

I had wondered who she was when I first noticed her. Only five years old – and there she was, a pretty little girl standing in the corner in her stained white dress, about twenty feet from where I sat. Tiny fists up in the air next to her head, blankly staring at nothing, not making a sound, and tears slowly rolling down her dirty cheeks. She was scared to death. A medic was holding onto the skirt of her dress to keep her there, and he was on the phone looking the other way. If I were an artist, I could paint that picture in detail even today; she was the poster child and epitome of what was wrong in Vietnam. That little child was the only person I ever cried for during the entirety of my stay in Vietnam. I have often prayed she somehow found her way to a better life. In that brief moment, I seriously thought maybe I had already seen and known of too much tragedy for any one person, and the vision of that little girl sometimes still haunts me today. I know many saw so much worse, but for me, this tragedy was the ultimate heartbreak.

14

A Sense of Duty

July 1968

Although it was technically the beginning of the rainy season, other than a couple scattered showers, the first couple of weeks of July were bright sunny days. I later learned this seventh month was a benchmark for many international happenings. On the 4th, yachtsman Alec Rose receives a hero's welcome home after sailing back to Portsmouth, England, successfully completing a 354-day round-the-world trip. On July 18th, a little company called Intel is founded. The first International Special Olympics Summer Games are held in Chicago on the 20th. Pope Paul VI publishes the encyclical titled *Humanae Vitae*, which condemned birth control, and this causes quite a stir.

Around Di An, things more or less had returned to their more peaceful ways – no more attacks and no more alerts. We were even allowed to wear civilian clothes to the office whenever we worked at night. In early July, I had an opportunity to make a supply run to Saigon and jumped at the chance. The next morning I hopped into a jeep without a canopy top along with three others, we left the base camp followed by two deuce and a half trucks with another jeep taking up the rear, and our small convoy headed south towards Saigon. The jeep had a section of L-shaped angle iron that stuck up about three feet above the hood which had been welded and braced to the front bumper, and a small "V" shaped notch facing forward had been cut into the vertical iron post. Another 8" long piece of angle iron had been welded to the top of the post slanted at a 45° forward angle to act as a guard. The purpose of this device was to break any strands of wire stretched across the roadway meant to decapitate any unwary travelers. The folding windshield was up and we all did our best to keep our heads down. What a country!

The countryside had remained pretty much the same since the last time I passed by; except for a few more bomb and mortar craters and a couple more destroyed buildings, all resulting from the Tet Offensive battles. Everything else was the same. The traffic, the people, and the lush greenery still graced the landscape. The roadway was pretty crowded but we successfully navigated whatever was in our path and made it to Saigon in record time. After a short stop at the supply depot, we left the trucks to be loaded and headed to the city. Tet had decimated Saigon and the evidence was all around us. It had been over five months since most of the fighting was over, but there were still bullet hole pockmarks in a many of the walls, and some of the buildings had been reduced to unrecognizable heaps of rubble.

We found our way to the PX, which for me was the real goal of the trip. First we had lunch and a quick beer, and then we went shopping. The Saigon PX put every other PX in the country to shame; it was like comparing a small convenience store to a large supermarket. I bought gifts for everyone in my family: a carved ivory statue holding an open ball containing two more, each inside the other, ancient knife money, old Vietnamese coins, an ornate doll, a transistor radio, clothing, a jungle hat, and more things than I can remember now. I also bought two bottles of CC (Canadian Club whiskey), which was all my ration card would allow, and two more bottles using my bunkmate's card. Everything was neatly packed into a cardboard box with a folding lid and I was ready to go. The other three also had one box each, and I can tell you it was no easy feat loading the four us and our boxes, into the confines of our jeep that somehow seemed to have gotten a lot smaller.

We headed back to the supply depot and found the trucks had no room for our boxes so they stayed in the jeep, and soon our little convoy was on its way back to Di An. The return trip was pretty much the same as the first, and it was uneventful until we had to go through one more little village just outside our base. The roads through town were crowded and hard to navigate until we made a right turn, finally on our way out of town. The street was completely empty – not one person, cart, chicken, or dog was there. I put a round into the chamber of my M-16, unlocked the safety, pointed it straight up into the air, then tried to hunker down, but that was impossible. Expecting an ambush, our driver hit the gas and our small convoy tore through the streets at breakneck speed. All of a sudden about a seven year old boy jumped out from behind a tree, pointing a stick at me like it was a rifle. In an instant I was aiming at him, and to this day I do not know why I didn't fire; if he had been a VC, I would have been just another statistic. Then he jumped up and down laughing and ran back to his house. Lucky boy – and lucky me.

Soon we were back at the Admin Company and I took my goody box back to the hootch. I sold one of my bottles of CC for double what I had paid and gave the other two to my buddy. Then I sat down and had a shot of whiskey to celebrate our safe return without any catastrophes. Since nothing had really happened I wasn't too shook up; but, even then, I occasionally still questioned my readiness but never once regretted my restraint that day.

OK, I know I've discussed guard duty before; but, just in case you were still wondering, I always had a love/hate relationship with that obligation. In the summer it was incredibly hot, too dusty, and whether outside or in the bunker, day or night, it was miserable. During the rainy season everything you had on you or wore got wet, the bunker sometimes flooded, the humidity was unbearable, and I never got used to sleeping on a cot that had been turned into a puddle. Then there was always that nagging suspicion that you were being watched, and that maybe something bad was about to happen.

If you added the critters such as snakes, rodents, mosquitos, flies, and fire ants to the mix, it could become more than a little uncomfortable. However, whenever there was an incident that did not directly affect you, it came as an almost welcome (although sometimes scary) relief from the monotony of it all. Guard duty was usually easy, mostly boring, presented very few problems, and sometimes was a pleasant escape from the tedious and sad realities of working in the office and constant scrutiny.

Guard duty came in a number of shapes and sizes: There was perimeter guard duty in a bunker, 24-hour bunker duty, gate duty at one of the three entrances to the base camp, special assignments like guarding the USO building, and tower duty about 30 feet in the air. Also, every morning around seven, there was a perimeter sweep outside the outer wires and minefield to see if there was any disruption to our defenses and to look for signs of activity. Admin Charlie, our local sniper, was of little concern; it seems he never stuck his head up for fear of losing it.

There's not too much I can tell you about the night-time bunker duty that I haven't already said. But beyond the discomfort, fatigue, and concerns, there were a couple of positive points. Although two people were to be awake at all times, you often found yourself alone to ponder your thoughts. Even with only the moon and starlight, you could see well enough to write a letter home or read your mail. Mostly, I just kept an eye on the perimeter, watched the ever-present intense bouquet of stars, and daydreamed about anything and everything. My thoughts usually centered on how to best improve my circumstance, what I should buy next, how everything was going back home, and how many days I had left in country. Pretty lackluster stuff actually, but I managed to keep myself occupied – and more importantly, awake.

Two things happened each night to help spice things up a bit. The Sergeant of the guard normally made at least one tour of our bunkers and he would give us updates if there were any concerns.

His true motivation was to make damn sure everyone was awake, but also probably wanted to "shoot the bull" to help pass the time. Every night around 8:00, the mess hall would send out a little dinner. This usually consisted of strong, thick coffee and a sandwich. Well, it looked like a sandwich wrapped in wax paper when delivered; but, as soon as you grabbed it, the bread turned into a gooey, slippery, doughy tortilla that made it almost impossible to hold or eat whatever the hell kind of meat was hidden inside. The coffee was very robust and usually not very hot, but it did the job. Afterward, for some reason, my next thoughts usually were centered on home and food.

Several times when I was on duty, our base camp was attacked by mortars and once by small rockets. Usually the attacks were centered on the infantry companies, the Korean compound, and engineering companies – all of which were a good distance away from the Admin defenses. Only once did the mortars crater a path between the hootches and the bunkers, and this was way too close for comfort (but it did keep my overconfidence in check). You felt the vibration and noise from the thumping impacts and heard the red-hot metal shards cutting through the air and anything else in their path. Thankfully, and sadly, the only building damaged was our shower – the Commie bastards. Shrapnel cut through a number of the barracks, but the good news was those slivers of death were too high to hit anybody since they were all hugging the floor. The guards were well protected in the bunkers; so the end result was no one got hurt, but it took over a week to replace the shower tanks. There were a number of additional attacks when I wasn't on guard duty, almost always in the middle of the night, and normally without result.

Right after Tet and for a couple of months after, our base camp was attacked sporadically. One week nothing would happen, and the next we might be hit two or three times. One theory was since we were pretty close to a branch of the Ho Chi Minh trail with the VC retreating from their nightly attacks on Saigon and the surrounding area they simply decided to lighten their load by the time they got to

Di An. And yes, I did know how to dive down from a top bunk and embrace the cement floor before actually waking up. Most of the hootches closest to the perimeter had been ventilated by shrapnel and I had a couple of slit-like holes high on the wall near my bunk.

It seems funny now, but the whole time I was in country I never once was in fear of losing my life – or anything else for that matter. I didn't feel invincible and took the necessary precautions and kept my head down when prudent to do so, but I was seriously not concerned. Maybe I had too much bluster or was in denial, too young, or too stupid; right now as I type these words, I'm more inclined to think it was the latter. As you know, ignorance is bliss.

Our normal response to any attack was always the same. First everyone took cover and then the flares began popping off every couple of minutes, illuminating our perimeter and focusing our scrutiny. The sirens repeatedly and loudly blared "RED ALERT," and reinforcements soon fortified our perimeter. Not one time did I ever see the enemy when I was on perimeter guard duty. I knew they were out there somewhere, but all I ever saw were the varying intensities of light and the shadows of darkness. Probably just as well because I wasn't a hand-to-hand combat kind of guy. Even with everything that I had already been through there hadn't been any close or face to face contact. I did wonder how I would react to a frontal attack. Would I cower and shake, run away, take too many risks, hesitate too long before I shot someone, or take care of business and worry about it later? I was more than halfway through my tour and still pondered my readiness

The perimeter needed to be guarded 24/7; so on occasion you were cordially invited to enjoy the bunker hospitality and amenities for 24 hours straight. Night or day, the responsibilities were still the same. The biggest difference when working the day shift was almost always nothing happened. The NVA and VC normally preferred the night shift for their attacks and ambushes because they rightfully feared the quick and awesome fire power the Americans always had ready to meet any challenge. So during the day, the only real excitement was when Admin Charlie took a couple of shots at the sun. There was some concern that one day he might take a vacation and be replaced with a more dedicated soul. Then, one day, a patrol found him in his spider hole. After that, no one shot at the sun anymore.

I had gate guard duty quite a few times and it was completely different. The perimeter barbed wire and minefield stopped short on either side of the roadway, and in-ground bunkers flanked both sides of our position left and right about 75 yards away. The gate had an above-ground sandbag walled hut which sported a M60 machine gun. The sandbags were piled about four and a half feet high, and four posts supported a slanted corrugated metal panel roof. The hut furnishings were sparse and consisted of a single folding canvas cot and a combo ammo cabinet and rifle rack with an M79, grenades, and handheld flares.

Across the road from the hut there was another above-ground sandbag bunker with a M67, a 90-millimeter recoilless rifle that was permanently mounted. A shell was sticking out of the rear of the chamber. All you had to do was push the round in, lock the chamber, aim, and pull the trigger. For backup, three additional shells in a wooden box leaned against one of the sandbag walls. It was an effective anti-tank weapon that would stop almost anything the VC could muster to ram the gate.

Each evening at 6:00 the gate was closed and two heavy-duty eight-inch diameter reinforced pipe pivoting gates were locked in place. Then we placed the two claymore mines in the roadway about 150 feet away, inserted the blasting caps, aimed them toward the outgoing road, and ran the wires down the middle of the road back to the gate hut. We stretched three rows of concertina wire in front of the gates and tied them in place. Afterward, and only then, we attached the claymore mine blasting cap wires to the clackers. The hut was adjacent to the road and about 20 feet back from the gate. Gate duty was about the same as bunker duty except, because of the road, there was no outer wire, no mine field, and a lot less barbed wire. I never saw any action at the gate but it had been hit a couple of times after Tet – attacked, but never breeched.

One night we were lucky enough to get C-rations for dinner but there were no heat tabs to warm the cans. One of the guys took an extra claymore mine and removed the back to expose the C4 plastic explosive. He used his fingertips and dragged them along the entire width of the explosive to gather a thin layer of C4. Then he rolled it into a ball about the about the size of a golf ball and reassembled the mine. Even though I knew the C4 was harmless unless detonated by a blasting cap, I still thought he was nuts. He used his *Zippo©* to light the ball. We huddled inside the bunker to conceal the flame, partially opened our cherished C-ration cans with a P38 can opener, then folded the lids back to form makeshift handles. A nice orange and blue flame with a not-so-aromatic chemical scent lit up the bunker, and each of us in turn heated our dinner. The fire was still burning, so the pyromaniac let it burn down then brushed enough soil on it to extinguish the flame. He warned us to never step on the burning C4 because compressing it when lit could cause an explosion. After it had cooled, he tossed the odd-gum shaped remnant over the barbed wire into the field to our right.

One evening an APC came rumbling up the road and approached our gate after our defensives had already been set in place. It had hit a mine and one of its tracks had been damaged, so it had to zig-zag back and forth across the road to move forward. It stopped way short of the claymore mines. When the crew shouted at us, we instantly knew they were U.S. simply by noting their accents and the number of F--- words used. Still, we had to call the duty sergeant to get permission to allow them to proceed. He rushed to the gate and asked who they were and if there were any casualties. When he found no one was hurt, he laughed and told us to open the gate. The light was beginning to fade so we quickly disassembled the blasting cap wires from the clackers, removed the concertina wire, opened the gates, and picked up the claymores. The APC tracked back and forth, passed through the gate, and went about a 25 yards beyond our position before stopping. We quickly secured the gate again. An hour later, a tank recovery vehicle towed the wounded warrior away.

Unfortunately I also witnessed something much worse. When exhausted men and dangerous weapons are in the same place at the same time, it is inevitable that something bad is going to happen. Shortly after the Fourth of July, one of my Finance buddies was also on gate duty, and he decided to take the claymore mines and blasting caps down the road to set them in place. As was the protocol, in one hand he had the mines and in the other he held the blasting caps. For some reason I'll never know, the blasting cap wires were still attached to the clackers and the wire lever safeties were not locked in place. As he walked down the road, the tangled wires pulled the clackers off the shelf and one of them compressed and detonated the blasting cap. We all rushed out to help him and I used my boot laces to make a tourniquet to stop the bleeding. He lost a thumb and two fingers from his left hand, and soon after he was on his way home. Stupid mistake, tragic consequences, and similar events were a daily occurrence; I never understood the "why" but always seemed to know the "what and where."

Guard duty in the tower was a real break from reality and rightfully so was the most requested guard post. Only once did I enjoy the views and remoteness of the tower which was maybe 30-feet high. Since nothing obstructed the view except for the other three distant towers, you could see forever, and I even thought I saw the curvature of the earth wherever I looked. It was a crystal-clear night, and with only the brilliance of a half moon and the stars, the only discernable views outside our base camp were Saigon and the Tan Son Nhut air base. In one easy panoramic glance, you had a full view of the perimeter, our company area, our base camp, and Vietnam as I knew it.

In the tower we were an easy target since we stuck out like a sore thumb, but we were far away from the perimeter and it was not all that easy to hit. My only real concern was the four flights of stairs necessary to negotiate before finding the ground and the distant outhouse (I always drank a lot of water). I never slept the whole night through and was intrigued every minute by the views. I used the starlight telescope to scour the perimeter and didn't see a thing except the hazy green silhouettes the scope provided, but nothing was moving. I checked out our base camp, the perimeter and beyond, and every image was amazing. Perhaps I was star-struck by the wonder of it all, but even now would love to have a chance to see it all again. Maybe I was easily entertained, but I still have those visions and feelings of tranquility whenever I think of that night.

Without a doubt, the morning perimeter sweep was the most dangerous assignment. Your resources were limited, support was far away, and, if anything happened, you were going to be on your own for a while – and most assuredly, you had a problem. Still, if you participated in that stroll through the boonies, your efforts were awarded with having the balance of the day to yourself, and this is what made this duty an attractive option – or so I thought. I had put in for the morning perimeter sweep maybe a dozen times, but I had to wait until my duty sergeant was in charge of the bunker guard before it actually happened.

The previous night's guard duty had been uneventful and, as usual, I was a little drained. Although I knew our journey through the wilds of Di An from gate to gate would take an hour or so, I was still looking forward to it. There hadn't been any problems with the sweeps for about at least a month so I had no concerns. I just hoped it would be over soon; I was really tired.

In preparation, I had cleaned my brand new M16 the day before and made sure I had a bandolier of 8 fully loaded magazines. I can't remember if I was told or volunteered to take the point position, but

I also chose to carry a M79 grenade launcher with a couple of bandoliers with 6 grenades each. The M16 was much lighter than my old M14 so the extra load wasn't much of a problem.

My duty sergeant and I with 6 others made up our squad, and soon we were bouncing around on the short ride to the South Gate in the back of a deuce and a half. We were a motley crew with six office clerks, a snooty Colonel's aide (he must have done something really wrong), and, of course, my office Sergeant. Not a real fighting man in the whole damn bunch (nor any wannabes for that matter). The gate defenses had not been cleared so we had a cigarette and "BS'd" while we waited. The gate guards told us they had heard rumors that there was a build-up of NVA forces in our area, but no one had actually seen anything and it had been quiet in our vicinity. I couldn't help but think this was just more crap to scare the office geeks.

As the gate defenses were being removed, a small convoy of three APCs and two tanks pulled up to the gate. As soon as the path had been cleared, they all roared past us each spewing black diesel exhaust and dust by the bucketloads shot out from under their tracks. We waited for the dust to settle, then I took point and started down the road about 20 yards in front of my sergeant and the others, all following in single file. Maybe 80 yards down the road, I turned left onto the path outside our outer perimeter wire.

The well-worn path varied from three- to six-feet wide. To my left, the brush entangled outer barbed wire fencing of our perimeter and the minefield behind it followed the pathway. On the other side of the trail, the shoulder areas were a mixture of assorted short grasses, weeds, small and taller trees, bushes, as well as an assortment of smaller rocks and a couple of fallen trees. Actually, the right side of the perimeter path was mostly a wide-open space with very few obvious places to hide. All the same, everybody intently surveyed every little bump, bush or tree, and the last one in line (also known as "tail end Charlie") was always watching behind us.

The thick, heavy dust coated everything. As we trudged along, we made ample impressions of our passing, but it had been a little windy that night so the path ahead was a blank slate. Being the point man, I had to look ahead for any signs of movement or danger but spent of the most time looking for booby traps more than anything else. It was very quiet and the stillness was only broken by the sarge a ways behind me updating the Command Post of our location and status on his walkie-talkie.

Our progress was very slow and deliberate and, even though I was anxious to get back inside our base camp, I didn't want to make the trip in a body bag. It was early morning; but as usual it was already bright and sunny and I could see everything in our path and a couple hundred yards to my right – except way up ahead, just short of the base camp perimeter corner where we turned left to head towards the east gate, where there was a small bunch of 30 or so trees and bushes less than 100 yards to the right of the turn.

I kept an eye on the tree line but was unexpectedly surprised by a footprint in the dust a short way up ahead. I stopped and had everyone squat or lie down and stay in place. I slowly crawled forward looking for any booby traps but didn't see anything. The footprint was walking away from our outer wire towards the boonies and looked like it had been made that morning. The deep impression was from a well-worn Ho Chi Minh slipper, a thong-type sandal made from an old tire, and popular with the VC. The Sarge called in and updated our status and was told to proceed with caution – easy for them to say.

I stood up and slowly walked down the trail, a little nervous, a little slower, and a lot more vigilant. We were less than 50 yards from the perimeter corner near that small collection of trees. I stopped dead in my tracks when I saw two Vietnamese soldiers in pith helmets turn and walk by the trees and take a path parallel to ours. Holy crap, they were NVA! They didn't see us because they were in a heated argument, and one spat at the other then took a swing at him. The only thing that immediately popped into my frantic mind was a drawing from an army manual I had read in basic training illustrating the correct manner to quietly point out an enemy position. I dutifully raised my M16 straight over my head and pointed it at the two men, and everybody looked at me like I had suddenly turned into Mary Poppins. They had absolutely no idea what was happening.

Before I could warn them, bullets whizzed by my head and I dove behind a fallen tree. Everybody hit the ground and found whatever cover was there. The Sergeant was the closest to me and he was on the horn asking for help. As I hunkered down, AK47 bullets zipped all around me and slammed into my favorite tree trunk sending chips of wood flying over my head. I decided to return the favor. I methodically loaded my M79, set the sight for 85 yards, stuck the barrel over the log, guessed at the direction, and fired without sticking my head up to properly aim. When I fired, there was a thump and the grenade exploded a couple of long seconds later. My sergeant went nuts and yelled "You can't fire your weapon here, we're in a no-fire zone." I stared in misbelief and shouted back "tell them that", inserted another grenade, and adjusted the sight for 100 yards just in case they had moved back and fired again without looking. I quickly loaded another grenade, set the M79 aside, grabbed my M16, chambered a round, and unlocked the safety. If I was going down, I wasn't going alone. I don't think I'd ever been so damned pissed off or that scared in all my life.

The Sergeant was still yelling and threatened me with a General court-martial if I fired again, something about disregarding a direct order under file. The incoming fire had stopped so I held my position, peeking around one end of the log then the other and looked for any movement – thankfully there wasn't any. It was then I realized that not one other person in my squad had fired and it was my turn to be dumbfounded. WTF would it take to get these guys into survival mode? I closed my eyes and prayed there were only two

NVA and that they had run away. I guess God was with us that day, and I thanked him profusely for that fallen tree.

I remained behind cover and started scanning the whole area through the sight on my M16 but didn't see a thing. The Sarge had called for choppers and he said they were due any minute; a full half an hour later they finally made an appearance. There were three Hueys and each took a sector and scoured the area, but there was nothing to see. After ten minutes they told us to pack it up and move on. I softly patted my lucky tree, stood up, and cautiously continued to lead our patrol. The choppers stayed with us but flew much higher and watched our progress as we turned the corner and headed for the east gate. Our pace was a little quicker than before, but I still took my time looking for trip wires, Punji Stakes, and Charlie. After another thirty minutes had passed, we walked through the East Gate and caught a ride back to the Admin Company.

Nobody was very talkative. When we returned everybody quickly went their separate ways. I was exhausted, still pumped up on adrenaline, mad at the whole damn world, and confused as hell. I was a mess. I got back to the hootch and dumped my stuff on the floor, took off my boots, and laid on my bunk still in my dusty fatigues. I just laid there, smoking like a chimney, staring up at the ceiling, watching spiders weave their webs and catch their prey. I remained there for hours with my eyes wide open, stunned by everything that had happened – and by what had not.

It had never once occurred to me before that it was even remotely possible at any time I could be shot and wounded or killed. I had never contemplated the concept of dying. I wasn't afraid but suddenly had become very apprehensive about just about everything. I never slept that day. Every time I closed my eyes, I saw those two guys turning and walking past those trees and, whenever I think about it now, I can still clearly see them arguing. I eventually concluded that my humanity was bruised but intact and it was time to move on. The anger slowly melted away and I guessed maybe I was in shock. I needed to hear some answers but also knew there were a lot of questions I would never ask.

Around two I got up and was lucky there was still enough water left in the tanks to be able to take a shower, then went for a walk around the Admin Company. Afterward I went up to the PX and bought a carton of cigarettes because I had already smoked the last three packs I had left. A haircut and shave followed as well as a massage and a manicure, and I got my boots polished. I usually felt much better about everything after all that – but not so much this day. I went over to the Di An Five & Dime and bought another *Zippo*© lighter and had it engraved, again; somehow I had managed to lose another one that morning. I trudged back to the hootch and picked up my gear that was still just piled in a heap on the floor, dusted off the fatigues and hung them on a nail, then disassembled and cleaned my M16. After that I picked up the M79 and the remaining grenades and returned them to the armory.

Although I hadn't eaten that day, I wasn't hungry. I went outside and set up my folding lawn-chair lounge behind the hootch, grabbed a warm beer, sat down, and stared at the perimeter bunkers. I didn't even notice when everyone got off work and went out back to exercise, play catch, and throw their *Frisbees*©. A 12" softball slammed into the wall to my right. I guess one of my buddies wanted to see if I was still alive. It did the trick. So after three warm beers and another pack of cigarettes, I finally got off my butt and discovered that now I was starving. I went to the mess hall and had a quick dinner.

Afterward I went to the office to write a letter home. My Sergeant was there. When I sat down at my desk he came over and asked if I was OK. I told him I was doing fine. He began to walk away but turned and put his hand on my back and said "thanks," and then he was gone. After that I had no more questions.

I started to write that letter home a dozen times and ended up rolling each attempt into a little ball and throwing it in the trash. I eventually decided to stop playing waste can basketball and to write that letter at another time. I covered my desk with a canvas tarp to keep everything clean and headed back to the hootch. It was movie night so I stopped and took a look. While standing, I watched the last half of the TV series "Wild, Wild West" episode before hitting the rack.

Before my eyes finally slammed shut, I thanked the Lord for saving our asses that day, then promised myself to never make a big deal of what had happened and to move on and live my life as best I could. And that has been my credo ever since what had proved to be a very eventful day. Oh, and I try to do my best not to get so damned angry anymore – but that aspect, then as now, still needs a little work.

15

Crazy

August & September 1968

In was early August and the wet season was adding more and more clouds to the sky each day. One day we had the most unique cloud cover I had ever seen, before or since. Right after work I was enjoying a semi-cold beer on my favorite folding chaise lounge smoking a cigarette and watching the show. A lot of guys were running around playing catch. We were all enjoying the weather since the rainy season was not into full gear yet.

It had started off being pretty sunny, but slowly the sun disappeared behind the billowing clouds. And this is the weird part: as if they were Broadway stage props, as they approached the churning clouds slowly drifted towards the ground. The lower they fell, the quieter it got. Eventually we were under a roiling canopy of clouds no more than twenty feet above the ground – twenty feet! We couldn't see the top of the tower. Everyone was staring at the phenomenon, eyes perplexed and mouths open. The guys started throwing their baseballs, footballs, and whatever up into the darkening, curling blanket of white and gray. Everything they tossed disappeared for a moment or two then returned to be caught. We were all intrigued by the phenomenon and having a great time.

And then in an instant it happened. There was a bright flash to my left and suddenly the entirety of our perimeter literally blew up. Every Claymore Mine shotgunned a widening path of total devastation through the minefield detonating some of the mines, and then those little ball-bearings of death cut through the outer perimeter barbed wire blockade. Most noticeably, all of the Foo Gas Cannons spewed forth in huge bright red and orange flames that quickly transformed into pitch black oily smoke. The flash was blinding. And the sound of all those ball bearings mowing the grass and the prolonged belching roar of the Foo Gas that seemed to linger combined to be the scariest thing I had ever heard. I was eating dirt by the time I heard the blast and I didn't move an inch for a couple of minutes. When I looked up, everybody was plastered to the ground and I was afraid there might have been some casualties. I thought maybe the long-anticipated frontal attack had finally become a reality. When I finally got back on my feet, the perimeter was all a blur of black rancid smoke spiraling toward the slowly rising, tossing layer of swirling light and dark gray-colored clouds. Nobody appeared to be injured and everyone ran back to the hootches. I followed them inside but kept the hootch door open so I could see if anything else was happening.

Not too much later we learned a lightning strike had detonated every hard-wired device on our perimeter. Why they all had exploded at the same time I couldn't figure out. As far as I knew, each individual bunker was in control of two Claymore Mines and one Foo Gas Cannon. Apparently I was wrong. For some unknown reason or mistake, they had all had been linked together. It took a week to replace the Foo Gas Cannons and all the barbed wire that had been blasted toward Saigon. There were some injuries but they were minor and had resulted from people hitting the ground. Pretty scary stuff, but a spectacular end of the day nonetheless. Just another day of shaken tranquility in paradise.

Sometime after the Tet Offensive, one of our company commanders thought the 1st Admin Company needed to take a more proactive role in our fight with the Vietcong. A memo asking for volunteers was posted in each of the company offices and a group of 30 or so signed up that day. They soon started training first thing every morning and again after work in the evening. An intense routine of exercises preceded a variety of classes teaching the use of booby traps, camouflage, tracking methods, and hand-to-hand combat. Then they went to the range to be re-educated in the proper use of weapons such as the M16 rifle, the M79 grenade launcher, and the M60 machine gun. They honed their proficiency for each of the weapons and added Claymore Mines, bayonet, plus smoke and fragmentation grenade use to their list of accomplishments. They also learned hand signals and radio communication. Then, after about six weeks of preparation, they were ready to go. And so was born our very own search-and-destroy specialist team: the 1st Infantry Division's "Admin Badmen."

I thought they were all nuts but admired their courage and dedication. At first, about once a week, they went out on patrol at dusk and set various types of ambushes which included the use of Claymore mines. In the beginning they were accompanied by infantry squads until they had passed a competency test, and after that were off on their own. Although they witnessed movement a couple of times, they never engaged in a fire fight but were able to supply some intel to MI. Everything was going along as planned until one morning when they were packing up after setting up an ambush. The found that three of the Claymore Mines they had set up the night before had been turned around 180 degrees and now faced their location. That could have been a disaster and it did in fact discourage a couple of the guys. They were still going at it when I left the Nam, but they had been reined in to only one or two operations a month. I was always amazed that nobody got hurt while I was in country. This was probably something that was done to break up daily monotony, or they simply wanted to see some action, and I sincerely hope they all fared well after I left. I think I'll always remember the Big Red One's rear echelon combatants, the one and only "Admin Badmen."

I had heard rumors about the Army replacing all the existing military scrip with a new design for as long as I had been in country. Well, that time had at long last come and "Conversion Day," or "C-Day" as it was called, was finally here. The United States had been using the existing design for about a year, and the countrywide exchange had been delayed several times due to all the hoopla surrounding Tet. The new currency was needed to stop its unintended use in the black market, to put a halt to anyone illegally selling U.S. supplies, and to thwart any ill-gotten gain. Greenbacks were forbidden for any U.S. personnel to have in their possession while in country; so the only cash normally available was the Military Payment Currency (MPC). If someone from home sent you a twenty-dollar bill for your birthday you could usually exchange it for about double that amount in MPC dollars. It was also illegal for any Vietnamese citizen to hold or use military scrip, but that didn't stop them.

There was a cap of $400 for enlisted men (I think this is correct but I don't remember the exact number) as the maximum amount of MPC any one person could exchange. To convert a higher amount required pay vouchers or some other kind of proof to substantiate that the total monies exchanged had been earned and saved (like for an upcoming R&R or tape recorder, for instance). Since MPC had in fact been used throughout Vietnam by everyone, the exchange was a devastating blow to many local entrepreneurs, bar girls, the black market, and all those enterprising soldiers of questionable character. For a lot of Americans and Vietnamese, this was a crippling economic event.

The date was not pre-announced so it came to as much of a surprise to us as it did to everyone else. The basecamp was locked down, no Vietnamese locals were permitted inside the camp that day, and no U.S. troops could leave. All U.S. personnel in the field had to return to their permanent bases if possible. Since some of the men in the field couldn't make back to make the swap, special chopper borne squads of Finance Specialists were dispatched and made their conversions in the boonies.

We rearranged a portion of the incoming processing office to accommodate the lines of people and expected to have a very long day, and it was. Troops stationed at Di An were first and came in company groups. The people that had been in the field came next in staggered clusters of 40-to-60 men. Since it was near the end of the month, the total average MPC exchange was decidedly less than $100. There were a few that maxed out the total amount possible to exchange, and they had some explaining to do. Most of those with too much to convert simply had others exchange their excess money for a finder's fee.

A lot of locals from villages around our basecamp came up to each of the three gates, walked past the Claymore Mines, moved the concertina barbed wire coils, approached the closed gate, and begged the guards to take their MPC. Some would take as little as ten cents on the dollar. Having anticipated this response, a cadre of MPs were stationed at each gate and sent the villagers all on their way. Those who protested too much were held for questioning. Some Vietnamese even tried to walk through our minefield but were discouraged when the bunker guards fired warning shots over the heads. I believe we closed up shop around 10:00 that evening. Any stragglers would be taken care of later, and they too had some explaining to do.

Later, around 1:00 AM that night, only the 1st Admin Company was hit by a mortar attack, and it didn't take a Perry Mason to figure out why. Luckily, once again, no one was hurt, but the surrounding countryside was pissed off as hell.

On July 31st, 1968, I left on my out-of-country R&R to Taipei, Taiwan for five nights and four days of fun and games. There were a lot of other locations I could have gone to including Hong Kong, Singapore, Tokyo, Bangkok, Kuala Lampur, Manila, Sydney, and Hawaii. Sydney and Hawaii were almost impossible to get, any destination with round-eyed girls was in great demand. A good friend was going to Taipei and had convinced me to join him. For me, the destination really wasn't all that important. Just escaping from the Nam, if only for a little while, was my real objective. We hopped onto a deuce and a half to Ton Son Nhut and caught a flight to Taipei. Before boarding the plane, we went through a thorough inspection of our paperwork and even our immunization records.

The flight was uneventful until we approached Taiwan. We were put in a holding pattern circling the island because we had been flanked by two jets from mainland China. China still disputed the independence of Taiwan and often harassed the incoming and departing flights. It was just a little reminder for us that Vietnam wasn't the only troubled spot on the planet, and another example of how much China hated the U.S. at that time. After the better part of an hour, our worrisome escort found someone else to bother and we landed a short time later. Luggage in hand, we were taken by a military bus to the U.S. Navy Exchange for R&R personnel at the Taipei reception area and schooled in the proper behavior expected of us. We chose the Hotel Golden Star as our destination and finally arrived at the hotel around 4:30 that afternoon. The building was very narrow and I think it was six stories tall, but it was a real hotel and not just another barracks – I was thrilled. We quickly checked in and then took the world's smallest, slowest elevator to our respective floors. The rooms were on the petite side and sparsely appointed, but they felt like a suite at the Waldorf to us. Not bothering to unpack, we met downstairs in the lobby, both anxious for our adventures to begin.

There was a tailor shop next door to the hotel and my buddy really wanted to get a custom-tailored silk suit. I thought maybe a new suit wasn't a bad idea and so we were both measured up, chose the style and fabric, and then we each put $5.00 down with $20.00 due when we picked up the suits two days later. I thought it was a little expensive but did it anyway. We had a nice dinner at a Chinese restaurant across the street, and I was pretty sure the steak I had wasn't water buffalo. There was a bar down the street that my buddy knew of so we went in to have a drink or two.

It was like no other bar I had ever seen; it was a very narrow room maybe 10 feet wide by 40 feet deep. Just inside the front door there were two six-foot-long bars, one on either side of the room, each with four backless stools. We were the only customers and were immediately greeted by the owner. The rest of the space was occupied by a single row of chairs completely covering the walls on both sides of the room, each occupied by a smiling Suzie Wong lookalike. I now knew why my friend had chosen this bar. He was off and running, but I wasn't so sure what I was going to do. I ordered a CC and ginger ale and watched as my friend went from one girl to the next – and he was having a great time.

Someone tapped me on the shoulder and I turned to find a pretty young lady holding a glass of ginger ale, and yes, her nickname was CC. She sat down next to me at the bar, and suddenly I didn't really care what my friend was doing. She had long black hair, was wearing a pristine white sun dress, and even in her high heels she only stood less than 5'2" tall. She wanted to know all about me. Where was I from, what did I do, how old was I, had I ever been in Taipei before, and, no surprise, did I want a date? About that time my friend strolled up to the bar with a gal on each arm. He said he couldn't decide so he had them stand side by side, one facing away and the other facing him. He took out a coin, flipped it into the air, and when it came up tails he chose the girl that was facing away. Crude, but still a little clever all the same.

He made the arrangement with the mama-san for his girl and we walked outside. CC followed me. When I told my friend I didn't understand, he said not to worry, he had taken care of it. So now we both had dates (each at the extravagant cost of $5 per day). We were all walking arm in arm and side by side, almost like in the Wizard of Oz (but no yellow brick road and no singing or skipping). We walked down to a park by a small lake, sat at a picnic table, and spent the next couple hours talking and laughing about everything and nothing. I was getting really tired and had just about all the adventure I could take in one day. We walked back to the bar and when I said I was going to return CC, my buddy said that she was mine for the night. I stood firm and without any more comments he and his gal walked away. I thanked her for her company, told the mama-san she had done nothing wrong, and returned to my room for some much-needed sleep.

About seven the next morning, my buddy was pounding on my door and yelling to hurry up and get moving, we were going to the coast to see the Queen's Head (and other rock formations at the Yehliu Geopark). The bus was just about to leave. I had already showered and shaved so I threw on some clothes, brushed my teeth, and then opened the door to find all three of my companions from the night before. I had to laugh, and then we rushed down the stairs, couldn't wait for the cramped elevator, and took a waiting cab to the bus station.

We made it on the bus only minutes before it left for the north coast of Taiwan. The girls had brought a few bags of chips with them and that sufficed for our breakfast. When we arrived at the park, I had to admit the views were absolutely spectacular. The wind- and surf-carved rock formations were sculpted in an amazing array of shapes and sizes. The Queen's Head was a stone pillar which was reminiscent of the profile of England's Queen Victoria, and I still have a picture me standing next to it. Close by was another formation that looked like a throne; so naturally there's another photo of me sitting on it, although admittedly I don't look all that regal.

We walked along the coast and took turns taking pictures of each other. Although it was the beginning of August, the cherry trees in the adjacent park were still in bloom, but the blossoms were starting to fade. Still, it was a another beautiful day and, for the first time in well over a year, I didn't think about Vietnam once that day. When we returned, we had a nice dinner, took another walk down to the park, and the sun was starting to rise before we returned for some sleep. The next two days were pretty much the same with sightseeing, shopping, and having fun being our only priorities. The last day we said our goodbyes, picked up our shiny new suits and after trying them on, and headed off to the airport. I never did get to wear that suit, after I returned home and re-discovered real food, I soon gained about 20 pounds in six weeks – and that was that.

The trip back was without any drama, and no Chinese fighter jet escorts harassed us as we departed the "land of Oz." It was a quiet, solemn journey back to the Big Red One, but I still had a smile on my face and memories that took a long time to fade.

Even in a combat zone it is easy to get bored, regardless of how much work there is to do. Every once in a while I'd play catch, softball, or throw a *Frisbee©*. But I was more often an observer than a participant; it was much easier to hold my beer that way. I had found a single dart stuck in the wall over the rear door and had thrown it my locker months earlier. When I first got the refrigerator it came with an ice pick. I think it was supposed to be used chop up ice so that little fridge could be used as a cooler.

Every so often I would sit on my bunk and play around with the ice pick, trying to stick it into a small target I had drawn on a piece of plywood. At six feet, I became pretty accurate at hitting the bull's eye and later decided to go outside and see how far away I could stand and still get it to stick. The target I chose was the plywood storm door to our hootch which was usually propped open during the day. I would stand back about twelve feet and practiced until the ice pick always stuck into the door, and the handle and tine were level with the ground. First I moved further back to sixteen feet, then to about twenty feet away, and practiced until I matched my earlier successes. The door was my only target so I decided to up the ante. I threw the dart I had found with my left hand and, before it hit the door, I'd throw the ice pick with my right hand, and I eventually became very accurate. When thrown and stuck, both the dart and the ice pick would fit inside a six-inch circle.

Of course some of the guys thought I had lost it. I really I couldn't argue the point – that is exactly what I was beginning to think. It seems there's always someone who needs to push the button as hard as possible, and there was one guy who was constantly making disparaging remarks. It probably didn't help much that I usually ignored his taunts like he wasn't there. One day, in the evening when I was at the office, he stopped by my desk and handed me the ice pick. He walked across the room and stapled the ace of diamonds to the wall. He told me if I could stick the ice pick anywhere into that card, he would stop complaining; if I missed the card, the ice pick was his. He then added a ten-dollar wager. I was getting tired of trying to be Daniel Boone so I readily agreed. Still seated, I turned and let the ice pick fly. Whether it was luck or skill I really don't know or care, but the tine of the pick had neatly pierced the center of the diamond in the middle of the card. He was speechless and all I could do was laugh, I was just as surprised as he was. I removed the card and the pick, handed them both to him, and said it wasn't fair – that I had just been lucky.

Still shaking his head, he left the office; but when I returned to the hootch, the ice pick was stuck into the wall next to my bunk through the middle of a ten-dollar bill. The next day I bought a couple of cases of beer and some bags of chips, got ice from the mess hall, and we had a hootch party. There were no more harsh words and no problems afterward. I never threw that ice pick again while I was in country and, when I tried again a few years after I got home, it seemed I couldn't hit the broad side of a barn.

One of the basic facts of life in Vietnam was, if you still had eyes and ears in your head, you were going to see and hear the consequences of war. Although our basecamp was sometimes a target, it never suffered an attack of any significance while I was still in country. Even during the Tet Offensive, the Big Red One base camp at Di An did not witness

any substantial action and sustained very little damage; but the surrounding area was a much different story – and it had been a killing
field many times before and after my tour of duty. We were right off
the Ho Chi Minh trail which warranted a lot of scrutiny and was in fact
the focus of many NVA and U.S. attacks.

While on guard duty, and even when working in the office, on
occasion you would hear the prolonged roar and growl of napalm
as it consumed everything in its path. Unless you were very close
by, you usually heard it before you saw it – first the low pitched
rolling rumble of thunder and then the inevitable trail of rising
pitch-black smoke angling towards the heavens. There were times
when I saw repeated air attacks using napalm resulting in staggered
ebony-colored ribbons of death spanning the horizon – it must have
been a nasty way to die. The smoke always reminded me of how our
basecamp looked each morning as the "honey dippers" plied their
craft. Many times the fighter planes also used rockets, Gatling-type
machine guns, and a wide variety of bombs; but, from where I sat,
napalm was our area's weapon of choice.

B-52 runs in our area were very rare since they almost always
concentrated their sorties in northern South Vietnam and most
of all North Vietnam. Once I did see their bombs explode to the
west of Saigon but, although I saw the smoke and felt the rumble
of their impact, I never saw the planes themselves. Their victims
never knew what was going to happen until it was too late. I believe
these big birds were all maintained outside Vietnam at airfields in
Thailand.

Shortly after Tet, they brought in a huge cannon, set it up on Di
An to use on the Ho Chi Minh trail, and they installed it up in the
middle of our base. It might have been a M107, a 175 mm self-propelled gun, but I don't know for sure. I never really saw it up close
and only got a glimpse of the enormous barrel. It seemed to defy
gravity, its barrel looked to be way too long not to fall to the ground
as it protruded over the sandbag enclosure. However, everyone on

our basecamp heard and felt it when it fired. I was told the rounds were better than 200 pounds each and that the range was up to 25 miles. It was a real behemoth of a weapon. When it was fired, the round cut through the air and sounded like a freight train engine passing through overhead. The ground shook, walls rattled, and the report was very, very loud; although sometimes we didn't even hear the impact. It was only there about a month but had reportedly had done significant damage to Uncle Ho's trail. And for all those targeted, just like with the B-52's bombs, they never saw or heard it coming.

Sometimes at night I would see the monstrous fire from "Puff, The Magic "Dragon," a Douglas AC-47 (AKA Spooky) aircraft that had been fitted with three 7.62 mm miniguns. Each could selectively fire either 50 or 100 rounds per second. These gunships could put a bullet or glowing red tracer (every fifth round) into every square yard of a football-field-sized target in potentially less than 10 seconds. Once again, the enemy never knew what was happening until it hit them. Whenever these airships were used, we never lost a battle. When fired, the stream of tracers looked like a molten solid red band of glowing lava that snaked and twisted its way to the ground – it was awesome. The sound reminded me of napalm's roar, but the growl never subsided and morphed into a continuous belch of utter destruction.

Then there were my favorites, the Huey gunships. Whether they were outfitted with Gatling guns, rocket pods, or M-60 machine guns, they were the workhorses and mainstays of every combat operation in Vietnam. Their brave pilots knew their choppers were sitting ducks for RPGs and machine gun fire, and they still did whatever was asked of them, regardless of the risks. Whether they were ferrying troops and supplies, evacuating the wounded, or in attack mode, each and every one of their pilots and crew was a hero whose daring efforts were directly responsible for saving so many lives. God bless them all.

Short exchanges of gunfire from our M-16s and the VC's AK-47s were heard in the distance almost on a daily basis. The gunfights were usually a short-lived event; Charlie much preferred the tactics of hit and run. He hated to become involved in a long, drawn-out battle, simply because we always won those. Some days I was much more aware of the silence than the sounds of war; many times I didn't even notice the gun fire or choppers flying overhead, unless someone said something about it. In so many ways and levels, that was and is a very sad circumstance.

Early in August, Richard Milhous Nixon is nominated by the Republicans to become their presidential candidate. On the 20th, the Soviet Union invades Czechoslovakia with 750,000 Warsaw Pact troops. On August 21st, the Medal of Honor is awarded to James Anderson, Jr. and he becomes the first black U.S. Marine to be so honored. The next day on the 22nd, police in Chicago start to have minor clashes with protesters at the Democratic National Convention, and in three days it gets so bad Major Daley supposedly gives the order "shoot to kill." Thanks to the raging rhetoric of socialist activist Jerry Rubin, the protests continue until the 28th. Major Daley later prophetically states: "The policeman isn't there to create disorder, the policeman is there to preserve disorder."

And the disjointed history continues. On September 1st, Hubert H. Humphrey starts his run for the presidency at New York City's Labor Day Parade. Later on the 7th, the "Women's Liberation" groups and members of "New York Now" protest the worthlessness of the Miss Universe Beauty Contest. Although none were burned, the New York Times later noted it was nothing more than "just symbolic bra burning," and this derogatory term lives on as a description for all future feminist protests. September 23rd marks the date the cornerstone from the famous London Bridge that had once spanned the River Thames in Great Britain, was installed in its new home in Lake Havasu, Arizona. On September 24th, the TV show "60 Minutes" debuts.

But back in Vietnam, on September 13, 1968, the 1st Infantry Division was engaged in a battle near Loc Ninh which was very close to the Cambodian border. The Big Red One experienced the unprecedented loss of lives of Major General Keith L Ware, three members of his command staff, the Division's Sergeant Major Venable, and the four-man helicopter crew; there were no survivors. While overseeing the battle, their chopper was hit by heavy anti-aircraft fire and it crashed.

General Ware had received the Medal of Honor during WWII for personally attacking and taking out four German machine gun nests on December 26, 1944 while he was a Lieutenant Colonel, eight days after I was born. Although wounded, he refused medical aide until the hill he attacked had been taken. He knew and was a close friend of Audie Murphy, another WWII Medal of Honor recipient. He had been drafted in 1941 and was selected to attend OCS (Officer Candidate School). After graduating the 12-week course, he had risen from being a platoon leader to the rank of Lieutenant Colonel in just three years. For his action in Vietnam, he was award the Distinguished Service Cross and was later buried in Arlington National Cemetery in Virginia. He was the first Major General killed in action (KIA) in Vietnam. He was 53 years old and had died with his beloved dog King. If you look him up on the internet his accolades go on and on. His death was a tremendous lost to the 1st Infantry Division and to America.

Division Sergeant Major Joseph A. Venable died along side of Major General Ware. He had also fought in WWII and participated in five major battles and had been wounded twice. He took part in three campaigns during the Korean War before returning home, and he later joined up with the General in Vietnam. Venable was a career soldier. When he died, he had served his country for over 28 years. He earned many awards including the Legion of Merit Award, the Distinguished Flying Cross, the Bronze Star, the Purple Heart, and the Combat Infantryman's Badge with two stars. He was laid to rest in Fort Sam Houston National Cemetery in San Antonio, Texas.

Each of those nine men who all died side by side when their Command Huey was shot down were and are the definitions and portraits of the word hero. They were not the only ones to die that day, nor were they the only heroes. The tens of thousands that followed all warrant the same respect and honor. Each and every man who has died serving our country to protect our freedoms is worthy of the admiration of every citizen in the United States of America.

16

Final Days

October to November 1968

had long debated and finally decided to extend my tour of duty in Vietnam to qualify for an "early out." After repeatedly double-checking my calculations, I extended my tour by 46 days on September 21st, 1968. By doing so, I met the requirement of having less than five months of active duty left when I returned home. I would be placed on inactive duty status, would never be assigned to another stateside post, and, in addition, there would be no future reserve duty responsibilities. I would be out of the army. My decision almost killed my mother, literally. She needed an operation and was waiting for my return. Had I known that, I never would have extended my tour; but she didn't want to worry me. What a dummy I was.

My original DEROS date was October 6, 1968, and I had been assigned to Fort Belvoir, Washington. After extending my time in country, the DEROS was extended to November 21st. On the first day of my extended tour, October 7, 1968, the 1st Admin Company suffered the first KIA that I had ever heard about. I had been there for about a year. In all that time our company had never had a loss of life due to hostile action. I was shocked beyond measure and could only think of his poor family and mine. He too was a short timer and only had a few weeks to go before returning home. His only mistake was trying to run to a bunker during a mortar attack, and that blunder changed his means of transport home. After that, for a short time (no pun intended), I think I qualified as the most paranoid person in country.

The days that followed held a few surprises but were almost exactly as I expected. However, I began to spend most of my spare time in the bunker in front of our hootch. I was unreasonable and bitchy and soon became very hard to be around. I read every letter I received over and over again, and each newspaper and magazine sent to me was devoured with newfound interest. I re-read every order associated with my departure, repeatedly re-calculated the length of my extension to make sure it was correct, and made sure I had "dotted all the I's" and "crossed all the T's." I found every excuse I could to stay in that bunker but knew that had to change. I hated what I had become and tried to show a better face; but each time, all too soon, I again retreated to the sanctuary of that bunker is search of solace. In time I realized all the worrying and paranoia in the world would not change my circumstance, and slowly but surely I became a human being again. I re-affirmed every friendship and tried to be the most upbeat person on the planet, and I think I fooled almost everyone except myself.

Every once in a while I asked myself what exactly was the true definition of depression and struggled to come up with a cohesive explanation. All I really knew is it became a part of my life in varying degrees of intensity throughout my tour in Vietnam and sometimes beyond. The simple truth is the entire time I was in Nam I was not happy and wanted to be somewhere else, just like the other 90 percent of the people in country including most of the South Vietnamese. It was not a crippling depression but was gloomy enough to cloud up a sunny day. Sometimes I felt like the Dustin Hoffman's character of Jack Crabb in the movie *Little Big Man*. I had seen so much and knew of so many things, yet I had done absolutely nothing to improve the circumstance and prevent the tenacious lunacy that surrounded me each and every day. Mostly my depression was short lived and quickly became a fleeting memory without lasting effects.

As I've said many times before, I believe almost everyone hides behind carefully crafted masks to obscure, deceive, and defend their persona, and I thought (and hoped) mine was still very much intact.

Talk about depression – being the company commanding officer of The First Administration Company was more than just a little complicated; it was daunting, loathsome, and frustrating. Supervising a company of more than 600 people was difficult enough, but it was even more twisted when more than a dozen of the company's personnel outranked the commander. As I remember, during my time in country, we had a total of six company commanders, and one of them served at two different times. The MOS of these captains were all field orientated and varied from Infantry to Engineering to Logistics. But not one of them was from Finance, Personnel Files, or any other type of office administrative discipline; otherwise they would have been part of that company specialty.

Once, one of the 201 file guys actually did a study and posted the results on a chart based on the military equivalent of an IQ score, then ranked the percentages of those with the best scores for the Officers, NCO's, and Enlisted men. Not all that surprisingly, the combined average scores of the Enlisted men were higher than the other two choices. I can't imagine what a challenge it must have been to manage a bunch of know-it-alls.

Almost every one of our commanders was able to successfully cope with all the complexities the First Admin Company presented and did a good job of maintaining order and control. All of the company's varied functions were administered and orchestrated in an orderly fashion. Still, from what I understand, every one of them started requesting a transfer soon after they arrived to another company that better suited their training.

Most of the commanders were very easy to get along with and, since it was a combat zone, they were not concerned with the stricter protocols of a stateside duty station. Drugs were never tolerated, but first offenders usually only got a slap on the wrist. Drinking was pretty much over looked unless there had been some trouble. The manner of dress had to be as was required but the rules were not very strict. The fatigues had to be clean but not necessarily pressed. If the name label was missing or the rank insignia was not in place, it really wasn't a problem. Generally speaking, saluting outside a building was not required. Some sharp-eyed sniper might find a priority target, and the interaction between the different ranks in the office was normally very casual. If you did your job and stayed out of trouble, that was all that was necessary to not have any problems.

Then there was that very special Captain. I don't remember his name because everybody simply referred to him as "the asshole"; so Captain A will have to suffice. I was told he had graduated from West Point ten years prior to making our acquaintance. Making it to only a Captain after 10 years spoke volumes of where he ranked in his class and what kind of leader he was. And lucky us, he was the one who commanded our company twice.

Captain A ran a very strict ship and demanded that everyone endeavor to be a perfect little soldier. Apparently he forgot where he was and insisted on a more traditional stateside Army environment. He demanded proper military haircuts and no moustaches; shined boots; wearing the appropriate headgear whenever outside; and the fatigues all had to have the proper insignia, indication of rank, and were to be clean and pressed. Swearing was not tolerated in his presence and every enlisted man had to salute every officer whether inside or outside of a building. Everyone's personal areas in the hootches had to be clean and orderly, and any open display of naked women was prohibited.

Maybe ten years had passed, but it seemed in his mind he was still at West Point and wanted everyone to act accordingly. No infractions were permitted and each error in protocol was met with distain – usually with the maximum penalty allowed by the military code of justice. He was a real sweetheart. Three people were found sleeping while on guard duty at the same bunker and each was charged with a general court-martial. Although dereliction of duty was a serious offence, it had never resulted in such severe discipline before. He was there both times during the dry season and without reserve handed out Article 15's one after another for anyone with dust on their boots. He was certifiably nuts and was not deserving of a command of any sort. To know him was to hate him.

Once, when we had a red alert because the tower had seen enemy movement, Captain A called for everyone in the entire company who was not on guard duty to gather around his office. Now that's about 600 people standing in the open, shoulder to shoulder. He proceeded to tell us he expected us to defend our perimeter with honor and to make him proud. He also warned us to be cautious because rockets had been spotted. Rockets! Christ Almighty, one of those rockets could have potentially wiped out our entire company. Shortly thereafter, two congressional investigations concentrated on Captain A and he was almost immediately replaced. When he returned for the second and final time he was only there for a week or two, then he was gone again. It appeared no one anywhere respected or wanted him around.

I found out later his last duty post was at a permanent listening post in the A Shau Valley, but commanding infantry in a very active combat zone did not curb his demeanor. The first grenade he found by his bunk had the pin in it and an attached note boldly stated: "Back F---ing Off!" Apparently he failed to comply because the grenade that followed a couple of nights later was not so encumbered. Although Captain A was an idiot and a nut case, he did not deserve to die; but then; neither did the many thousands of KIA who followed. The Army didn't necessarily agree with me; but for the record, I think anyone who died in Vietnam was a KIA regardless of the circumstances – whether fragged, fighting, in a traffic accident, working a desk, or asleep in your bed, you had died in action in an active combat zone.

Not even a month after I had received my promotion to Finance Specialist Fourth Class (E4), I decided to try out for E5. I had started to hate guard duty and KP with a passion but could not afford to have someone else take my place very often – besides, that was pretty much frowned upon. Supervising a Company Detail and CQ were also a pain in the butt. So I filed my application with the appropriate signatures and waited for the opportunity to move on. I had been promoted to E4 on the 29th of February and applied for E5 on March 27th.

While it was true that moving up in rank in Vietnam was incredibly easier than in the States, the process could also be painfully slow. Many weeks later I was notified and told I would be interviewed by a board of officers and NCOs and was given a list of categories to study. I needed to know the Army chain of command from the Commander in Chief through the 1st Admin Company Commander. Also required was knowledge of the sequence of Presidential succession and their names, all the local politicians from my state of Illinois, and up-to-date knowledge on all current events. Piece of cake. I studied as hard as I ever had for anything before and soon realized I was probably doomed. When I went before the board, I answered all the questions as best I could in a firm, assured manner – even when I didn't have a clue of what was the correct answer. A couple of weeks later, the list of successful candidates was posted. Somehow I had qualified for the promotion to E5 on May 30, 1968 – be there no doubt, the Army always found a way to surprise me.

All I had to do was wait for an allocation to open up. So I waited and waited and waited. Finally, well into the term of my tour extension to get an early out, I was officially promoted to Specialist Fifth Class along with two of my teammates on October 28th, 1968 (less than a month before I was to go home). Apparently all the allocations had gone back to the states for four months so my promotion and all the others had been in limbo. Not exactly the break from guard duty I had hoped for, well anyways, it looked good on the DD-214.

Shortly before I went home, I had to be interviewed by the re-enlistment officer. I kind of felt sorry for him because I could only imagine the nasty responses he had to endure. After I sat down, he told me what a great job I had done and how much the Big Red One needed me. Then he offered me another immediate promotion to E6 if I would extend my tour for 6 months. I just sat there and stared with my mouth open and question marks in my eyes. He took offense and told me to shut my yap. I thanked him for the offer and explained my shock at the possibility of another promotion less than a month after the last one. I shook my head "no" and said I could not extend my tour again and put any more strain on my family than I already had done. We parted on good terms, and the only thing I wondered about was how successful he had been with all my fellow short-timers.

Once I had finally gotten over that plague of a cough I had for those many months when I first arrived in country, I had stayed relatively healthy until about six weeks before I was to go home. While chasing a softball I found the only tent stake within a hundred miles when it sliced through my thong cutting my foot. After six stitches, a hefty tetanus shot, a couple of weeks of hobbling around, I was good to go. Right after that, my vision became a little blurry. I figured it was due to too much detail work under a dim lightbulb, but went to the medics and saw an eye doctor just in case. I returned with two lovely pair of black plastic-rimmed reading glasses that were OK for a couple of days. Then the headaches started and I began to run into the office furniture. I was not an optometrist but I knew exactly what to do. I put the glasses in my foot locker, donated them to the Salvation Army when I got back to the "World," and that was that. My ability to see perfectly fine remained unhampered for another 25 years or so.

Another two weeks passed and I had a toothache, I thought for sure that I was beginning to fall apart. Army dentists had always scared me because I remembered poor toothless Bob back at Fort

Knox, Kentucky, while back Basic Training had his encounter with the boogieman. Still, the sensitivity to hot and cold finally overruled my objections – so off to see the tooth doc I went. I needed a small filling that was pretty much painless and at the time I never gave it another thought – that is, until it fell out three weeks after I got home. At least it got me there. There were no more health problems for me while in country, and I eventually went home (more or less) realitively whole and well.

As my departure date neared, I took a look at was happening back in the "World." On October 10th, the Detroit Tigers won the World Series after a miraculous comeback. On the 12th, the Summer Olympics started in Mexico. Jacqueline Kennedy, wife of the President assassinated in September of 1963, married the Greek shipping magnate Aristotle Onassis. Yale University announces it will begin admitting women on November 14th; on that same day, protesters proclaimed "Turn In (and burn) Your Draft Card Day" at college campus protests across the country. I always marveled at the diversity and robust pursuits of my country.

On Halloween I appropriately celebrated the day by watching the *Peanuts©* movie *The Great Pumpkin*. The next day I packed up a wooden crate and sent the remainder of my things home. I tried to pack some Vietnamese cigarettes but was told they probably contained marijuana (oops, I had forgotten about that). I also tried to send home two field jackets, but since I was not going home to a duty station that was also a big no-no. The tape recorder and everything that went with it were also packed into the crate. They nailed the crate shut and told me it would take four-to-six weeks to be delivered to my home (but it actually got there just before I returned).

Two weeks before my DEROS, my Staff Sergeant came up to me and said he had secured an R&R allocation for me to go to Australia. Oh, my God, Australia! I couldn't believe my luck. I had dreamed about it, and I would rather have gone to visit the Aussies than go to Hawaii. Of course, this is after I had heard there was still a shortage of men in Australia. I had $650 saved up and that would have paid for an excellent time "down under." I told the Sarge to give me a couple of minutes to think about it – then I took a short walk, and that's when reality stuck its ugly head in. Sure I had the money, but what was I going to do when I got home? I had figured on taking some time off before looking for a job. I was so "short" and still a little paranoid and wasn't so sure I wanted to travel that much before going home.

Finally, I reluctantly talked myself out of taking the R&R and went back and said "thanks but no thanks." The Sarge was genuinely disappointed and said he could loan me some money if I needed it and that he really wanted me to go. I shook his hand and told him I really, really appreciated everything he must have done to get me that allocation but I just couldn't go. Later it occurred to me that maybe this was his way of trying to make things right after our perimeter sweep ordeal. I had been angry with him at the time but had long since stopped being upset and now considered him a friend. Without a doubt, not going to Australia was probably the number one wrong decision I had made while in country. I should have gone, money be damned.

Days before I was to board that freedom flight back to the "World," I went over every piece of paperwork and official order I had to make sure everything was correct. As I scanned my personnel file I noticed an new order indicating I had been nominated for a Bronze Star by my Staff Sergeant. I was confused and didn't know what that meant. Was further approval required and was there any question about its validity? I knew I had a couple of questions about it. The Sergeant wasn't anywhere to be seen; so I asked the WO4 what he thought, and he told to go over to the Awards and Decoration office to check it out.

When I showed the paperwork to the first clerk I found, he offered his congratulations and said it was a done deal. I was stunned to say the least. A Warrant officer came over to the desk and said to wait a couple of minutes. I watched him pull out a vinyl portfolio, rubber stamp a couple of signatures on the official document, then trace over the stamped names with a thin felt-tipped marker. When done, he placed everything in the binder and handed it to me along with a black case containing the Bronze Star. For me this was such an anti-climactic event that I still sometimes even today wonder about its authenticity. Since the award was also noted on my DD-214, I decided I had no choice other than to believe it was official. I was stunned.

Later, when I asked my Staff Sergeant about it, all he said was I deserved it for being a good role model, for doing a great job, and that I had made his life easier. I knew there were two types of Bronze Stars, and the one I was awarded was for meritorious service. The other one more insignificantly has a V Device for heroism and bravery. I was not the best Finance Specialist by any stretch of the imagination, and know many others on my team who were much better than me. The only justification I could come up with was that this too also related to that perimeter sweep he and I had been on so many months before. Since there was no record of nor any award nomination for a response to hostile action under fire, it appeared the only option left was to nominate me for a meritorious award.

I felt so very undeserving and a little embarrassed but in time decided to let it pass, and it took me better than four decades to display this medal. I now do so with pride – not for myself, but as a tribute to all those who served and gave so much. An imprinted copy of the medal now adorns my car's vanity license plate. Every time I'm thanked for my service, I think of it as a gentle reminder and tell all those who take notice to be thankful for all the sacrifices made by so many others.

One of my teammates and I were going home on the same day. The day before we departed, our section group held a finance office party in our honor. I had a lot of mixed emotions. I was really happy to be going home, but I also realized in all likelihood I would never see any of these guys again. I had literally spent every day I was in country for the last year plus 46 days with each of these men, and now that was about to end. I didn't know what to do or say, so I didn't hang around too long; but I made sure to thank each of them for their friendship and everything else before I left the party and went back to my hootch. I told the Sarge I would miss him, then shook his hand and thanked him for his support.

I had previously returned my M-16 and the bandolier of ammo to the armory, and now it seemed a little daunting to not have it around anymore. I had already packed up almost everything I owned and then stuffed my duffle bag full with the remaining miscellaneous things I had. I laid out the uniform I would wear home, shined my shoes, and double-checked to make sure I had all the paperwork needed to guarantee my journey would be without a hitch. I walked around the hootch and gave away my refrigerator, chairs, and plastic fringed bookcase (it was the only one I had ever seen) and said my goodbyes. I left a stack of magazines and newspapers on one of the chairs. It all seemed so surreal, and suddenly I felt very detached.

I grabbed the chaise lounge and a couple of beers, joined a few of the guys outside behind the hootch, looked at the perimeter, and boastfully toasted goodbye to the F---ing Nam. We talked for a long time cursing the war, Vietnam, and expressing hope for the future. After dark, I was the last to go back inside, I was tired but wasn't sleepy and didn't know what to do. Later I wrote down a list of the names of all my friends with every intension of writing to each of them and see how they were doing. Somehow I managed to lose that list and much later realized I had never written a word to anybody. I guess when I left, I didn't want to have anything to do with Vietnam ever again – but I do regret not keeping in touch with any of those guys.

Early the next morning, I took care of the three S's, dressed, closed my duffle bag, and hauled my ass down to the departure area. I was a little early, maybe three hours or so. I left everything where it was and slowly walked down to the mess hall for my final meal. I took my time and walked back through the office and said my last goodbyes. When I got back to the departure area, I found five other guys waiting, and we still had an hour and a half to go. The clocked ticked slowly, then all of sudden the truck was there. The crowd had grown to about a dozen people, half going home and the others headed across the globe for R&R, and then we were on our way to Tan Son Nhut airbase. The ride probably took about an hour and a half, but I really didn't know how much time had passed; my mind was thousands of miles away, and all I knew or cared about was that I simply had get home ASAP.

When we arrived at the airbase, we were shuttled to the waiting area. Our departure orders were reviewed and our "luggage" was taken away to later be placed on the appropriate airplane. Of course, I had to wait four hours to board my flight. There was a small snack shop and PX nearby next to rows and rows of seats already filled with anxious escapees. I grabbed a candy bar and a *Coke©*, but would have preferred a hot dog and a nice cold one. "So sorry, no can do."

There wasn't an empty seat in the place, so I walked around looking for my buddy who was also going home but never saw him again. So I sat down along one wall on the floor with a couple of other guys. This was not my first prolonged experience of people watching, but I was still fascinated by the diversity. Every human sensation and emotion was portrayed on the faces of those all around me. Happy, worried, stoic, scared, sad, thoughtful, fearful, paranoid, oblivious, serious, shocked, and thrilled faces were everywhere. It was easy to pass the time by making up a short story for each expression. This one had run away from an insane asylum (actually quite a few met that description). Another was a bigamist returning to three wives and upon returning needed to discuss the fourth one he had taken on during his tour. So many others appeared to be so happy it was hard to assign a narrative to their tale. All superfluous BS, but still entertaining and it helped to pass the time.

Finally, I couldn't believe it, it was time to board the Flying Tiger jet airliner and take our seats. We boarded as if off to a gold rush and, even though we were packed in like sardines, there wasn't a single complaint. I had a middle seat but didn't care. I bent over, looked out the window to catch my final glimpse of Vietnam, and smiled as I watched all the vehicles and people rushing around like ants on an ice cream cone. I sat back in my seat, closed my eyes, and loudly said out loud "Thank you, God."

A few moments later, the engines came to life and soon we were rolling down the runway. All the cheering had stopped and, other than the roar of the engines, the silence was deafening. Slowly we rose into the air and banked starboard to start our journey home, back to reality, back to the "World." We waited until we thought we were out of missile range and suddenly you couldn't hear yourself think. All the anticipation, the worry, the hardship, and the long wait, transformed into to a continuous righteous screaming shout of happiness. It took a little while for things to quiet down but there were delirious smiles everywhere. It was about then I realized apparently I hadn't been dreaming, I was actually on my way back to the "World," and couldn't stop smiling.

Frankly I do not remember much about that trip back to the States other than it took too long. I don't know if or where we stopped, if I got any sleep, or if I ate anything. It was and still is all a blank page in my mental diary. I do remember arriving in Oakland, California mid-morning on November 21, 1968. Processing out of active duty from the Army was another blur and I struggle to recall the details. I'm pretty sure I waited in line at each out-processing station, then waited some more to complete very simple tasks, then hurried to the next station, and then waited some more. This went on for hours and hours.

Ultimately we turned in all our army clothing and got new dress greens and shoes. Our orders were double-checked, and we had to stand on one foot then the other to prove we were physically fit (really?). Then we were handed our DD-214s and given travel vouchers good to go anywhere in the continental United States. Lastly, after zeroing out my last payroll voucher, I was handed all the monies due me in greenbacks, American – wow. I only know most of this because I still have much of the paperwork associated with my convoluted mustering-out experience, and I seriously remember that I had never held that much cash in my hands before.

After suffering through another longest day, all we wanted to do was complete our journey home. There was one little problem: it was now almost 5:00 PM and last flights out of Oakland took off around 6:00 PM. We quickly found a ride (bus or cab I don't remember) and rushed to the terminal, but then we were told we were probably too late. However, if we could make it to the gate in time, we just might make it on the flight. As each of us got our tickets and flight's gate number, we took off running, our belongings dangling from outstretched hands. There was no intense security to cope with back then, so it was a simple foot race to the gate. I got there just in time to see my plane slowly heading toward the runway. Crap!

Later we regrouped and found two of our tardy crew did not return to the lounge area. We hoped that they had made their flights or maybe they had simply decided to go back to town. I debated about heading back to the city myself; but, with almost $700 in my pocket, I decided to spend the night at the airport with a couple of the other similarly disheartened travelers. We were all hungry, but there were no open restaurants or snack shops. Even the newsstand was closed. I found three vending machines, one each with pop, snacks, and candy bars. The only soda left was strawberry, which I hated – but I got it anyways because it was better than nothing. There were no snacks left and the only candy bar available was a *Snicker's*©. So I sat down on the floor and enjoyed my first meal as a civilian finally back in the "World" (I mean the United States).

Afraid to sleep and miss our flights in the morning and more than a little worried about all that cash, we sat on the floor and shared our experiences the whole night through. Finally, the sun rose, people appeared out of nowhere, and the race was on again. We wished each other happy days and disappeared, all in different directions.

I made a quick stop at the newsstand and grabbed another *Coke©* and package of potato chips. Then I called home and gave them the flight information; although I talked to my father, I could hear my mother crying softly in the background. When I got to the gate, I was told the plane wouldn't accept passengers for another hour or so. Damn!

I asked if I could board the plane early and take a nap, and a nice young lady escorted me down the gate steps to the tarmac and we walked over to the waiting plane. I thanked her for letting me board so early, then I scrambled up the stairs. Before boarding, I took a quick look around figuring it would be a long time before I would see California again; but all I could see was a fuzzy sunrise and the low-hanging fog. I went inside, stored my gear, and then took the first seat on the port side closest to the door by the window. I pulled the window shade down and closed my eyes for just a second; but, since I only had a couple of hours sleep the last two days, I was soon off to dreamland.

A pretty stewardess shook my shoulder to wake me up to tell me we were leaving and to fasten my seatbelt. I told her this was the final leg of my trip back home and that I would really appreciate a CC and ginger ale, and she readily promised to bring it in a couple of minutes. I smiled at the thought, remembering my R&R in Taipei, then buckled up and closed my eyes for another second or two.

The next thing I knew was that very same pretty girl was shaking my shoulder again. She was smiling when she told me to wake up; we were about to land at O'Hare International Airport. I opened the shade, looked out the window, and saw that the plane was getting closer to Chicago, and soon we were slowly gliding serenely over the city as the plane descended and approached the runway. It was about then I looked to my right and noticed the folding tray was down. It held a clear plastic glass of ice that was joined by a tiny bottle of CC that sat next to a can of ginger ale; and under the glass, there was a nicely penned note simply saying: "welcome home."

17

AS PAUL HARVEY ALWAYS NOTED IN HIS POPULAR RADIO BROADCASTS:

"And Now, The Rest of the Story"

The "World"

Like so many other things I have experienced, my prolonged trip back to the "World" was "a hurry up and wait" ordeal; each step along the way had been both anti-climactic and hopeful. Still, on November 22, 1968, I had officially finally made it home. My personal experiences in Vietnam were really not all that traumatic and, in the entirety of my life's journey, that 412-day experience in country had only been a brief detour. That may all be true, but it is a rare day indeed that a memory or two from that time aren't a part of my day.

I seriously thought about not mentioning this, but it is an important part of the pain of that era. When soldiers returned from Vietnam they were emphatically often not welcomed home or appreciated by most people other than by their families. So many hated the war and blamed the troops. When I disembarked that plane in Chicago, my family was all over me and there were smiles, hugs, kisses, and tears everywhere. It was really great to be home.

But, as we walked back to pick up my luggage, I was greeted by some of the passersby with frowns, scowls, taunts of "baby killer," and a litany of swear words. Some simply turned their backs to me as we passed. I was shocked and confused, and I didn't know how to respond. That is, until a long curly-haired hippy type, wearing a *Stetson*©, a fringed tan suede jacket, and snakeskin cowboy boots decided to spit at me; then I knew exactly what to do. I dropped my bag, cursed, and lunged at him. Every fiber of my being was ready for battle. My father and brother grabbed me and held me back; my antagonist just smiled, pretended to spit again, and walked away. My dad and brother had to redouble their efforts to hold me back. Given the chance, I would have beaten that doper to a pulp or died trying. I yelled "enjoy Canada, you f---ing coward" but he just kept on walking away.

It took a while for me to calm down; then I apologized to my family for my reaction. That moment stayed with me for a long time, and I would still like to have a little chat with that pompous ass. Many of the anti-war protesters thought it was their duty to disrespect anything connected to the Vietnam War, and returning soldiers were a convenient and frequent target. It made no difference whether the veteran had pushed a pencil, carried a litter for the wounded, pulled a trigger, or where he was stationed for that matter (many had never even been to Vietnam). Regardless, we were all too many times treated with anger and disrespect; or even worse, were looked at with a mixture of pity and disdain. Most of the veterans didn't take it personally and simply shook it off, but for a few it became a lifetime ton of guilt to bear.

It took a lot of years for the unjust contempt to subside, before all the memorials were built and the heroes recognized. For some, it was much too late since they had already found their own tragic escapes. Ironically, these same self-righteous grandiose accusers had absolutely no problem voting for the politicians who had actually orchestrated the war. The media and all those political hacks had done a good job of gutting our country. There was very little justice, support, help, or compassion for the veterans who returned; even if they were not physically injured, many were still walking wounded. When you look around even today, you can still see the pain, shame, and confusion in the eyes of the elderly homeless veterans, and there is no remedy I know of; for many it is too late for compassion to soothe the soul.

Unfortunately, I know a couple of people who even today are afraid of Vietnam Veterans, and they still fear something bad could happen if an older vet is nearby. Perhaps these people still carry some kind of guilt for their previous contempt and antagonistic reactions, regardless, it is just another sad footnote.

I have not lived an extraordinary life, but I have known exceptional times. In the brief span of my lifetime, I've seen the world evolve through an astonishing array of triumphs and trials and have witnessed the incredible metamorphosis of my generation and all those that followed. The impact of all the amazing inventions, surprising world events, space exploration, advances in medicine, and tragic confrontations, only means to me that our evolution will always be a continuing work in progress. Whether the end results of our ever changing advances ultimately has been for the better or not, I do not know. What I do know is that I have survived incredible and troubled events and with pride I still have unbridled hope in the future for our county. With any luck, my optimism will prevail and the motto I admire most for the United States will forever be "God Bless America."

Halleluiah! I had finished my tour of duty, was still physically intact, had made it safely home, and had been discharged from active duty. Simply said, I was ecstatic. As soon as I walked into our house, I tried not to think about Vietnam or my arrival home anymore, and eventually those memories started to fade. Still, Vietnam was making news daily and it was almost impossible to ignore. The catastrophic history of America's involvement continued until April 30th, 1975 when the last of our troops, ten Marines, boarded a "Jolly Green Giant" chopper atop the crumbling U.S. Embassy.

In chapter 9 I wrote about how America became involved in Vietnam and how fast things escalated. Now I think it is important to understand how our departure from chaos evolved. Today the only ones who really remember the Vietnam era are the survivors; it has not become an object lesson, used as an example, nor chosen as a warning to do better. Hopefully, the story of the consequences of America's involvement in Vietnam will someday help the world understand the importance of peace. I hope so, but still fear it will never be the case. I will continue to pray that one day everyone will understand you really do not need to "destroy a village to save it."

NOVEMBER & DECEMBER 1968

After I left for home, the situation remained pretty much the same, but there was some hope things were gradually starting to change for the better. Unfortunately, it was a long, painfully slow, and costly process. On November 5th, 1968, Richard Milhous Nixon wins a very close election to become the 37th American President. By the end of the month, Henry Kissinger accepts his offer to be the National Security Advisor.

At the end of 1968, there were 495,000 troops in country and a total of 36,956 young men up to that date had departed the country in coffins, surpassing the total of all those killed (36,506) during the Korean War. The highest number of Americans killed in a single year occurred in 1968 with 16,899 dead, that means over 1,400 Americans had died each month. It is estimated that more than 150,000 NVA troops had used the Ho Chi Minh trail to continue the fight in the south. America conducted over 200 air strikes on the trail each date of that year, yet about 10,000 NVA trucks were on that road every day.

It seems fitting to take a break from the saga of Vietnam and note that the Big Red One still continued to be an active participant in many operations and battles, and the following statistics list the combat history for the First Infantry Division in Vietnam for the year of 1968.

1968 COMBAT OPERATIONS

1. Quyet Thang   (Mar. 11 – Apr. 7)   Body count: 429
2. Toan Thangs I   (Apr. 7 – May 31)   Body count: 1739
3. Toan Thangs II   (Jun. 1 – Jan. 1969)   Body count: 2549

1968 MAJOR BATTLES

1. Xom Bung	(Jan. 6)	Body count: 100
2. An My	(Feb. 1-2)	Body count: 372
3. Xom Moi I	(Feb. 2)	Body count: 46
4. Tan Hiep	(May 4)	Body count: 257
5. Xom Moi	(May 5)	Body count: 40
6. Loc Ninh III	(Aug 18)	Body count: 200
7. Loc Ninh IV	(Sep. 7)	Body count: 216
8. Julie	(Oct. 26)	Body count: 86
9. No Name	(Nov. 1)	Body count: 27
10. No Name	(Nov. 8-11)	Body count: 70
11. Junction City	(Dec. 1)	Body count: 44
12. Not Named	(Dec. 1)	Body count: 43

The total enemy body count added up to 6,218 killed. Just as noted in chapter 7 concerning the 1967 battles, I do not know the total 1st Infantry Division sacrifices made for this sad tally; but the cost was undoubtedly very substantial. And the Big Red One battle stats continued to add up for the balance of their stay through April of 1970 when the Division honorably returned to Fort Riley, Kansas.

The following is a quote from General Vo Nguyen Giap's memoirs, found in the Vietnam War Memorial in Hanoi; he was a brilliant, highly respected leader of the North Vietnamese Military: "What we still don't understand is why you Americans stopped the bombing of Hanoi. You had us on the ropes. If you had pressed us a little harder, just for another day or two, we were ready to surrender! It was the same at the battles of Tet. You defeated us! We knew it, and we thought you knew it. But we were elated to notice your media was definitely helping us. They were causing more disruption in America than we could in the battlefields. We were ready to surrender. You had won!"

It is more than apparent that the strategy of the Rolling Thunder mission to continuously bomb North Vietnam was a very successful tool which should have resulted in the end of hostilities in 1968. Bombing is an indiscriminate killer that has no concern for innocent victims; but it is an effective means to hasten the end of a war. Just ask the survivors of the Allied bombing missions in Germany and Japan why they lost WWII. Had we been more dedicated in our purpose and not swayed by all the grandiose idiots who knew nothing about war we would have saved tens of thousands of American lives.

I know this is a rhetorical question, but just how fucking (sorry, just couldn't hold back anymore, and will hold back on the "F" word in the future) stupid were we? It is the purpose of the media to report the news – not to direct it, make it, or to become some kind of self-ordained moral compass. Yet the media seemed to be in control, using their limited understanding of what was really going on, to impose their faulty perspective as fact and direct our military decisions. The only thing the media really accomplished was to empower the enemy into thinking they were winning the more important psychological war back in the States, and this conclusion resulted in an ever increasing total of Americans coming home in body bags. The North Vietnamese were certain they could lose every battle in the South and still win the war.

All that said, how could 1968 have been anything but a disaster?

1969

Late in 1968, "lame duck" President Johnson made a budget proposal to use the assets of the Social Security funding to help balance the national budget. So Social Security was to be added to all the other government assets and trust funds to create a "unified budget" to effectively offset the deficits created by the Vietnam War. Johnson presented this budget concept to Congress in January of 1969; later, after President Nixon took office, it was adopted as the united budget approach. And so the misdirection and misuse of everybody's retirement funding became a mainstay in how our government would fund itself from that point forward. Although the budget processes were changed again a number of times starting in 1983, the end result was Social Security funds would always be available to offset any budget deficits. I consider this to be an illegal remedy to balance our politician's over-indulged and self-serving budgets; thus, by simple deduction, this action is a monumental governmental FUBAR.

It would appear our country used the nation's retirement funds the same way Illinois used the pension reserves for its state employees. As a result, neither the Social Security reserve nor the Illinois State Pension plans are properly funded. This is part of the reason our national debt continues to grow by the trillions of dollars and our only remedy is to print more money. Anybody know the definitions of inflation and bankruptcy? All this treachery and deceit is deserving of a double WTF.

Now back to the continuing history of Vietnam. After successfully campaigning to bring "peace with honor," on January 20, 1969 Richard Milhous Nixon is officially sworn in and becomes the 37th President of the United States and also becomes the fifth President with the dubious honor of overseeing the Vietnam War. On January 22nd, the U.S. Marines launch Operation Dewey Canyon in the A Shau and Song Da Krong Valleys; it is their last major offensive in Vietnam. Although the 56-day operation was a considered a victory, it did not stop the return of the inevitable stream of North Vietnamese troops and supplies. At the end of January, peace talks renew in Paris.

The Tet celebration in 1969 proved to be a repeat of 1968. Later in February, just like clockwork, the Viet Cong attack 110 different objectives in South Vietnam including Saigon. In early March 1969, President Nixon threatens to resume bombing of the North. Although threats never once worked against North Vietnam, we seemed to be obsessed with the concept; but then again, we never seemed to comprehend that they used our bold talk and lack of commitment as a weapon. Even now I still cannot understand just how stupid (not to mention ineffectual and sacrificial) we really were.

In March of 1969, a disheartened veteran writes a letter to General Creighton Abrams, revealing the real story of what happened in the 1968 My Lai Massacre. For the first time it becomes the subject of a U.S. Army investigation. March also sees clandestine "Operation Menu" unfold as we secretly bombed Cambodia. In April, American troop levels reach a new benchmark of 543,000 in country; and 39,120 had died to date.

In early May, the New York Times breaks the story of the secret bombing of Cambodia. President Nixon orders the FBI to install wire taps on the journalist involved to find the source of the leak. On May 10th through the 20th, the 101st Airborne fights its way up Hill 937 which later becomes known as the infamous "Hamburger Hill" – 46 die and over 400 are wounded. Once again we had been victorious; and as we had done so many times before, after our victory, we quickly abandoned the hill and the NVA resumed control of the site totally unchallenged. Just exactly what was the game plan?

The madness of fighting and dying for vantage point in the middle of nowhere, then giving it back to the enemy unopposed, defines the genocidal battle strategy that shackled our ability to "win the war." Without a doubt, it all stank to high heaven. Washington orders General Abrams to avoid any senseless confrontations in the future and to only get involved in smaller group actions. It was about time we looked at the reality and results of our indecisiveness. What they really needed to do was to pull their heads out of their collective asses and either fight to gain control of an area, then hold it, or don't fight at all; but this is a stratagem that would never be implemented by our country.

The orchestration of this war was a tragic comedy of errors and one of constant redirection. There was no overall consistent plan of attack. We were more of a reactionary and retaliatory force. Because of this there was no hope for victory. If we had applied the same tactics we used in WWII, no doubt we would have won the war in Vietnam. Instead, we chose to fight like a Chicago street gang – kill a lot of people, destroy multiple targets, over-react to aggression, have no long-term plan to adhere to, be in lots of firefights with untold collateral damage, seriously not value life, and the only plan of our leadership was a revolving door of ever-changing priorities and politics. WTF. The morale and discipline of the troops began to disintegrate, drug use was out of control, and the hospitals treated significantly more drug-related cases than war causalities. A very sad ending was slowly coming into focus, but it seemed no one wanted to look at it or do much about it.

On May 14th, President Nixon offers to pull out of Vietnam if the NVA will do likewise. Later Hanoi rejects the offer. In June, Nixon tells South Vietnam's President Thieu we are proceeding with the "Vietnamization" of the war and announces the withdrawal of 25,000 U.S. troops. On June 27, 1969, the issue of Life Magazine contains 242 pictures of each American killed in Vietnam the previous week, including the 46 who gave up their lives on "Hamburger Hill." The smiling face of each young man who had died needed no script and made a heartbreaking statement. The very first of 14 planned troop withdrawals soon commences.

On July 20, 1969, the legacy and challenge of President John F. Kennedy is finally fulfilled. At 02:56:15 UTC (Universal Time Coordinated, similar to Greenwich Mean Time), Neil Armstrong was the first man to set foot on the moon. As his foot first touched the surface, his words were "One small step for (a) man, one giant leap for mankind." It was a benchmark unequaled in the history of the world. I remember staring up at the full moon that night in awe and wonder, then pondered the state of our humanity and accomplishments to date. It has always been an ironic postscript for me to know we had the technology and united effort to send men safely to and from the moon but lacked the elementary common sense to stop shooting and killing each other.

On July 30th, President Nixon visits Vietnam for the first and only time after becoming President. Later in August, the VC choreographs 150 attacks throughout South Vietnam. On September 2nd, Ho Chi Minh dies and leaves a will urging the NVA to continue fighting "until the last Yankee has gone." On September 5, 1969, the U.S. Army charges Lt. William Calley concerning the My Lai massacre in March of 1968. On September 16th, Nixon orders 16,000 soldiers home and reduces the numbers drafted each month. Things are really starting to move now.

Anti-war protests and confrontations continue at home. On November 3rd, President Nixon tries to solidify the county's views on Vietnam in an attempt to improve his chances of negotiating a lasting peace. In his "Silent Majority" speech, he tells the country "Let us be united for peace. Let us also be united against defeat. Because let us understand: North Vietnam cannot defeat or humiliate the United States. Only Americans can do that." A growing number of peace demonstrations continue, and on the 15th, an estimated 250,000 protest the war in Washington. On the 16th, the U.S. Army publicly discusses the My Lai incident for the first time.

The first draft lottery since WWII takes place in New York on December 1st. Random numbers are assigned for each birth date and are later drawn to determine the sequence of those to be drafted. Once the results are known, some of those first on the list to be inducted drop out of school and debate their options and a number of them decide not to stick around. Many of those lowest on the list also drop out and pursue more leisurely endeavors.

On the 15th, President Nixon orders 50,000 U.S. troops out of Vietnam. By the end of 1969, over 115,000 men had come home and the number killed in action totaled 48,736. Admittedly, 1969 was another disaster; but at least it seemed that a dim light at the end of that imaginary tunnel was beginning to shine a little brighter.

1970

In February of 1970, U.S. B-52 bombers wreak havoc on the Ho Chi Minh Trail in response to VC raids in the South. Peace talks in Paris continue to go nowhere. Meanwhile in Cambodia, Prince Sihanouk of Cambodia is overthrown by General Lon Nol. Sihanouk joins up with Cambodian Communists known as the Khmer Rouge in hopes of regaining control. Pol Pot heads the Khmer Rouge and later violently expels Lon Nol, then attempts to create a farming paradise. This utopian goal ultimately results in 25% of the country's population dying of starvation, overwork, or by methodically organized executions. In March, Lon Nol counterattacks Pol Pot, and Nixon's top aides discuss how to best assist Lon Nol. I guess since Vietnam was starting to fall from the limelight, our country felt the urge to stick our communal noses in somebody else's business once again. In late March, charges are brought by the U.S. Army against the other participants in the My Lai massacre.

In mid-April, President Nixon announces the withdrawal of another 150,000 troops. On April 15, 1970, the Big Red One returns to Fort Riley, Kansas; had I known I would have been there to greet them. While serving in Vietnam, 11 had been awarded the Medal of Honor, 20 had been taken as prisoners of war, 16,019 had been wounded, and 6,146 had died for their country. I still ask myself why there was so much sacrifice for so little gain and know that the answer will forever elude me.

April 30th, Nixon shocks the nation when he announces the U.S. is getting involved in Cambodia to help end the war in Vietnam. True to his word, the very next day on May 1st, a combined force of U.S. and South Vietnamese troops attack NVA supply bases in Cambodia. Also on that same day, President Nixon says student protesters were "bums blowing up campuses." With unbridled enthusiasm college campuses around the country burst into angry protests the next day. Two days later on the 4th, four students at Kent State are shot and killed and nine others are wounded by distraught National Guardsmen. After that, there were angry protesters everywhere and in Washington D.C. about 100,000 of them surrounded government buildings. Meanwhile on the 6th in Saigon, 450 civilians were killed by the Viet Cong, more than any other week in the war. It seems the carnage will ever end.

On June 22, 1970, the use of Agent Orange (a jungle defoliant, and another of my favorites) is finally stopped. Two days later, the Senate repeals the 1964 Gulf of Tonkin Resolution. On the 30th, all U.S. troops withdrew from Cambodia after they had suffered a loss of 350 American souls. September 5th, 1970 is the date the last U.S. offense in Vietnam begins in the Thau Thien Province. In a televised speech on October 7th, President Nixon offers a "standstill" ceasefire and, like so many times before, Hanoi does not respond. On the 24th, the South Vietnamese Army starts a new offensive in Cambodia – and, for the first time, it is all by themselves.

On November 12th, two and a half years after the event, the military trial for Lt. William Calley commences. On December 22nd, the Cooper-Church Amendment to the U.S. Defense Appropriations Bill forbids the use of any U.S. ground forces in either Laos or Cambodia.

By the end of 1970, the total troop levels have been reduced to 280,000 people. It has been estimated that fully 25% of those still in country had experimented with drugs and that over 200 incidents of fragging had occurred, but I firmly believe these totals fall far short of the mark. Fragging was the act of trying to kill someone, usually an unpopular officer or sergeant, with a hand-thrown fragmentation grenade. The most common targets were second lieutenants who were in charge of infantry platoons and squads; their jobs were considered by many to be the absolute most hazardous duty in Vietnam. Racial unrest also plagued our troops in reaction to the bitterness felt by people of color back home. It was no picnic in Vietnam.

In 1970, America lost a total of 6,173 soldiers, had 24,835 wounded, and 101 were missing in action. The casualty counts had been lowered significantly but were still at an unacceptable level for anyone whose loved ones came home wounded, in a casket, or did not come home at all. The tally of those who died in Vietnam now exceeds 54,900.

1971

On January 4, 1971, Nixon announces "The end is in sight." But on the 19th, U.S. fighter bombers launch air strikes on NVA camps in Laos and Cambodia. No U.S. troops were on the ground, but we were there all the same. On the 30th, the South Vietnamese Army (SVA) launches Operation Lam Son with a ground force of 17,000 people. They plan to attack Laos in hopes of destroying the Ho Chi Minh Trail. Although they were initially successful (due to all of the American air support), after better than three months, the South Vietnamese Army finally limps home with only 8,000 men. The U.S. lost 215 killed; 100 helicopters were destroyed and another 600 were damaged in that action. Even though the NVA death toll was estimated to be somewhere around 20,000, they still controlled the trail, had ultimately been victorious, and nonetheless remained very much a constant threat.

Nixon's approval rating continues to slide and most Americans consider the war immoral. On March 10, 1971, China again pledges to help North Vietnam win the fight with the U.S. On the 29th, Lt. William Calley is found guilty of murdering 22 My Lai innocent civilians. Originally he was sentenced to life imprisonment. In subsequent appeals, his sentence was first reduced to 20 years and later lowered to 10 years, and he kept on submitting appeals. Five others were also court-martialed, but only Calley was found guilty. On April 1st, President Nixon orders Calley released pending his most recent appeal.

On April 22, 1971, John Kerry became the first Vietnam veteran to testify before congress. He served three tours of duty in the Navy and had been awarded a Bronze Star, a Silver Star, and three Purple Hearts. Although the circumstances of his service and his awards then and even now are somewhat suspect by a few people, he was and still is considered a war hero. He was violently opposed to the war and reportedly had been quoted as saying "Someone has to die so that President Nixon won't be the first President to lose a war." In a later demonstration, he and 800 other Vietnam veterans threw their medals and ribbons at the U.S. Capitol building. In an ironic twist of fate, he much later becomes Secretary of State for the 44th President. Is he a Hawk or a Dove? I don't know, but I do applaud his service.

The madness and senseless inhumanity continue…

By April 29th, 1971, the total of those Americans killed in Vietnam reached 56,102. The next day, the last of the Marine Vietnam combat units leave the country. The anti-war demonstrations continue and in early May, 12,000 protesters are arrested in Washington D.C. On June 13, 1971, the *New York Times* begins to publish the "Pentagon Papers" (just what President Nixon needed). The publishing of classified documents really upsets Nixon and he tries to use the U.S. District Court to put a halt to anything else being released. It gets more interesting on the 18th when the *Washington Post* follows suit and also begins to publish of the "Pentagon Papers."

Both the *Times* and the *Post* end up in the Supreme Court. Sometime later, they win the right to publish the papers. And if all that wasn't enough, on June 22nd, a non-binding resolution was passed by the Senate which urged removal of all U.S. troops by the end of the year. Also, on June 28th, Daniel Ellsberg (the source of the "Pentagon Papers" leak) surrenders to the police. There was so much happening, almost nobody could figure out what's going on. What a pathetic mess. Our state of affairs was an embarrassment to our legacy and, personally, I don't think we've changed all that much since.

On July 1st, a total of 6,100 military personnel depart Vietnam, a new one-day record. On the 17th, the "Plumbers unit" is established in the White House by John Ehrlichman and Charles Colson to investigate Daniel Ellsberg.

I apologize if all this history is confusing; even now, my head is spinning. I've tried to present the events more or less in the order of occurrence. The disjointed sequence of this much information can be all too bewildering; but I believe each of these events had a direct impact on the decisions being made which affected everything that went on in Vietnam. Most of those who ran the show seemed to be concerned only with their personal images, power, and legacy (if ever they had any positive achievements).

On October 3rd, President Thieu of South Vietnam (running unopposed) is re-elected. On the 9th, members of the U.S. 1st Cavalry Division refuse to go out on patrol, saying they had "a desire not to go." Although they could have all been court-martialed, more "combat refusals" follow. By December 17th, troop levels have dropped to 157,000. The U.S. bombs military sites in North Vietnam for violating a previous agreement. In 1971, a total of 18,109 U.S. troops have been wounded, 16 are missing in action, and 2,414 have been killed.

Please note that not all deaths in Vietnam were the result of hostile action. For instance, in 1971 there were 1,446 people killed in combat and another 968 people killed by a host of other causes such as traffic accidents, disease, drug overdoses, accidents with explosive ordinance, etc. Each and every single death was tragic, and a combined total of 2,414 had died that year. By year's end, a total 57,323 had been slain in Vietnam.

I have always been a little confused about the word casualty; it is normally defined as either being (1) dead or (2) wounded. In my mind, you are simply one or the other, and there is no common ground. My guess is the term was the result of someone who could not tell the difference and needed to go back to "Triage School" or perhaps they had something to hide. Regardless, it is a confusing and stupid word; hopefully one day it will be dropped from our vocabulary.

1972

Things seemed to be improving – but, then again, maybe not so much since the firefights continued to produce more needless victims. Late in January of 1972, Henry Kissinger presents yet another peace agreement, but Hanoi once again refuses the offer. From February 21st to the 28th, Nixon goes to China in an effort to improve on our diplomatic association. The meetings do improve our relationship, and Hanoi fears China's agreement to open discussions with the U.S. might in fact reduce North Vietnam's negotiating power during future peace discussions (xin loi). On March 10th, the 101st Airborne Division (The Screaming Eagles) finally gets to go home.

Starting in late March, the NVA send 200,000 men south during the Eastertide Offensive in a mammoth effort to triumph over all of South Vietnam. NVA General Giap reasoned the reduced U.S. troop strength and the many failures of the South Vietnamese Army would assure victory. The NVA also hoped their show of power would destroy President Nixon's chances of winning the upcoming presidential election, just as Tet had done to President Johnson. With Nixon gone, they thought American aid to South Vietnam would stop. President Nixon immediately authorizes massive B-52 bombing raids on all NVA positions and tells the U.S. Navy to target the Demilitarized Zone with air strikes and naval gunfire. Hanoi and Haiphong are also attacked. It is a very determined NVA attempt for a conclusive North Vietnamese victory, and the intense Eastertide Offensive would go on for six months.

More protests break out across America; but, as a result of the quick U.S. retaliatory response to Eastertide, peace talks are soon scheduled to resume in Paris. At the same time, U.S. troop strength in Vietnam had been reduced to 69,000. In May, and in my opinion much too late, America mines Haiphong harbor. The NVA were starting to rack up many victories, but they paid a very heavy price in mortality for each of their successes. President Nixon travels to

Russia and meets with Leonid Brezhnev to improve diplomatic relations. Again, just like with China, Hanoi is worried about the consequences. Back in Washington on June 17, 1972, five intruders are arrested inside the Watergate building trying to plant microphones in the Democratic National Committee offices. Ties to Nixon and the White House are uncovered sometime later. On July 13, the Paris peace talks begin one more time.

On July 18th, Jane Fonda, a self-professed and peace-loving zealot (who was a young movie actress with questionable Communist ties) travels to Hanoi. Believing she can singlehandedly rescue Vietnam and the United States, she broadcasts anti-war speeches on Radio Hanoi. She also meets and supposedly rebukes American POWs at the Hanoi Hilton. When she returns to the U.S., she is justifiably singled out as being a traitor to her country and, in the end, all her rhetoric only made things worse. I personally don't know of a single Vietnam veteran who can find anything nice to say about Ms. Fonda. In Vietnam her name soon becomes a common term referencing someone who is a traitor. Apparently because of her famous actor father's connections and status, she was never formally punished for her stupid, adolescent behavior. Although she apologized too many years later, I seriously doubt she ever really cared what anyone else thought. And for many Vietnam veterans the judgement still remains the same, treason is treason, no matter how you color it.

Hollywood, just like the media, should never be the voice of authority for any military stratagem. There have always been great entertainers, but being a good actor, singer, comedian, magician, or whatever, does not qualify one for a leadership position. It certainly is OK to criticize and protest, but by no stretch of the imagination does memorizing a script or singing a song make you a decision maker and a leader. The goals and perspectives of the entertainment industry are often self-inflating, ultraistic, and many times are counterproductive.

If you really want to impact the policy of our country, run for a government office, support a politician you agree with, or join the military and earn your stripes. Everybody in the United States enjoys the freedom of free speech. By law you can protest all you want; but that does not license nor certify any one person to dictate military strategy – no matter who you think you are. It is so much easier to point your finger and condemn, complain, and cajole than it is to get off your butt and actually do something constructive.

On August 23, 1972, the last American combat soldiers leave Vietnam although many thousands of U.S. advisors remain in country. The United States still keeps an active presence in the battlefield via air support and, later in September, ten percent of the NVA air force is obliterated by U.S. forces. On October 8th, Henry Kissinger and North Vietnam's Le Duc Tho at long last come to an agreement. The proposal would allow North Vietnam to have the NVA troops already there remain in the South and, side by side with President Thieu, and they would share joint power.

The thought of allowing the NVA to stay in South Vietnam is appalling to President Thieu, most U.S. statesmen, and anyone with a functioning brain in his head. In response, Kissinger simply says "I want to end this war before the election." Did he really care about all the consequences or was he only focused on winning the next presidential election? – You be the judge. Negotiations are not always about what is best; mostly they are simply about power.

When Kissinger and President Thieu meet in Saigon, Thieu totally rejects the agreement. Even after Nixon threatens to cut off all aid, Thieu does not back down. Allowing NVA troops to remain in South Vietnam is not only crazy, it is suicidal. In October, after suffering 100,000 NVA casualties (40,000 had died), it is more than apparent the Eastertide Offensive has failed. North Vietnam's General Giap is inauspiciously replaced after losing the biggest offensive of the war, and General Van Tien Dung takes command. On October 24th, President Thieu lets everyone know how much he hates and rejects Kissinger's peace plan. On the 26th, Radio Hanoi releases the peace proposal details and accuses the U.S. of disrupting the process.

One week before the U.S. Presidential election, Kissinger is quoted as saying "We believe that peace is at hand. We believe that an agreement is in sight." On November 7, 1972, President Nixon is re-elected by the biggest margin in history of our country up to that date. On the 14th, Nixon sends Thieu a note and assures him the U.S. will "take swift and severe retaliatory action" if the NVA violate the treaty (remember that empty promise).

At the end of November 1972, there are still 16,000 American administrators and advisors in country. On December 13th, the peace talks between Kissinger and Le Duc Tho fall apart after Kissinger presents the 69 changes stipulated by President Thieu. Nixon demands that the North Vietnamese must resume negotiations in 72 hours. What a surprise – Hanoi does not respond. In response, President Nixon initiates 11 days of intense bombing of Hanoi.

The sad truth is bombing does work, but only if you are committed. On December 26th, the North Vietnamese agree that peace negotiations need to start again. At the end of 1972, those killed in Vietnam for that year total 759 troops; 3,936 have been wounded, and 11 are MIA. Although significantly smaller, these tallies are still heart wrenching. Over 58,000 had been killed in Vietnam as the year ended. Everyone, everywhere, demands that this seemingly never-ending senseless slaughter come to an end. It is now finally apparent that the war will end in the foreseeable future, but the actual date and the cost to mankind remained a mystery.

1973

On January 8, 1973, Henry Kissinger and Le Duc Tho meet in Paris and the very next day they somehow overcome every objection. President Thieu, still under threat of losing all U.S. aid, finally reluctantly accepts the agreement but feels the terms for South Vietnam are "tantamount to surrender." On the 23rd, President Nixon proclaims the agreement will "end the war and bring peace with honor." My only question is peace and honor for whom; the whole mess is (brace yourself) a clusterf--k. Why would anyone in his right mind ever trust the North Vietnamese? How stupid were we? Please don't answer this. Although valid, it's only a rhetorical question (and by now you already know the answer).

On January 27, 1973, the Paris Peace Accords are signed by the United States, South Vietnam, North Vietnam, and the Viet Cong. The U.S. agrees to remove all military personnel and stop every military action. The North Vietnamese agree to an immediate cease fire and again emphasize that 150,000 NVA will remain in South Vietnam. Vietnam will still be considered two separate countries. It's just that South Vietnam will have two governments: one headed by President Thieu and the other by the Viet Cong. I mean, what could possibly go wrong? It seems almost everyone in Washington D.C. were insane, mindless, and idiotic buffoons, but they were running the show. I do not understand why we allowed this to happen. I don't know the answers, but this type of self-inflating political reasoning has been going on forever and it only serves to prove to the world our word and bond are sometimes meaningless, worthless promises.

Also on the 27th, Washington announces the end of the draft, and on that same day the last American soldier dies in combat. His name is Lt. Col. William B. Nolde and his death is a sad epitaph to the Vietnam saga. On February 12th, Hanoi releases 591 prisoners of war. On March 29th, the last remaining combat troops leave the country and Nixon announces "This is the day we have all worked and prayed for has finally come."

In April, Presidents Nixon and Thieu meet in San Clemente, California and Nixon once again agrees to respond militarily if the NVA violates the Peace Accords. On April 30th, Nixon aides Haldeman and Ehrlichman resign due to the Watergate scandal. On June 19th, Congress passes the Case-Church amendment forbidding any further military involvement is Southeast Asia. That's all well and good, but this gives the NVA the green light to organize yet another offensive in the South. "No good deed (ever) goes unpunished," a quote attributed to American Author Clare Booth Luce, and I think she would agree that her quote really seemed to be most appropriate just about then.

In July of 1973, the U.S. Navy is ordered to remove the mines we had placed in the seaports in North Vietnam. On October 10th, political scandal forces Vice President Agnew to resign and Gerald R. Ford becomes Vice President and takes his place. On December 3rd, the Viet Cong destroy a huge fuel dump just outside Saigon. As 1973 comes to a close, many are concerned about the ramifications of the Paris Peace Accords, and rightfully so. Only 68 U.S. troops died that year, one every five days or so. If this was truly the legacy of "peace with honor," just where were we headed? It seemed the only goal was for the U.S. to get out of Vietnam, regardless of the pain that would follow, both here and there.

The United States had been seriously involved in Vietnam for over 15 years, and it is the first war we had ever lost (although never formally declared a war, the Vietnam Conflict was undeniably a war by anyone's definition). Well over two and one half million Americans had served in country with 500,000 seeing actual combat. By the end of 1973, 47,364 U.S. troops had been killed in hostile action and there were another 10,786 non-combat deaths, for a total of 58,150 killed since the war began. 153,329 had been seriously wounded and over 2,400 Americans were still missing in action. These were very heavy prices to pay, and for what reason? There will never be a logical answer. What a waste, what a loss, what a shame, what a crime!

1974

On May 9, 1974, Congress starts impeachment proceedings against Nixon for his involvement in the Watergate scandal. On August 9,

1974, a humiliated President Nixon resigns. Gerald R. Ford is sworn in as the new President of the United States. He was the sixth and last U.S. President involved in the Vietnam War.

In September, Congress cuts appropriations for South Vietnam leaving it seriously under-funded. On September 6th, Ford offers clemency for draft dodgers; of the estimated 124,000 men eligible, only 22,500 take advantage of the program. No surprise, it seems few trusted the government.

In November, William Calley is freed after serving only three and a half years under house arrest following his conviction for murdering 22 My Lai civilians. I am at a loss for words. Even cloaked in the insanity of war, this sad chronicle and the punishment rendered were just more examples of how much America was spinning out of control. Fear, anger, and mistakes sometimes combined in the midst of battle and resulted in catastrophic collateral damage to both innocent Vietnamese civilians and U.S. troops alike. I wasn't there, so I don't know what really happened; but, undeniably, genocide was the end result in My Lai. As had occurred many times before, justice would never be served. Just another tragic Vietnam War postscript added to a very long accusatory and painful list.

On December 13, 1974, the North Vietnamese once again violated the Peace Treaty and attacked Phuoc Long Province in South Vietnam. No surprise it appeared they never really planned to comply with the peace accords they had agreed to, something they had demonstrated more times than not. President Ford's only response was a weak, ineffective diplomatic protest and absolutely no military support or funding was ever provided. At the time the North Vietnamese Army was then the fifth largest in the world and was confident in nothing less than total victory. The NVA had planned on a two-year offensive to take over the South. In reality, once the invasion got rolling and started its advance southward, it only took 55 days (139 days after breaking the treaty in Phuoc Long Province).

1975

Speaking before Congress on January 15, 1975, Secretary of Defense James Schlesinger tells them that the U.S. was not honoring our pledge for "severe retaliatory action" if the NVA ever violated the Peace Treaty. On the 21st, President Ford says that the United States will not get involved in the war again. The South Vietnamese valiantly fight on but are no match for the North. President Thieu starts to abandon sites in northern South Vietnam and the roads are soon filled with SVN soldiers and refugees, all running for their lives. The NVA shows no mercy and continuously fires shells and rockets into the unorganized retreating masses. The throngs of escapees soon become known as the "Convoy of Tears." Cities and province's fall one after the other and in no time Saigon is in big trouble.

On April 20, 1975, the U.S. Ambassador meets with President Thieu and urges him to resign. On the 21st, Thieu gives a heartfelt speech concerning what he feels is the undeniable betrayal by America. He reads the letter from Nixon who had promised to respond with "severe retaliatory action" when needed. He goes on and on and condemns the Paris Peace talks and America's broken promises. He resigns an abandoned and broken man, saddened and justifiably angered. He is then ushered into exile to Taiwan by the CIA. I have always been appalled by this action, right or wrong; we gave our promise to protect democracy and had failed miserably.

South Vietnam still fought on – they really had no choice. By April 23rd, Saigon is surrounded and overflowing with many tens of thousands of refugees plus 30,000 South Vietnamese soldiers. On that same day, President Ford is speaking at Tulane University and says "Vietnam is a war that is finished as far as America is concerned." How prophetic. What a visionary. What a sad memorial to the sacrifices made by so many.

The NVA bombards Saigon with rockets and the city becomes shrouded into a chaotic, smoldering, insane throng of humanity, all scared to death. The NVA also shells Tan Son Nhut air base on the 29th killing two American Marines. More than a little late President Ford eventually orders Operation Frequent Wind, which starts with a radio broadcast of the song "White Christmas." This signals the beginning of the end and the remaining 7,000 Americans and their Vietnamese counterparts rush to escape by helicopter.

Everyone who attempts to use Tan Son Nhut air base soon finds there is too much bedlam; so the evacuation point is moved to the U.S. Embassy as their primary escape route. The Embassy is surrounded by sturdy walls and is guarded by a cadre of Embassy Marine security guards. Soon the scene becomes extremely frenzied and the evacuation continues as best it can until everyone who could had escaped Saigon. There were so many choppers, the Navy Aircraft Carriers didn't have enough room for them all on their flight decks. Unavoidably, many of the Hueys were grudgingly and dutifully dumped into the Saigon Sea. The last Americans to depart were ten U.S. Embassy Marines who lifted off on April 30, 1975 at 8:35 AM. By 11 AM, the Viet Cong flag flies over the Presidential Palace of South Vietnam. The war was over; but the pain, shame, and agony still linger and probably always will.

The Final Tally

Vietnam had some very interesting statistics. Only 24 men were ever reported as being deserters, an amazingly low number considering all the discontent. The United States dropped three times as many bombs on Vietnam as it did in all of World War II. Perhaps the most unbelievable stat of all was that we had without a doubt won every significant battle but still managed to lose the war. Tragically, 58,213 U.S. troops had died, in excess of 304,000 had been wounded, and more than 2,330 were still missing in action. A total of over 2,650,000 had served America in Vietnam from 1960 to 1975; this included about 7,500 women of whom about 85% were nurses and 8 of them had died while in country. There are so many more depressing statistics that I find it emotionally impossible to list them all, but I think the totals listed speak for themselves.

In Conclusion

When I left Vietnam in 1968, the average American had an entirely different lifestyle than we enjoy today. The population of the United States was about 201 million people and now there are about 322 million. By year's end, the Dow Jones average still had yet not closed in excess of 1,000 points (and would not until November 14, 1972). A new house only cost a little over $26,000, rent was $130 per month, a new car would set you back about $2,825, and gas cost $0.34 per gallon. The average income per year was $7,850 and many more families than not lived on one income. The minimum wage was $1.60 per hour. A postage stamp cost $0.05. There were no cell phones. Most homes had only one phone and it had a dial on it, and long-distance calls were costly. Personal computers did not exist so there were no emails and no internet. TV's had very few stations; those TV's with color pictures were still rare; and, if it had a remote, it was connected to the TV with a cord (most TVs only had a dial on the front next to the screen which needed to be turned by hand). It was not just another point in time; it was an entirely different planet. The cultures of then and now are worlds apart. To me, it is somewhat debatable which is really better – 1968 or 2017.

Whether you were a witness to the Vietnam era or are a student of history, if you believe the ethics of the men fighting in Vietnam was a big problem, you are very wrong. The average age of the combat troops in Vietnam was 22, but so many were only in their teens. 8,283 of those who died were only 19 years old or younger. Think about that. Only God knows how many of our youth were wounded and decimated. Far too many had their lives forever ruined. The maturity levels and psyche of everyone in Vietnam were constantly bombarded with stresses no one should ever have to endure. You didn't have to be in a firefight; just knowing what was going on all around you could raise your anxiety and impact any sense of reality. But actually being in combat and witnessing people you knew being horrifically injured or killed with abandon would exagerate the definitions of fear, anger, and desire for revenge into uncharted territory. One more thing to remember, when one person shoots another there are two victims, two who suffer the consequences.

All that said, I firmly believe all Americans in Vietnam simply wanted to do their jobs, stay well, and come home whole. All too many arrived home figuratively or literally "walking wounded." It is the only war I know where all the heroes and combatants were blamed for every atrocity when they returned home. They were no parades, no welcome-home speeches, no pats on the back; the best most could hope for was that nobody noticed their tans. As a country, we should be very ashamed.

The average age of a college graduate was older than most of the Americans who served in Vietnam. How many truly mature college (or high school) graduates do you know? There was nothing wrong with the integrity and loyalty of those who served our country in Vietnam or of those now serving across the globe. The same thing cannot be said about the leaders of our country then and most assuredly now. We need to replace all those transparent politicians who are all too willing to "give away the store" in order to achieve personal gain and more power for their party affiliation. We need leaders of integrity working for a better America; to reinstate the Judeo-Christian values this country is based upon, and to put the concept of "political correctness" where it belongs – in the toilet.

This is America. For the most part, all are welcome; but we need to maintain and preserve our heritage. We should not attempt to transform our country to meet every newcomer's demands and wants. They came here to enjoy our freedom, and each and every one of them needs to respect and remember our motto is and will always be: "God Bless America!"

The war had ended, and now this book has also reached its conclusion. I'm not sure whether this story should be considered an epilogue or an epitaph – and it may very well be both. I've tried to be faithful to the history of the United States and Vietnam and have told my story as I remember it.

Hopefully, the entirety of this chronicle will serve its purpose to honor every United States Veteran. Americans have always respectfully and dutifully served our country to protect the integrity of our ideals. Whether you like it or not, our rights, freedoms, and safety all hinge on the security our nation's military ensures. Ultimately, the leadership, resolve, and strength of our armed forces are the linchpins that hold everything in place. You don't have to use force, but you damn well better have it in place and be prepared to use it when it is needed. The sad history of America's impact on the Vietnam era bears testament to our country's unstable, wavering, questionable direction and purpose. To me it appears this very same lack of resolution and dedication continues to plague us to this day.

I know we can do better.

Epilogue

This book is solely the result of my research, personal documents, reminders from the Army's Big Red One Vietnam Books (volumes 1 and 2), and the resurrection of my fading memories. Although much of the material I have researched has conflicting statistics and dates, I've sincerely tried to make sure this story is as factual as possible. But confirming the validity of America's involvement in Vietnam's history was never my primary objective. Whether the chronology is accurate or if the names, events and references are exaggerated or incorrect, none of these things were the real goal of this work.

What I originally hoped and strived to achieve was to successfully portray the emotions that grew from my experiences; all in an effort to share some of the awkward realities of the Vietnam War. However, as soon I started to take a closer look, I realized my story was inconsequential compared to the evolution into madness America experienced during that era. So my real purpose quickly metamorphosed into a need to reveal the sad history that dragged America down a spiraling path into the painful and deadly bedlam that resulted in the Vietnam War. I have high hopes that this narrative will inspire a select few to make more positive contributions to better serve our country and mankind than our predecessors were able to achieve. Then as now, America must do better.

It is amazing how much impact a simple decision or minor mistake can make, endlessly changing and challenging your direction and destination as you navigate life's twists and turns. I really don't believe in fate or destiny but sometimes wonder at how very fortunate my storied past has been, and I am more than just a little thankful. Although not preordained, my life has enjoyed an ample supply of good luck and fortune. I am not a historian, just an average traveler in amazing times, much more so a long time ago; and I still have memories I want to share. Undoubtedly somebody else would have done a much better job of telling my tale and writing this book, but this chronicle was simply something I needed to do for and by myself.

Everybody has a story; don't ever hesitate to tell yours.

MILITARY RANK CHART

ENLISTED MEN

GRADE	COMMAND RANK	SPECIALIST RANK
E1	RECRUIT	N/A
E2	PRIVATE	N/A
E3	PRIVATE FIRST CLASS	N/A
E4	CORPORAL	SPECIALIST 4TH CLASS
E5	SERGEANT	SPECIALIST 5TH CLASS
E6	STAFF SERGEANT	SPECIALIST 6TH CLASS
E7	SERGEANT 1ST CLASS	N/A
E8	MASTER SERGEANT	N/A
E8	FIRST SERGEANT	N/A
E9	SERGEANT MAJOR	N/A
E9	COMMAND SERGEANT MAJOR	N/A
SPECIAL	SERGEANT MAJOR OF THE ARMY	N/A

OFFICERS

GRADE	COMMAND RANK	INSIGNIA
O-1	SECOND LIEUTENANT	SINGLE GOLD BAR
O-2	FIRST LIEUTENANT	SINGLE SILVER BAR
O-3	CAPTAIN	TWO SILVER BARS
O-4	MAJOR	GOLD OAK LEAF CLUSTER
O-5	LIEUTENANT COLONEL	SILVER OAK LEAF CLUSTER
O-6	COLONEL	SILVER EAGLE
O-7	BRIGADIER GENERAL	ONE SILVER STAR
O-8	MAJOR GENERAL	LINE OF TWO SILVER STARS
O-9	LIEUTENANT GENERAL	LINE OF THREE SILVER STARS
O-10	GENERAL	LINE OF FOUR SILVER STARS
SPECIAL	GENERAL OF THE ARMY	CIRCLE OF 5 SILVER STARS
SPECIAL	COMMANDER IN CHIEF	PRESIDENT OF THE U.S.

PHONETIC ALPHABET

LETTER	CODE WORD *	LETTER	CODE WORD *
* THERE ARE MANY OTHER PHONETIC WORDS, BUT THESE WERE THE MOST COMMON.			
A	ALFA	N	NOVEMBER
B	BRAVO	O	OSCAR
C	CHARLIE	P	PAPA
D	DELTA	Q	QUEBEC
E	ECHO	R	ROMEO
F	FOXTROT	S	SIERRA
G	GOLF	T	TANGO
H	HOTEL	U	UNIFORM
I	INDIA	V	VICTOR
J	JULIET	W	WHISKEY
K	KILO	X	X-RAY
L	LIMA	Y	YANKEE
M	MIKE	Z	ZULU

MILITARY ORGANIZATIONAL CHART

UNIT NAME	CONSISTS OF (QTY)
SQUAD	12 SOLDIERS (12)
PLATOON	4 SQUADS (48)
COMPANY	4 PLATOONS (192)
BATTALION	5 COMPANIES (960)
BRIGADE	5 BATTALIONS (4,800)
DIVISION	3 BRIGADES (14,400)
CORPS	4 DIVISIONS (57,600)

THE BREAKDOWN OF THE ABOVE UNITS WAS OFTEN TIMES LARGER OR SMALLER THAN NOTED ABOVE. THE 1ST ADMIN COMPANY HAD WELL OVER 600 MEN, DIVIDED INTO 12 PLATOONS OF 4 SQUADS EACH, WITH 12 TO 15 MEN PER SQUAD. OUR 1ST ADMIN COMPANY HAD MORE THAN THREE TIMES AS MANY PEOPLE AS WAS THE NORM.

1967-1968 - 1st INFANTRY DIVISION COMPANIES

1st BRIGADE   (ACE OF SPADES)
1st BATTALION, 2ND INFANTRY   (RAMRODS)
2nd BATTALION, 2ND INFANTRY   (RAMRODS)
2nd BRIGADE   (READY NOW)
HEADQUARTERS AND HEADQUARTERS COMPANY   (HHC)
HHC & BAND SUPPORT COMMAND
1st MEDICAL BATTALION   (READY FOR EVERYTHING)
1st BATTALION, 5th ARTILLERY   (ALEXANDER HAMILTON'S CANNONEERS)
1st BATTALION, 16th INFANTRY   (RANGERS)
2nd BATTALION, 16th INFANTRY   (RANGERS)
3rd BRIGADE   (IRON BRIGADE)
1st SQUADRON, 4th CAVALRY   (QUARTERHORSE)
1st SUPPLY & TRANSPORTATION BATTALION   (LET US CARRY THE BURDEN)
8th BATTALION, 6th ARTILLERY   (QUICK AND BOLD)
1st BATTALION, 18th INFANTRY   (VANGUARDS)
2nd BATTALION, 18th INFANTRY   (VANGUARDS)
DIVISION ARTILLERY   (CAISSONS)
1st AVIATION BATTALION   (ABOVE THE FIRST)
1st ENGINEERING BATTALION   (ALWAYS FIRST)
1st BATTALION, 7th ARTILLERY   (PHEONS)
1st BATTALION, 26th INFANTRY   (BLUE SPADERS)
SUPPORT COMMAND
121st SIGNAL BATTALION   (DO IT WELL, DO IT NOW)
701st MAINTENANCE BATTALION (SERVICE AND COURAGE OF HEART)
2nd BATTALION, 33rd ARTILLERY   (GOLDEN LIONS)
1st BATTALION, 28th INFANTRY   (BLACK LIONS)
2nd BATTALION, 28th INFANTRY   (BLACK LIONS)
1st ADMINISTRATION COMPANY   (ADMIN)
1st MILITARY POLICE COMPANY

1967-1968 - 1st INFANTRY DIVISION ATTACHED UNITS

35th AND 41st SCOUT DOG PLATOONS
304th AVIATION DETACHMENT
243rd ARTILLERY DETACHMENT
17th MILITARY HISTORY DETACHMENT
242nd AND 266th CHEMICAL DETACHMENTS
5th TRACKER TEAM
43rd AND 44th PI (PUBLIC INFORMATION) DETACHMENTS
1st MI (MILITARY INTELLIGENCE) DETACHMENT
61st INFANTRY COMBAT TRACKER PLATOON

1st INFANTRY DIVISION MOTTO

NO MISSION TOO DIFFICULT
NO SACRIFICE TOO GREAT
DUTY FIRST

LISTING OF U.S. ARMY AND OTHER UNITS IN VIETNAM - 1967 & 1968

UNIT	DESCRIPTION
1st	1st AVIATION BRIGADE
1st	1st FIELD FORCE
1st	1st INFANTRY DIVISION (BIG RED ONE OR BRO)
1st	1st LOGISTICAL COMMAND
1st	1st SIGNAL BRIGADE
2nd	2nd FIELD FORCE
3rd	3rd MARINE DIVISION
4th	4th INFANTRY DIVISION
4th	4th TRANSPORTATION COMMAND (IVY)
5th	5th INFANTRY DIVISION
5th	5th TRANSPORTATION COMMAND
9th	9th INFANTRY DIVISION
11th	11th AIR ASSAULT
11th	11th ARMORED CAVALRY REGIMENT (BLACK HORSE)
11th	11th LIGHT INFANTRY BRIGADE (ALSO AMERICAL)
15th	15th SUPPORT BRIGADE
18th	18th ENGINEERS
18th	18th MILITARY POLICE BRIGADE
20th	20th ENGINEERS
23rd	AMERICAL, 23rd INFANTRY DIVISION
24th	24th CORPS
25th	25th INFANTRY DIVISION
44th	44th MEDICAL BRIGADE
82nd	82nd AIRBORNE DIVISION
101st	101st CAVALRY DIVISION, AIRBORNE
124th	124th TRANSPORTATION COMMAND
125th	125th TRANSPORTATION COMMAND
151st	151st INFANTRY, LONG RANGE PATROL (NG)
173rd	173rd AIRBORNE BRIGADE
196th	196th LIGHT INFANTRY BRIGADE
198th	198th LIGHT INFANTRY BRIGADE (AMERICAL)
199th	199th LIGHT INFANTRY BRIGADE
AMERICAL	23RD INFANTRY DIVISION

LISTING OF U.S. ARMY AND OTHER UNITS IN VIETNAM - 1967 & 1968

UNIT	DESCRIPTION
I CORPS	NORTHERNMOST MILITARY REGION IN SOUTH VIETNAM
II CORPS	CENTRAL HIGHLANDS REGION IN SOUTH VIETNAM
III CORPS	REGION BETWEEN SAIGON AND THE HIGHLANDS
IV CORPS	MEKONG DELTA, SOUTHERNMOST MILITARY REGION
I FFV	I FIELD FORCE VIETNAM
II FFV	II FIELD FORCE VIETNAM
MACV	MILITARY ASSISTANCE COMMAND VIETNAM
S-1	PERSONNEL
S-2	INTELLIGENCE
S-3	OPERATIONS
S-4	SUPPLY
S-5	CIVIL AFFAIRS
U.S. ARMY COMBAT	U.S. ARMY COMBAT DEVELOPMENTS COMMAND
U.S. ARMY ENG COM	U.S. ARMY ENGINEER COMMAND VIETNAM
U.S. ARMY MATERIEL	U.S. ARMY MATERIEL COMMAND
U.S. ARMY MEDICAL	U.S. ARMY MEDICAL VIETNAM
U.S. ARMY REP VN	UNITED STATES ARMY REPUBLIC VIETNAM
U.S. ARMY SECURITY	U.S. ARMY SECURITY AGENCY GROUP VIETNAM
USAF	U.S. AIR FORCE
USARPAC	U.S. ARMY PACIFIC
USASTRATCOM	U.S. ARMY STRATEGIC COMMAND, SOUTHEAST ASIA
USAVN	U.S. ARMY VIETNAM
USMC	U.S. MARINES
USN	U.S. NAVY

NOTE: I'VE TRIED TO LIST THE NAMES OF ALL OF THE U.S. ARMY & SOME OF THE OTHER U.S. MILITARY UNITS THAT WERE IN VIETNAM DURING MY TOUR OF DUTY, BUT IF THERE ARE ANY ERRORS OR OMISSIONS I OFFER MY SINCEREST APOLOGIES.

GLOSSARY - DEFINING VIETNAM*

*For adults only!

NAMES, PHRASES, AND TERMS USED IN VIETNAM FROM 1954 TO 1975 AND BEYOND

> Fair warning: Much of the content of this robust glossary is profane, harsh, stupid, boring, and distressing; it contains insulting slurs, amusing terminology, tragic consequences, mundane nonsense, and colorful commentary; and it includes graphic vocabulary that is all too often demeaning or sad, some of which may prove to be painful
> - but then again, so was the duty.

1ST - 1ST Infantry Division, the Big Red One (AKA BRO).

4-F - Low wellness rating, unfit for military service.

11 Bravo - MOS 11B, Infantryman.

11 Charlie - MOS 11C, Indirect Fire (Mortar) Infantryman.

12 Bravo - MOS 12B, Combat Engineer.

17th Parallel - North and South Vietnam dividing line per 1954 Geneva Conference.

33 - (Ba M'ba) Vietnamese beer.

38th Parallel - North and South Korea dividing line per 1945 Potsdam Conference.

73 Charlie - MOS 73C, Finance Specialist.

201 File - File containing all the military records for a soldier.

A-Team - 12-Man Green Beret unit.

A-Wall - (AWOL) Absent without leave.

A Shau Valley - (Awe Shaw) entry point from the Ho Chi Minh Trail into South Vietnam.

AAA - Triple A, Anti-Aircraft Artillery.

AAR - After action report.

Above My Pay Grade - Not my responsibility.

Abrams, Creighton - U.S. Commanding General August 1968 until 1972.

AC - Aircraft Commander

Ack-Ack - Anti-Aircraft fire, flak, or shrapnel.

ACR - Armored cavalry Regiment.

Admin. - Administration Company.

Aft - To the rear of a vehicle or craft.

AFVN - Armed Forces Vietnam Network (U.S. military radio and TV network).

Agency, The - CIA, Central Intelligence Agency.

Agent Orange - Defoliant used throughout Vietnam, later found to cause cancer. There were other colors such as Blue, Green, Pink, Purple, and White.

Air America - CIA-sponsored airline for clandestine operations.

Air Bear - MP (Military Police) security in an airplane.

Air Cav - Air cavalry, helicopter-borne infantry.

Air Evac - (Evac or Medevac) evacuation of the wounded by helicopter.

Air Mobile - Helicopter-borne Infantry.

Airborne - Paratrooper or parachutist.

AIT - (8-week) Advanced Individual Training, follows Basic training.

AK-47 - Communist Kalashnikov assault rifle.

AK-50 - An AK-47 with a special bayonet designed to inflict a sucking wound that would not close.

AKA - Also Known As.

Alpha Alpha - (AA) Automatic Ambush by Claymore mines or similar types.

Alpha Bravo - (AB) Ambush.

Americal - Vietnam Unit: 23rd Infantry Division.

Amerasian - A person of mixed American and Asian ancestry.

American Legion - American military veterans' fraternal organization.

AMF - Adios Mother F--ker.

Ammo - Ammunition.

Ammo Dump - Ammunition Storage facility.

Amtrac - Large armored enclosed personnel carrier on tracks.

And a Wake Up - Last day in country, i.e., 6 days and a wake up (= 6 days).

Angle Track - APC used as an Aid Station.

Ao Dai - Vietnamese-style long flowing silk dress, usually with long pants.

APC - Armored Personnel Carrier (Open-Top) on tracks.

APO - Army Post Office.

AR - Army Regulation.

Arc Light - B-52 Bomber strikes along the Cambodian and Vietnamese borders.

Arcom - Army Commendation Medal.

Army Reserve - Volunteers, provides a reserve of trained military reserve.

Army Strawberries - Prunes.

Article 15 - Military punishment, a fine and/or temporary reduction in rank.

Arty - Artillery.

ARVN - Army of the Republic of Vietnam, a Vietnamese soldier.

As You Were - Command to continue whatever you were doing or to be at ease.

ASAP - As Soon As Possible.

Ash & Trash - Non-combative mission.

Asses and Elbows - Everyone is busy, cleaning something, loading a truck, etc.

Astern - To the rear of a vehicle or craft.

At Ease - Command to relax in place.

ATC - Armored Troop Carrier.

Au Contraire - (French) To the contrary.

Aussie - An Australian.

AWOL - (A-Wall) Absent Without Leave (without permission).

Azimuth - The vector (trajectory) from an observer to a point of interest.

B-52 - Large military high-altitude long-distance bomber.

Ba M'ba - (Bom Di Bom) Vietnamese beer brand, AKA "33."

Baby San - (Pidgin English) Child.

Bac Bac - (Pidgin English) To shoot.

Bac Si - (Vietnamese) Name for a doctor or medic.

Ballgame - Hostile operation or enemy contact.

Balls to the Wall - Popular saying indicating extreme effort, based on the balls on the governor which control the speed of a steam engine. As it goes faster, the balls spread out and get closer to the wall.

Bamboo Viper - AKA "two step." If bitten, after you take 2 steps, you're dead.

Banana Clip - High-capacity banana-shaped curved assault rifle magazine.

Band Aid - Radio call sign for a medic.

Bandoliers - Canvas or cloth ammunition belts.

BAR - (WWII weapon) Browning Automatic Rifle, replaced by M-60 machine gun.

Baseball Cap - Similar to today's popular cap except for the army drab green color and a slightly different shape.

Base Camp - Normally a Brigade or Division Headquarters and re-supply base, AKA "Rear Area."

Basic Training - (8 weeks) MOS evaluation, introduction to military protocols, and initial training in the maintenance and use of weapons.

Battalion - A military unit usually consisting of 4 to 6 companies.

Battery - Artillery unit.

Battle Fatigue - (AKA PTSD and Shell Shock) Post-Traumatic Stress Disorder. The combined effects of danger, shock, fear, pain, trauma, and physical and emotional loss, can cause a wide variety of mental disorders.

Bayonet - A stabbing blade affixed to the business end of a rifle barrel.

Bazooka - WWII shoulder-fired rocket – see LAW.

BCD - Bad Conduct Discharge, (DD) Dishonorable Discharge.

BDA - Bomb Damage Assessment.

Beans & Dicks - (C-Ration meal) Beans and hot dogs.

Beans & MotherF--kers - (C-Ration Meal) Beans and lima beans.

Bearcat - Early 1st Infantry Division Base Camp, later re-named Camp Martin Cox.

Beaucoup - (French) Boo Coo, many or much.

Beehive - Artillery round with steel darts.

Belching Buzzards - 101st Airborne Division.

Belligerents - Persons or nations involved in a war or conflict, the enemy.

Berm - Protective earthen mound.

BFD - Big F--king Deal.

BFE - (Bum F--k Egypt) Isolated or remote location.

Betel Nut - Vietnamese tooth pain remedy, turned teeth black.

Bien Hoa - (Ben-Wah) One of the 1st Infantry Division Base Camps.

Biere Larue - (AKA Tiger Beer) Vietnamese beer, still brewed today.

Big Boys - Tanks.

Big Red One - (BRO) Nickname for the 1st Infantry Division.

Bingo - (Air Force term) Point when there is only enough fuel to return safely to base.

Bird - A helicopter or any other aircraft, also nickname for a Full Colonel.

Bird, Ball, and Chain - Nickname for the Marine Emblem.

Bird Barn - Aircraft carrier.

Bird Dog - Forward Air Controller.

Bivouac - Temporary military camp.

Blanket Party - Punishment, covered with a blanket and beaten by your peers.

Blasting Cap - 3"-long pencil-sized igniter for explosives.

Blood Trail - Trail of blood left by the wounded, used to find them.

Blue Falcon - (BF) Buddy F--cker.

Blue Leg - Infantryman.

BN - Battalion.

Body Bag - Heavy rubber bag used to transport bodies.

Body Count - Number of enemy dead, counted to prove we had won the battle.

BOHICA - Bend Over Here It Comes Again.

Bok-Bok - (Pidgin English) Bac-Bac, fight or fighting.

Bolo - Inept or useless trooper.

Bomblets - Small bombs, part of a firecracker artillery round.

Bong - Water pipe used to smoke tobacco or marijuana.

Boo Coo - (French: Beaucoup) Many or much.

Booby Trap - Trip wire or mechanically fired anti-personnel weapon.

Boom Boom - To have intercourse.

Boondoggle - Work that is worthless or useless.

Boonie Rat - Combat Infantryman.

Boonies - (Boondocks) Jungle or remote area outside base camp perimeter.

Boot - Soldier just out of boot camp, inexperienced, untested.

Boot Camp - Military training camp or school.

Booze - (AKA Hootch) Any alcoholic beverage.

Bought the Farm - Died.

Bouncing Betty - Booby trap shoots a grenade straight up 18" to 24"; then it detonates. It is designed to maim and not kill, taking two people out of action.

Brain Bucket - Helmet.

Brain Sponge - Soft baseball cap or jungle hat that offers no protection.

Brasso - Commercial polish used to polish brass belt buckles, etc.

Break - To rest or stop.

Break Squelch - (Break) Stop talking on a field radio, listen.

Brigade - Consists of 2 to 5 battalions.

Bring Smoke - Use a smoke grenade to identify a location.

BRO - Big Red One, 1ˢᵗ Infantry Division.

Broken Arrow - Urgent call for help from all the air support in the region.

Brother - (Bro) Your buddy, companion, or slang for a black trooper.

Bronze Star - Medal for heroism or meritorious accomplishment.

Brown Water Navy - River patrol boats.

Buck Sergeant - Sergeant rank E-5.

Bug Juice - Insect repellant (about 100% DEET).

Bug Out - To hurry away.

Bulkhead - Dividing wall between compartments of a ship or aircraft.

Bum F--k Egypt - (BFE, Bravo Foxtrot, Echo) Isolated or remote location.

Bummer - Bad luck or bad day.

Bunk - Bed or cot.

Bunker - Fortified foxhole or other position to provide permanent security.

Bunker Box - Heavy timber box filled with sandbags to protect bunker entry.

Bush - Boonies or the field.

Butter Bar - (Brown Bar) Second Lieutenant insignia.

C & C - Command and Control.

C-4 - A type of plastic explosive.

C-7 - A small cargo plane known as a Caribou.

C-123 – A larger version of the C-7 cargo plane.

C-130 - A very large propeller-driven cargo plane named Hercules.

C-141 - Another large cargo plane known as Star-lifter.

C-Rations - (AKA "C's," "Charlie Rats," and "Combat Rats") Prepared meals in packages containing cans and condiments. Today's version is MRE: Meals, Ready to Eat.

CA - Combat Assault.

Caca Dau - (Vietnamese) I'll kill you.

Cache - Stash, stored, or concealed supplies.

CIA - Central Intelligence Agency.

Cam On Bay - (Vietnamese) Thank you.

Cam Ranh Bay - One of two places the 1st Infantry Division arrived in country in 1965, became a large supply depot and primary entry and departure point for U.S. troops.

Cammies - Camouflage clothing.

Camo Band - Elastic band used to hold the fabric camouflage cover on a helmet, also used to hold bug juice, cigarettes, etc.

Camo Cover - Camouflage-printed cloth used to cover a helmet.

Camouflage Hat - (AKA Jungle or Bucket Hat) Large soft-rimmed cloth hat.

Camp Zama - Hospital in Japan that treated seriously wounded troops.

Campaign Hat - Stiff broad-brimmed felt hat worn by drill sergeants and instructors.

Can Sa - (Vietnamese) Marijuana.

Canidiot - Slang for an office candidate or cadet.

Cannibalize - Take from one place and use in another.

Cannon Cocker - An artilleryman.

Cannon Fodder - Sadly, infantrymen sent into battle with low survival expectancy.

Cap - A rifle bullet or (olive drab) headgear.

Capping At - Shooting at.

Caribou - (C-7) Small cargo plane.

CAS - Close air support.

Casing - The (brass) case of a spent shell or cartridge (bullet).

Casualty - Means either wounded or dead, this term is often confusing.

CATFU - Completely and totally f--ked up.

Cav - Air cavalry, helicopter-borne infantry.

CC - Command Center, also short for Canadian Club (whiskey).

CH-54 - Largest American helicopter, AKA Sky-crane and Flying-crane.

Chain of Command - The sequence of command positions starting with the President (Commander in Chief) down to your individual officer in charge.

Chamber A Round - When a bullet is placed in a weapon in position to be fired.

Charge - The amount of explosive needed to perform a task.

Charge of Quarters - (CQ) In charge of an area, an administrative task.

Charlie - (VC) Viet Cong, the enemy.

Charlie Foxtrot - Cluster F--k.

Charts and Darts - Artillery target map with pin markers.

Cheap Charlie - GI who is very frugal with his money, usually in a bar.

Check (Watch) Your Six - Watch your back (Air Force term based on a clock face). Twelve is forward (or up) and six is aft (or down).

Cherry - Untested, a new trooper never under fire, or a virgin.

Chest Candy - Military medals and ribbons worn on a uniform.

Chicken Colonel - Full Colonel, rank insignia is an eagle.

Chicken Plate - Protective chest body armor for chopper door gunners.

Chicom - Chinese Communist.

Chieu Hoi - (Vietnamese) Open arms, name of a VC amnesty surrender program.

China Beach - In-country R&R location, location of Marines landing in Vietnam.

Chinook - Large helicopter with two sets of top rotary blades.

Chop Chop - (Pidgin English) Food, or to move faster.

Chopper - Any helicopter.

Chow - Army food.

Chuck - (Charles or VC) Viet Cong.

Church Key - Beer or soda can opener.

CIA - Central Intelligence Agency.

CIB - Combat Infantry Badge, a genuine badge of courage.

Circus Battery - Service battery of an artillery battalion.

Civvies - Civilian clothing.

Clacker - Claymore mine detonator.

Clearance - Permission to engage the enemy, or an individual's intelligence security status or ranking.

Click - (Klick) The distance of one kilometer, or 0.62 of a mile.

Cluster Bomb - A bomb that breaks up into many small ones that then shower an area.

Cluster F--k - Totally screwed up.

CMAC - Capitol Military Assistance Command.

CMB - Combat Medic Badge.

CMO - Congressional Medal of Honor, the highest and most prestigious U.S. military decoration. For heroism above and beyond the call of duty, more often than not awarded posthumously.

CO - Commanding Officer.

Co Cong - (Vietnamese) Female Viet Cong.

Cobra - Attack helicopter AH-1G.

Code of Conduct - Military rules for U.S. troopers should they become prisoners of war.

Colored Map - Color-coded map used to delineate fire and no fire zones.

Command Private Major - Derogatory term for a private first class (E3) who attempts to command others.

Combat Engineer - Soldiers who built the fortifications, the hootches, the roads, and the airports, and they were also considered infantrymen.

Combat Operation - Joint action by U.S. forces reacting to a hostile event.

Combat Pay - Hazardous duty pay. In 1967, it was an extra $65 per month.

Combatant - Anyone engaged in armed conflict.

Comic Books - Color-coded military maps.

Comm Check - Check communication capability.

Command Center - (CC) Location of Operations and Logistics control.

Command Post - (CP) Commander of operations.

Company - Usually consists of 4 to 5 platoons.

Compound - Fortified military installation.

Concertina Wire - Razor-sharp coiled barbed wire.

Conex - Corrugated shipping container.

Cong - Viet Cong.

Cong Bo - (Vietnamese) Water buffalo.

Cong Khi - (Vietnamese) Monkey.

Cong Moui - (Vietnamese) Mosquito.

Congressional Medal of Honor - (CMO) Congressional Medal of Honor, the highest and most prestigious U.S. military decoration. For heroism above and beyond the call of duty, more often than not awarded posthumously.

Conscientious Objector - Someone who refused to fight for religious reasons. Many served as medics and other non-combat support positions.

Conscription - Compulsory enlistment into the U.S. Armed Forces, being drafted.

Contact - To engage the enemy.

CONUS - Continental United States.

Cook-Off - When a weapon's barrel is too hot, the gun can continue to fire by itself.

Cordite - Smokeless explosive used in bullets, replaced gun and black powder.

Cords - Civil Operations and Revolutionary Development, pacification.

Cork - Slang for drug used to create constipation while in the field.

Corps - Two or more Divisions, or a specific military branch or organization.

Corpsman - Medic or Doc, provided first aid in the field.

Counter-Insurgency - Anti-Guerrilla warfare.

Court-Martial - Highest judicial court used to try members of the U.S. Armed Forces.

Cover - Any headgear (hat, cap, or helmet), or a concealed hiding place.

Cowboy - A show-off, someone seeking fame and recognition.

CP - Command Post.

CQ - In charge of quarters, office administration.

Cracker Box - Field Ambulance.

Crapper - The latrine, named after John Crapper, who was acclaimed to be the inventory of the flushable toilet but was not. He was just a plumber who installed 1,000's of them.

Crew Chief - Person in charge of maintaining an aircraft.

Crispy Critters - Burn victims.

Crosscheck - Quality control, everyone double-checks everyone else.

Crumb Catcher - Your mouth.

CS - A powerful form of tear gas used for crowd control and to evacuate tunnels.

Cumshaw - Unofficial trading, bartering, or stealing from another unit.

Cush - Easy.

CYA - Cover your ass, protect yourself.

Cyclo - Three-wheeled bicycle taxi, AKA pedicab.

D-Ring - D-shaped link used as a handle, to hang something, or to connect gear.

Da Nang - (Vietnamese: Dnang) A military camp in Vietnam.

Daily-Daily - Anti-malaria pill.

Daisy Chain - Multiple explosive devices connected with detonation cord.

Dap - A stylized handshake ritual, there were many unique and complicated variations.

Dapsone - Pill given to the troops supposedly to fight malaria, but it was actually to protect against leprosy.

Day The Eagle Shits - Payday.

DD - Dishonorable Discharge resulting from a court-martial.

DD-214 - Military document with a record of a trooper's military service and accomplishments.

De-Americanization - An early term for Vietnamization, an effort to have the South Vietnamese take over all of the combat operations.

Dear John Letter - Letter from a lover who found another.

Debarkation - (Debark) To leave a ship or aircraft.

Deep Shit - (AKA Deep serious shit) The worst possible situation.

DEET - Commercial insect repellant chemical used in bug juice.

Delta - Land that forms from river sediment, see Mekong.

Demarcation Zone - Boundary area of a defensive zone that presumably has no military presence, oftentimes not the case.

DEROS - Date Eligible to Return from Overseas.

Deserter - One two runs away to avoid doing his duty, usually considered a coward.

Det Cord - (Detonation Cord) Instantaneous explosive fuse.

Deuce & a Half - Two-and-a-half-ton truck.

Dew - Marijuana.

DI - Drill Instructor.

Di An - (Pronounced Zee-On) Headquarters base camp for the 1st Infantry Division.

Di-Di Mau - (Vietnamese) Move quickly of go away (pronounced Dee-Dee Mowe).

Diddy Boppin' - To move about carelessly without any concern.

Dink - (Pidgin English) Derogatory slang for Vietnamese peasant or Viet Cong.

Dinky Dau - (Vietnamese) Stupid or crazy.

Discharge - To fire a weapon, or released from military service.

Dishonorable Discharge - Resulting from a court-martial a person is dismissed from active duty in disgrace.

Ditty - A song or a poem.

Ditty Bag - A bag or box with mementos and miscellaneous odds and ends.

Ditty Boppers - Radio operators who used Morse Code.

Division - Usually consists of 3 brigades.

DMZ or DZ - Demilitarized zone, front line area without fortifications or permanent troop installations.

Doc - Medic, corpsman, or doctor providing first aid in the field.

DOD - Department of Defense.

Dog Tags - A pair of rectangular aluminum tags hanging from a ball chain imprinted with the soldier's name, serial number, blood type, and religion. To be worn around the neck at all times.

Domino Theory - Theory or fear that if a country becomes communistic its neighbors will surely follow, popular from 1950 through the 1980's.

Dong - Vietnamese coin and currency value.

Donut Dolly - Female American Red Cross volunteer.

Doobie - Marijuana Cigarette.

Dope - Marijuana and other illicit drugs.

Dope On a Rope - Air assault parachutist.

DOR - Date of Rank.

Doubtfuls - Wounded casualties expected to die. Also, uncertain if the local people were friendlies, VC, or NVA.

Dove - One who opposes war, a peacenik, or pacifist.

Drafted - Compulsory conscription, induction into military service.

Dragon Lady - (Hanoi Hannah) Infamous North Vietnam radio personality.

Dragon Wagon - Tank transporter.

Dress Greens - Army formal dress uniform.

Dry Season - Vietnam's dry season ranges from October to June.

Du - (Vietnamese) F--k.

Du Ma - (Vietnamese) F--k you.

Du Mi Ami - (Vietnamese) Mother F--ker (Doe Mammie).

Dud - Something or someone that fails to work properly.

Duffle Bag - Long cylindrical canvas bag, a soldier's luggage.

Dung Lai - (Vietnamese) To stop.

Dust Off - Medical evac via helicopter.

Duty - Responsibilities.

DX - Direct exchange, equipment or item to be discarded, cancelled, or discontinued.

E & E - Escape & Evasion.

E-Tool - Entrenching tool, a folding shovel.

Eagle Flights - Large assault by helicopter.

Early Out - To end your remaining active duty requirement, you could extend tour in Vietnam until only 5 months of your obligation remained after your DEROS. You simply went home without any active or inactive duty obligation, and you were out of the Army.

Echo, Tango, Suitcase - (ETS) End Term of Service.

ECM - Electronic counter-measures, used to disrupt enemy radio transmissions.

Egg Beater - Helicopter.

Eisenhower - (Ike) Dwight D. Eisenhower, 34th President 1953 to 1961.

Eleven Bravo - MOS 11B, Infantryman.

Eleven Charlie - MOS 11C, Mortar squad infantryman.

Elephant Grass - Up to seven-foot-tall razor-edged tropical grass.

EM - Enlisted Man.

Embarkation - (Embark) To go on board a ship, plane, or vehicle.

EOD - (AKA: Eve of Destruction) Explosives Ordnance Disposal.

ER - Efficiency Report or Emergency Room.

ETA - Estimated Time of Arrival.

ETS - Expiration term of service (so go home already).

Eurasian - A person of mixed European and Asian ancestry.

Evac - (Medevac) Evacuation of the wounded, usually by helicopter.

Eve of Destruction - (EOD) Explosives Ordnance Disposal.

Extraction - Withdraw troops from an operational area.

Expectants - Casualties expected to die.

FAC - Forward Air Control.

Fag - A cigarette, or a homosexual.

Fairy Dust - Opium.

Fart Sack - Sleeping bag.

Fat Albert - C-54 Aircraft.

Fatigues - Military work clothes topped with a baseball cap or helmet. This is what everyone wore about 99% of the time.

FB - Fire base.

Field Strip - Knock the live ash off a cigarette, empty the tobacco, and conceal the butt.

FIGMO - F--k It, Got My Orders.

Finis - (French) Finished, or the end (Fin-Nee).

Fire - To shoot a weapon: rifle, machine gun, artillery, etc.

Fire Base - Semi-permanent artillery firing position.

Fire For Effect - Once the range has been verified, continuous fire at the enemy.

Fire Mission - Artillery target mission.

Firecracker - Artillery round with many small bomblets.

Firefight - Exchange fire, active combat with the enemy.

First - 1st Infantry Division. Should <u>always</u> be written as "1st" and <u>never as</u> "First."

First Shirt - First Sergeant (E8).

Fitty - 50-Caliber machine gun.

Five - Radio call sign for an executive officer.

Five-Sided Squirrel Cage - Slang for the Pentagon in Arlington, Va., Headquarters of the Department of Defense.

Flak Jacket - Heavy armored jacket to protect against enemy fire.

Flakey - In a state of mental disarray or stupidity.

Flamethrower - A gun that sprays a burning stream fuel, a very cruel weapon.

Flank - The outer left and right sides of a patrol.

Flare (Handheld) - Nighttime illumination flare, hangs from a small parachute when fired.

Flip-Flops - A sponge rubber thong sandal.

Flying Crane - CH54, Largest American helicopter, AKA Sky-crane.

FNG - F--king New Guy, or F--king National Guard.

FO - Forward Observer.

Foo Gas - Buried Napalm canister, creates a fireball when ignited.

Ford - (Jerry) Gerald R. Ford, 38th President 1974 to 1977.

Fore - The front of a craft or vehicle.

Forward - Advance to the front.

Foxhole - Shallow hole in the ground used to provide cover from the enemy.

Frag - Hand-thrown fragmentation grenade, or the use of it to murder someone, usually an officer.

Fraternization - Socialize with another group, i.e., enlisted men and officers at a party.

Free Fire Zone - You can fire at will, every enemy is a legitimate target.

Freedom Bird - Nickname for the plane that transported you back to the world.

French Fort - An observation base or structure built by the French 1946 to 1954.

Freq - (Freak) Radio frequency.

Friendlies - U.S. troops, our allies, and Vietnamese supporters.

Friendly Fire - (Not so friendly) U.S. fire mistakenly aimed at U.S. troops, this was and still is a frequent problem.

Front Leaning Position - Push-up position.

Front Line - Troops or position closest to the enemy.

Fruit Salad - Colorful collection of medals and ribbons worn on a dress uniform.

FTA - F--k The Army.

FUBAR - F--ked Up Beyond All Reason (Recognition, etc.).

FUBB - F--ked Up Beyond Belief.

F--k - Early puritan acronym: Forbidden and Unlawful Carnal Knowledge.

F--k - Used as a noun, verb, adverb, preposition, etc. to express anger, contempt, emphasis, used as an insult, or crude expression for making love.

FUGAZI - F--ked Up, Got Ambushed, Zipped in.

Funny Papers - (Funny Books) Color-coded topographic maps.

G-1 - Personnel Officer.

G-2 - Military Intelligence.

G-3 - Tactical Operations or staff officer.

G-4 - Supply Officer.

G.I. Joe - Nickname of an infantryman.

Gaggle - A group of choppers on a mission.

Galloping Dandruff - Head lice.

Ganga - (Pidgin English) Marijuana.

Garrison Cap - Flat folding semi-formal felt military cap.

Geek - An inept person who performs disgusting acts for alcohol.

General Quarters - Battle stations.

Ghosting - Goldbricking or sandbagging, screwing off, pretending to work.

GI - Government Issue, or General infantry.

GI Party - Cleaning or scrubbing the barracks, office, etc.

Glad Bag - Body Bag.

Gofer - (Gopher) Someone who runs errands.

GOFO - Grasp Of the F--king Obvious, AKA GTFO.

Goldbricking - Ghosting or sandbagging, screwing off, pretending to work.

Gomers - (Pidgin English) Viet Cong or VC.

Gone Elvis - Missing in action.

Goofy Grape - Purple smoke grenade.

Gook - (Pidgin English) Derogatory slang for Vietnamese peasant, or Viet Cong.

GP - General Purpose.

GQ - General Quarters, Battle Stations.

Grass - Marijuana.

Greenbacks - U.S. currency, replaced with military scrip while in Vietnam.

Green Beret - Army Special Forces.

Green Eye - Starlight night vision scope.

Grids - Map broken down into 1,000 meter squares.

Grunt - Infantryman.

GSW - Gun Shot Wound.

GSW-TTH - Gunshot Wound - Through and Through.

GTFO - Grasp The F--king Obvious, Get The F--K Out, GOFO.

Gun, The - M-60 Machine Gun.

Gung Ho - (Chinese) - All together, patriotic, overzealous, enthusiastic.

Gun Ship - Any armed aircraft.

Guerrilla - Soldier in a resistance group, usually indigenous people.

GVN - Government of South Vietnam.

H & I - Harassment and Interdiction, random artillery fire used to confuse and destroy the enemy.

Hai Phong - Primary seaport in North Vietnam.

Halftrack - M16 Light armored vehicle with M-50 machine gun(s), half on tracks and half on wheels.

Halo - High-Altitude Low-Opening, paratrooper tactic.

Hamburger Hill - (Hill 937) Hard-won battle to take the hill in 1969, but we promptly abandoned it and the VC simply walked in to retake the observation point.

Hamlet - Small rural village.

Hand Grenade - Hand-thrown fragmentation grenade.

Hand-to-Hand Combat - Face-to-face fight without firing a gun.

Hanoi - (Ha Noi) Capitol of North Vietnam until 1975, afterward became the capitol of a Unified Vietnam.

Hanoi Hannah - (Hanoi Jane, Dragon Lady, etc.) North Vietnam radio personality AKA Trinh Thi Ngo.

Hanoi Hilton - (Hoa Loa) Infamous prison for U.S. troops in Hanoi.

Hat Up - To change your location.

Hawk - One who supported the war.

Hazardous Duty Pay - In 1968 it was an extra $65 per month for all troops based in a combat zone.

HE - High Explosives.

Heart - Purple Heart Medal, received for being wounded or killed.

Heart Marker - 18th Infantry patch supposed to be worn on the left breast pocket making it a target, most did not comply.

HEAT - High Explosives Anti-Tank.

Heat Tab - Fuel pellets used to warm C-Rations, always in short supply, and they did not work in the boonies especially during the rainy season.

Heavies - High-ranking officers and commanders.

Heavy - (LRRP, LURP) Long-Range Reconnaissance Patrol.

Hellfire - A non-relenting constant rate of automatic weapon fire, also the everlasting fires of hell.

Helipad - Permanent helicopter station.

Helmet - A hard metal protective head covering.

Helmet Liner - A fiberglass liner required to wear a helmet.

Helo - Helicopter.

HHC - Headquarters and Headquarters Company.

Higher Highers - The Command group or commanders.

Highway 1 - Route North from Saigon, through Di An, up to Hanoi and beyond.

Highway 13 - Thunder Road, route from Saigon to Loc Ninh.

Hill 861 - Location of the battle for Khe Sanh.

Hill 875 - Location of a 1967 bloody battle which produced 3 Medals of Honor.

Hill 937 - Location of a 1969 bloody battle, better known as Hamburger Hill.

Hindquarters - Slang for Headquarters.

Hit the Silk - Parachute jump.

Ho - (Uncle Ho) Nickname for Ho Chi Minh.

Ho Chi Minh - Revolutionary communist leader of North Vietnam 1954 to 1969.

Ho Chi Minh City - Second largest city in Vietnam, previously known as Saigon.

Ho Chi Minh Slippers - Sandals made from rubber tires.

Ho Chi Minh Trail - Primary NVA road routed through North and South Vietnam, Cambodia, and Laos.

Honcho - Squad leader.

Honey Dippers - Unfortunates chosen to burn outhouse waste.

Honky - (Honkie or Honkey) Derogatory slang for any white person, perhaps derived from 1920's term "Honky Tonk" meaning a cheap or disreputable bar or dance hall.

Honorable Discharge - Formal document confirming one served his county honorably.

Hootch - U.S. Army barracks in Vietnam, also slang for alcohol (booze).

Horn - Field radio.

Hose Down - Massive automatic weapon fire from a gunship to the ground.

Hostiles - The enemy.

Hot - Under fire, dangerous.

Hot LZ - Landing Zone under hostile fire.

HQ - Headquarters.

Hue - Site of the month-long 1968 TET attack by the NVA and VC on the ancestral city.

Hue Motto # 1 - Fighting for piece is like f--king for virginity.

Hue Motto # 2 - (My favorite) We are the unwilling, led by the unqualified, doing the unnecessary, for the ungrateful.

Huey - Bell UH1 Iroquois helicopter.

Hump - Slogging through an area or carrying supplies.

Hurricane - Typhoon.

I & I - Intoxication & intercourse, substitute term for R&R.

I & R - Intelligence and Reconnaissance patrol.

I Corps - Northernmost military region in South Vietnam.

II Corps - Central Highlands region in South Vietnam.

III Corps - Region between Saigon and the Highlands.

IV Corps - Mekong Delta, southernmost military region in Vietnam.

IG - Inspector General.

Ike - Dwight D. Eisenhower, 34th President 1953 to 1961.

Immersion Foot - Cracking and bleeding feet due to overexposure to water.

Immersion Heater - (M-67) Gas-fired water heater, fit neatly inside a 55-gallon drum.

In Country - In Vietnam.

In The Shit - (In Vietnam) Make contact with the enemy.

Incoming - Hostile enemy fire on a friendly location.

Indian Country - Enemy Area.

Indochina - The original French colonies: Vietnam, Laos, and Cambodia.

Insert - Deployed to a tactical area by helicopter.

Insignia - Metal badge, ribbon, or cloth patch signifying a soldier's rank, unit affiliation, and job type.

Intel - Intelligence, clandestine information.

Iodine Tablets - Used to purify water.

Iron Triangle - VC area from Thi Tinh to the Saigon River in Cu Chi District (included Di An), the shape roughly resembled 1st Infantry Division's insignia patch.

Irregulars - Vietnamese armed groups not part of the South Vietnamese armed forces.

Jacked Up - Screwed up or in trouble.

Jag - Judge Advocate General, the Army's legal department.

Jane Fonda - Anyone thought to be a traitor.

Jarhead - U.S. Marine, in respect to their "high and tight" haircut.

JCS - Joint Chiefs of Staff.

Jeep - Military open-topped, 4-passenger, all-terrain vehicle.

Jerry - Gerald R. Ford, 38th President 1974 to 1977.

Jesus Nut - Retaining nut that holds the rotor blades to a helicopter.

JFK - John F. Kennedy, 35th President 1961 to 1963.

Jody - Anyone who steals a military man's wife or girlfriend, see Dear John letter.

Joe - (G.I. Joe) A soldier.

Joint - Marijuana cigarette.

John - The latrine, named after John Crapper, who was acclaimed to be the inventory of the flushable toilet but was not . He was just a plumber who installed 1,000's of them.

John Wayne - Someone thought to be a hero.

Johnson - (LBJ) Lyndon B. Johnson, 36th President 1963 to 1969.

Jolly Green Giant - CH/HH CH-3 Sikorsky Helicopter.

Jungle Boots - Military boots with canvas sides.

Jungle Fatigues - Fatigues with a camouflage print.

K - Kilometer (0.62 miles).

K-Bar - (Ka-Bar) Combat knife.

KBA - Killed By Artillery.

Kennedy - John F. Kennedy, 35th President 1961 to 1963.

Kent State - (University in Ohio) In 1968 a nervous National Guard unit shot and killed 4 Vietnam anti-war protesters.

Kerry, John - (See VVAW) A Vietnam veteran who was an anti-war protester, he addressed the Senate in 1971; later he becomes Secretary of State 2013 to 2017.

Keypunch - To create reports with a computer in 1968 you had to have a typist keypunch small rectangular slots in about 3" X 7" card stock (in varying colors); the cards were then run through a sorter which then printed spreadsheets.

KHA - Killed in Hostile Action.

Khakis - Semi-formal beige military uniform.

Khe Sanh - Marine base camp in northern South Vietnam which came under a long fierce fight during the TET offensive in 1968.

Khong Biet - (Vietnamese) I don't understand or don't know.

Khong Lau - (Vietnamese) It will never happen.

Khung Xau - (Vietnamese) Don't worry about it.

KIA - Killed In Action.

Kill Zone - Area around an explosive with a 95% kill ratio.

Killing Zone - Area within an ambush where everyone is killed or wounded.

Kit Carson Scout - Former VC who became a scout of the U.S.

Kiwi - New Zealand Military Forces.

Klick - (Click) Kilometer (0.62 miles).

Kool-Aid - Killed in action.

Koon Sa - (Vietnamese) Marijuana or Wacky Weed.

KP - Kitchen police, mess hall duty.

L - L-Shaped ambush set-up.

Lager - Nighttime defensive perimeter.

Lai Dai - (Vietnamese) Come here, or bring it to me.

Lai Khe - One of the 1st Infantry Division's base camps.

Land Line - Wired ground communications.

Landwehr, Duane - 2nd Lieutenant KIA June 6, 1969. He was my Basic Training Sergeant and he died a hero.

Latrine - Communal toilet or outhouse.

LAW - M-72 Light Anti-tank Weapon, a disposable shoulder-fired rocket. Sometimes the VC would take the discarded tubes and turn them into makeshift mortars.

Lay Chilly - To lay on the ground motionless.

LBJ - Long Binh Jail (stockade). Also Lyndon B. Johnson, 36th president 1963 to 1969.

Leatherneck - Nickname for a Marine. Suggest you look up the origin of this term.

Leg - Paratrooper nickname for the ground troops.

Lego - Infantry unit.

Life - Best defined by John Wayne: "Life is tough, and it's tougher if you're stupid."

Lifer - Career Military man or woman.

Lima Charlie - Load and clear (your weapon).

Lit Up - Fired upon.

Light Up - Order to open fire on the enemy, or permission to have a cigarette.

Lima Lima - Land line, ground communications.

Listening Post - Usually a temporary position near enemy lines to detect movement.

Litters - Stretchers use to carry casualties.

Little People - The enemy.

Little Pink Pill - Anti-malaria pill.

Loach - Light operations helicopter.

Loc Ninh - Vietnam battle location.

Lock & Load - Chamber a round in your weapon and prepare to fire.

LOH - OH-6 Light observation helicopter.

Long Knife - Air cavalry.

Long Nose - Vietnamese slang for an American.

Long Time - All-night sex.

Loran - Long range radio navigation.

Louis Lime - Green smoke grenade color.

LP - Listening Post.

LPC - 2-Week Leadership Preparation Course.

LRRP - Long-Range Reconnaissance Patrol, AKA LURP.

LSA - Small arms (pistol) lubricant.

LT - Lieutenant.

LURP - Slang for LRRP.

LZ - Landing Zone.

M-1 - 30-caliber rifle.

M-3 - Small medical bag.

M-5 - Large medical bag.

M-11 - Large pink malaria pill (diarrhea always followed).

M-14 - Full automatic rifle, 7.62 caliber.

M-16 - Lightweight full automatic rifle, 5.56 caliber.

M-18A1 - Claymore Mine.

M-50 - Machine gun, 99 mm 50 caliber, 50 BMG – Browning M2.

M-60 - Machine gun, 7.62 caliber.

M-67 - Gas-fired immersion water heater, fit inside 55-gallon drum.

M-72 - Disposable LAW, Light Anti-tank Weapon.

M-79 - Large mounted grenade launcher.

M107 - Self-propelled cannon, shot 200 pound rounds 25 miles.

M203 - Over/under combining a M-16 rifle and a M-79 grenade launcher.

MA - Mechanical Ambush, booby trap.

MACV - Vietnam unit: Military Assistance Command Vietnam.

Mad Minute - (AKA: Red Splash) Concentrated fire of all weapons.

Magazine - (Mag) Ammunition supply device or chamber, holding 8 to 30 or more cartridges (bullets).

Mail Call - Daily delivery of personal mail and packages.

Maim - To wound, dismember, or disfigure.

Major Battle - Planned decisive attack to inflict the most harm to the enemy.

Mama San - (Pidgin English) Any mature Vietnamese woman.

Mandate - Official order or commission to do something.

Marker Round - The first round fired, used to adjust fire or designate a target.

MARS - Military Affiliated (or Auxiliary) Radio Station.

Marxism - Early form of Communism.

Mary Jane - Marijuana.

MASH - Mobile Army Surgical Hospital.

MAT - Mobile Advisory Team.

Mat Tran - (Dan Toc) Vietnamese Liberation Front, a Communist organization.

Meat Wagon - Ambulance.

Mech - Mechanized infantry, usually in tracked vehicles.

Medal of Honor - (Congressional) Medal of Honor, the highest and most prestigious U.S. military decoration. For heroism above and beyond the call of duty, more often than not awarded posthumously.

Medcap - Medical civil action program, medical aid for the local population.

Medevac - (Evac) Evacuation of the wounded by helicopter or airplane.

Media - Newspapers, magazines, plus TV & Radio Stations (and now you can add the internet, smart phones, etc. to the list).

Medic - (Doc) Medical personnel who provide first aid in the field.

Mekong Delta - The largest river area in Vietnam. The river delta area was formed from river sediment and is about 4,000 miles long and very convoluted.

Menu - List of military operations in Vietnam.

Mess Hall - Military dining room area or tent.

MFW - Multiple frag wounds.

MI - Military Intelligence, gathered and evaluated enemy information.

MIA - Missing In Action.

Mic - (Mike) Microphone.

Midnight Requisition - To steal something after dark.

Mig - Soviet-made fighter jet aircraft.

Mighty Mite - A type of fan used to inject tear gas into VC tunnels.

Minh Oi - (Vietnamese) Sweetheart or lover.

Mike - Microphone or minute.

Mike Mike - Millimeters.

Military Assistance Command - (MACV) Joint service command center Air Force, Army, Marines, and Navy.

Military Scrip - Military currency (replaced greenbacks).

Million Dollar Wound - Injury severe enough to send you home but not debilitating, sometimes self-inflicted.

Mini-Gun - Rapid fire remotely controlled machine guns, usually mounted to an aircraft.

MK-II - (AKA: Brown Water Navy) River patrol boat, sailors were called River Rats.

Moped - Two-wheeled motor scooter.

Monopoly Money - Military Scrip.

Monsoon Season - Rainy or Wet Season, usually July to September.

Montagnard - Tribe of mountain people from central and northern Vietnam.

Moonbeam - Aircraft with large searchlights.

Moose - (Pidgin English) Mistress.

Mortar - (Vertical Cannon) Fires rounds at a high angle that then fall vertically.

MOS - Military Occupational Specialty, a number specifying your job responsibilities, i.e., MOS-73C20 was a Finance Specialist.

MP - Military Police.

MPC - Military Payment scrip, currency, replaced greenbacks.

MR-IV - Military Region 4, Mekong Delta around Saigon.

Mr. Charles - The Viet Cong, VC.

MRE - Current military meals for the field now known as "Meals Ready to Eat." In Vietnam, we had C-rations.

Muck Yi - (Vietnamese) F--k you.

Mule - 4-Wheeled all-terrain vehicle.

Murphy, Audie - WWII hero awarded the Medal of Honor, later he became a movie star. Many soldiers, most rightfully so, were nicknamed Audie Murphy.

Mustang - Officer promoted from the enlisted ranks.

Muster Out - Discharged from Active military Service.

Mutt - A type of Jeep.

Muzzle Flash - Bright flash (light) emitted from the end of a weapons barrel when it is fired.

My Lai - Vietnamese village where hundreds of civilians were murdered.

Nam - Vietnam.

Napalm - Jellied incendiary that ignites and then clings to any surface when fired, a very effective but brutal anti-personnel weapon.

National Guard - Primary reserve military force available for federal service.

NCO - Noncommissioned officer, a corporal or sergeant.

NDP - Night Defensive Position.

Net - Radio frequency setting.

Newbie - Basically, anyone in country with more time left than you had.

Next - Soldiers about to return home.

NG - Serial number prefix for the National Guard, many served in Vietnam.

Nickel - The number five, or half an ounce of pot.

Nixon - (Tricky Dick) Richard M. Nixon, 37th President 1969 to 1974.

Night Scope - (Starlight or Green Eye Scope) Nighttime light-amplifying telescope.

NLF - (Dan Loc) National Liberation Front, Communist organization.

No Sweat - (Pidgin English) No problem, easy, simple.

Non Lai - (Vietnamese) Conical straw hat worn by the local people.

Number 1 - (Pidgin English) The very best, good, etc.

Number 10 - (Pidgin English) The very worst, bad, etc.

Number 10 Thou - Number 10 Thousand (Pidgin English) The absolute very worst, terrible, etc.

Nung - Northern Vietnamese person of Chinese origin.

Nuoc Man - (Vietnamese) Fermented fish sauce for rice, AKA armpit sauce.

NV - North Vietnam or Vietnamese.

NVA - North Vietnamese Army.

OCS - Officers Candidate School.

Off & On - Off your butts and on your feet.

OJT - On-the-Job Training.

Old Man, The - Commander.

Olive Drab - The Army's favorite green color.

On the Double - Quickly, hurry.

Opium - Strong narcotic derived from the opium poppy, highly addictive.

OP - Observation Post.

OR - Operating Room.

Oscar - Slang for RTO, Radio transmission Operator.

Oscar Mike - On the Move.

OSS - From WWII, Office of Strategic Services (forerunner of the CIA).

Over the Fence - Crossing into Cambodia or Laos.

Over the Hill - Missing in action, desertion, or too old to rely on.

Out Country - Asian conflict outside Vietnam in Cambodia or Laos.

P-38 - Small folding can opener that came with C-Rations, AKA: John Wayne.

Padre - Chaplain.

PAP - Pierced Armored Plate, used to pave roads, chopper pads, runways, see PSP.

Papa San - (Pidgin English) Mature Vietnamese male.

Papa Sierra - (PS) Platoon Sergeant.

Paratrooper - Member of an airborne unit.

Pathet Lao - Laotian Communists.

Patrol - Troops sent out to search an area.

PAVN - People's Army of North Vietnam, AKA: NVA.

Pay Grade - Income based on rank and years of service.

PBR - Patrol Boat River, also known as Pabst Blue Ribbon (Beer), or the Brown Water Navy.

Peanuts - Wounded in action.

Pedicab - (Pidgin English) A tricycle taxi, AKA: a Cyclo.

Pentagon Papers - Secret government document detailing Vietnam War policies.

Perimeter - Boundary and outer limits of a permanent or temporary military position.

Peter Pilot - Helicopter co-pilot.

PF - (North Vietnamese) Popular Forces.

PFC - Private First Class.

PFCIC - Private First Class In Charge, less than likely.

Phoenix - Military intelligence-based program to eliminate the Viet Cong.

Phonetic Alphabet - For clarity, words are used instead of letters, i.e., Alpha = A.

Phu Loi - One on the 1st Infantry Division Base camps.

Phuoc Vinh - One on the 1st Infantry Division Base camps.

Piasters - (AKA: P's) Vietnamese currency.

Pidgin English - Oversimplified form of language used to communicate with those who do not share a common language.

Pig - M-60 Machine gun.

Pill Pusher - Medic or doctor.

PIO - Public Information Officer.

Pith Helmet - Lightweight sun helmet made from dried pith, a non-protective hat.

Platoon - Usually consists of four squads, but can vary as needed.

Plebe - Freshman at a military academy.

POG - Person Other than Grunt, rear echelon personnel.

Pogue - Derogatory term for rear echelon personnel.

Point - (Point Man) First man far in front of a patrol, the first to see action.

Police - Maintain, clean up, or search an area.

Police Action - Inaccurate media driven "politically correct" term referring to Vietnam War because war was never formally declared.

Politically Correct (1) - Media-driven terms used to justify and authenticate their agenda.

Politically Correct (2) - Pervasive theology to embrace the insanity of a whitewash.

Politically Correct (3) - Make it smell better no matter how bad it stinks.

Politically Correct (4) - Good label for bad medicine, or vice versa.

Politically Correct (5) - Mandate to avoid offending someone deemed important regardless of the cost to the truth.

Politically Correct (6) - (And my favorite) This is a quote from a telegram sent from President Truman on September 1, 1945 to General MacArthur and Admiral Nimitz just prior to the formal surrender by the Japanese at the end of WWII. "Political Correctness is a doctrine, recently promoted by a sick mainstream media, which holds forth the proposition that it is entirely possible to pick up a piece of shit by the clean end."

Political Correctness, A Little Ditty - "Round and round, and round we go. Up is down, in is out, tell me what it's all about. Tell me, tell me." (Please feel free to add your own words to this little ballad.

Poncho - (Poncho Liner) Military rubberized rain poncho and blanket.

Poo Tang - ("Pussy") Crude slang for any eligible female.

Poor Man's Subway - VC tunnel system.

Pop a Flare - To launch a handheld flare at nighttime. When used a bright flare floats down from a small parachute which illuminates the area for about a minute.

Pop Smoke - To throw a smoke grenade to indicate a location.

Port - To the left side of a vehicle or craft.

Port of Entry - Harbor, border town, or airport which is an entry point into a country.

Potpourri - A mixture of different things.

POW - Prisoner of War.

Prick 6 - PRC-6 Radio carried by platoons.

Profiled - One who is selected or stands out, usually capable of limited military duty due to injury or other limitations.

Protocol - Code or mandate of proper behavior.

PSDF - People's Self-Defense Force, South Vietnamese.

PSP - Perforated Steel Plate used to pave roads, chopper pads, and runways, see PAP.

Psyops - Psychological Operations.

PT - Physical Training.

PTSD - Post-Traumatic Stress Disorder, often misunderstood and mistreated, formerly known as "Shell Shock" and "Battle Fatigue."

Pucker Factor - Fear Factor, the measure of difficulty or risk.

Puff the Magic Dragon - (AKA: Spooky) AC-47 plane with high rate of fire machine-driven Gatling guns and it also fired large flares for illumination.

Puking Chicken - 101st Airborne Eagle Crest.

Pump & Dump - To have sex.

Punch Card - Cards used to run computer reports and programs, see keypunch.

Punji Stakes - Concealed pit with bamboo or wooden spikes covered with feces, a dangerous booby trap.

PX - Post Exchange, one-stop, all-in-one store, they have everything.

QC - (Quan Canh) South Vietnamese military police, AKA: White Mice.

Quad 50 - Four 50-caliber machine guns permanently mounted to a vehicle, boat, or defensive position. Used to protect ground installations and to attack fixed enemy positions. In WWII this was used as an anti-aircraft weapon.

Quan Loi - One of the 1st Infantry Division's Base Camps.

Quarter Ton Truck - A jeep.

Que Sera, Sera - (Italian or Spanish) Song title meaning "whatever will be, will be."

R&R - Rest & Recreation, a vacation.

ROTC - Reserve Officers Training Corps (classes), these mandated classes were located in most state-funded colleges and universities.

RA - Serial number prefix indicating enlistment into the Regular Army.

RAC - Royal Ass Chewing.

Rack - Cot or bed.

Railroad Tracks - Captain's Bars, rank insignia.

Rainy Season - Vietnam's wet season, June to October.

RAP - Rocket-Assist Projectile, extended range of artillery shells.

Rappel - Descend by rope.

RBF - Reconnaissance By Fire, firing weapons or starting fires to locate the enemy.

Rear Area - Base camp.

Rear Echelon - Non-combat supply, service, and administrative support troops.

Recon - Reconnaissance in the air or on the ground.

Rectal Cranial Inversion - Head up your ass, a common problem back in 1968 with the military leaders, and with politicians everywhere at any time, including today.

Red Alert - Most urgent warning of imminent attack. Must wear a flak jacket, helmet, and carry a weapon with a bandolier of ammo.

Red Bird - Cobra Helicopter.

Red Cross - International humanitarian organization providing relief to victims.

Red Legs - Artillerymen.

Red LZ - (Hot LZ) Landing zone under hostile fire.

Red Rain - Heavy fire with a stream of red tracers.

Red Splash - (Mad Minute) Concentrated fire from all weapons.

Reefer - Marijuana.

REMF - Rear Echelon Mother F--ker.

Remington Raider - (Remington Rider) Clerk Typist.

Repo Depot - Troop Replacement Depot.

Retarded Over-Trained Children - Slang for ROTC, Reserve Officers Training Corps.

Revetment - Sand-bagged or earthen barrier.

RF/PF - (Ruff & Puffs) Slang for regional and popular forces in South Vietnam.

RHIP - Rank Has Its Privilege.

Rice Paddy - Flooded field used to grow rice.

Rice Paddy Racers - GI foam rubber shower shoes (thongs).

RIF - Reduction In Force - Forced retirement used to eliminate excess or senior cadre, oftentimes disqualifying those chosen from a pension.

River Rat - Navy river patrol boat and crew.

Rock-N-Roll - To fire your weapon on full automatic fire.

Roger - Radio communication term signifying you understand or agree.

ROK - (ROKs) Republic Of Korea ground troops.

Roll call - While in platoon formation, attendance is taken and any important notices are given.

Rolling Thunder - Prolonged (1965 to 1968) mission to systematically bomb North Vietnam into submission. It was stopped so many times in an effort to negotiate a peace agreement, it became totally ineffective. Had we continued non-stop, we would have won the war in 1968 and saved many thousands of American and Vietnamese lives. Basically the media and the "Doves" deserve all the credit, and all the responsibility.

Rome Plow - Large heavy-duty armored bulldozer.

RON - Remain Overnight.

Rotate - To return home after your tour of duty was over.

ROTC - Reserve Officers Training Corps, located in state colleges and universities.

Rotorhead - Chopper (Helicopter) pilot.

Round - A bullet, cartridge, or artillery shell. Based on the original musket rifle's round bullet.

Round Eye - American or European Woman.

RPG - Rocket Propelled Grenade.

RTO - Radio Telephone Operator.

Ruck - (Rucksack) Backpack carried by the infantry.

Rules of conduct - Mandates for U.S. behavior should a soldier become a prisoner of war.

Rules of Engagement - Directives for fighting a battle.

RVN - Republic of (South) Vietnam.

S-1 - Personnel.

S-2 - Intelligence.

S-3 - Operations.

S-4 - Supply.

S-5 - Civil Affairs.

S & D - Search & Destroy mission.

Sad Sack - To be unhappy.

Saddle Up - Prepare to deploy.

Saigon - Previous Capitol of South Vietnam. It is now called Ho Chi Minh City.

Saigon Sea - South China Sea.
Saigon Tea - Weak tea sold in bars to scam soldiers.
Salad Bar - Medals and ribbons worn on a dress uniform.
Salvo - Battery of weapons firing in unison.
SAM - Surface to Air Missile.
Same Same - (Pidgin English) Surprisingly it means "the same."
Sampan - Vietnamese low-draft boat.
Sandbagging - Screwing off, AKA: Ghosting or Goldbricking.
Sapper - Demolition commando.
SAR - Search and Rescue.
Sarge - Sergeant.
Sat - Satisfactory.
Satchel Charge - Anti-personnel pack of explosives or bomb in a bag.
SC - Support Command.
Screaming Eagles - 101st Airborne Division, AKA: The Belching Buzzards.
Screw the Pooch - To mess up.
Scuttlebutt - Gossip, rumor, or BS.
SDS - Students for a Democratic Society, zealous, destructive, and violent protesters.
SEA - Southeast Asia.
SEA Huts - Southeast Asian huts.
Seabees - Navy construction engineers.
Seal - (Sea, Air, & land) Navy Special Forces.
Search and Destroy - Offensive to destroy enemy positions, AKA: Zippo Raids.
SEATO - Southeast Asia Treaty Organization.
Selective Service System - (SSS) Government group responsible for overseeing the notification and conscription of draftees.
Semper Fi - (Semper Fidelis) The Marine motto, Latin for always faithful.
Set - A party.

Shake & Bake - A 2ⁿᵈ Lieutenant right out of Officer Candidate School (OCS).

Shamming - Goofing off.

Shaped Charge - Curved (Concave or Convex) explosive charge with shrapnel, focused in one direction. A claymore mine meets this description.

Shave-Tail - 2ⁿᵈ Lieutenant.

Shawnee - CH-21 Helicopter.

Shell - Artillery rounds and projectiles, also the act of bombarding a position.

Shell Shock - Battle fatigue or PTSD.

Shit - Basically anything unpleasant: combat action, a nasty chore, your stuff, problems, something that either figuratively or actually really stinks.

Shit on a Shingle - Creamed chipped beef on toast.

Shit Patrol - Latrine Duty.

Shithook - Chinook CH-47 twin-rotor cargo helicopter.

Short - Less than 30 days before DEROS.

Short-Time - (Quickie) Quick sex.

Short-Timer - One who has less than 30 days until DEROS.

Short-Timer Stick - Carved wooden stick with a dragons head, symbolic swagger stick.

Shotgun - Armed guard in a vehicle or door gunner on a chopper.

Shrapnel - Devastating explosive fragments, sharp shards of torn metal sent flying.

Sierra, Tango, Foxtrot, Uniform - (STFU) Shut the F--k Up.

Silent Heroes - Troopers who did their jobs and went home without boasting.

Silent Majority - Those with strong opinions who do not say much or actively protest anything; but they make themselves heard in other ways, usually with their votes.

Silver Bullet - Rectal thermometer.

Silver Star - Medal for extreme heroism.

Sit-Rep - Situation Report.

Six - (Six o'clock) Aviation slang, means to watch your back.

Skate - To goof off and get away with taking it easy.

Sky Pilot - Chaplain.

Skycrane - Chinook CH-54 largest American helicopter, AKA: the Flying Crane.

Slackman - Man right behind the point man, takes over point position whenever necessary.

SLAM - Search, Locate, Annihilate, Monitor.

Slant Eye - Derogatory slang, usually referred to any Asian woman.

Sleeper - Undercover agent, a mole.

Slick - Huey chopper used to move troops and cargo.

Slope - Derogatory nickname for a Vietnamese peasant or Viet Cong.

Smoke - Smoke grenades used to specify a location, or a cigarette or a doobie.

Smoking Lantern - Figurative term, when "lit," it is OK to smoke a cigarette, if not "lit," no smoking is permitted.

Smokey Bear - Drill instructor.

SNAFU - Situation Normal, All F--ked Up.

Snake - AH-1G Cobra attack helicopter; also slang for someone new in country.

Snake Eaters - U.S. Army Special Forces or Rangers.

Sneaky Petes - U.S. Army Special Forces or Rangers.

Snoop & Poop - Search & Destroy.

Snoopy Blanket - Camouflage poncho liner.

Snot Locker - Your nose.

Snuffy - Marine Grunt.

Soldier - Any member of the U.S. Army or Marines.

Solid - Help or a favor.

Song - (Vietnamese) A river.

Sortie - Aircraft conducting a mission.

SOP - Standard Operating Procedure.

SOS - Shit on a shingle, or destress call: "Save Our Ship."

Soul Brother - Any African American.

South China Sea - Ocean area east of Vietnam, AKA: Saigon Sea.

SP - C-Ration packet containing cigarettes & toiletries.

Special Forces - Army Green Berets or Airborne Rangers.

Specialist - Rank of Specialist 4th to 6th Class, rank without command authority.

Spider Hole - VC sniper foxhole with a grass lid or cover.

Spit Shined - Shoes or boots polished to a reflective shine.

Spook - CIA secret service agent.

Spooky - AC-47 Gunship, AKA: Puff the Magic Dragon.

Squad - A military group of 8 or more men, usually 4 squads to a platoon.

Square - A cigarette.

SSS - Selective Service System, or the three S's: Shit, Shower, & Shave.

Stand Down - Period of rest, take it easy.

Stand Tall - To be proud, or strict, correct military appearance.

Starboard - To the right of a vehicle or craft.

Starlight Scope - (Night Scope, Green Eye) Night vision light-amplifying telescope.

Stars & Bars - The Confederate flag.

Stars & Stripes - The American flag, or the military newspaper.

Steel Pot - Helmet.

Sterilize - Restoring an area to its original condition, or an immaculate cleaning.

Stratofortress - B-52, long-range, subsonic, jet-powered strategic bomber.

Stretcher - (Litter) Canvas sheet with two poles used to carry casualties.

Stripes - (NCO) Non-Commissioned Officer ranks E-4 to E-9.

Stupid O'clock - Too early in the morning.

Suck It Up - Brace yourself or get prepared.

Super Constellation - C-121 Aircraft with sophisticated radar and listening devices.

SVN - South Vietnam.

Sweat Rot - Fatigues that are falling apart, were worn too long and not washed.

Sweat Towel - Olive drab green-colored bath towel, often worn around the neck by the men in the field.

Swinging Dick - Lower ranking enlisted men.

Syrette - Disposable single-dose syringe with morphine for use in the field by medics.

T&T - Through-and-Through wound.

TAC - Tactical Air Command.

TAC Air - Tactical air strike.

Tail-End Charlie - Person or unit last in line, or the last person in a patrol.

Take a Knee - Take a break, relax.

Tan Son Nhut - Air Force base just north of Saigon.

Tangle Foot - Ankle-high meshwork grid pattern of single-strand barbed wire.

Tango - Target.

Tango Boat - Armored Troop Carrier (ATC) boats that patrolled the Vietnamese waters.

Tango Mike - Thanks much.

Tango Uniform - Tits Up, dead body.

Tarmac - Hard surface of aircraft landing strips, runways, and helipads.

TC - Tactical Commander.

TDA - Temporary Duty Away.

TDT - Temporary Duty Travel (orders).

TDY - Temporary Duty.

TET - Vietnamese (Buddhist) Lunar New Year Celebration.

TET Offensive - 1968 (and 1969) Major NVA clandestine attack under the guise of a cease fire during a religious holiday.

Thang Cho De - (Vietnamese) Son of a Bitch.

Thermite - Powdered aluminum & metal oxide mixture that creates extreme heat.

Thieu, Nguyen van - The last president of South Vietnam, resigned in April 1967.

Those People - Enemy forces.

Three-Quarter - Three-quarter-ton truck.

Threes - Shit, Shower, and Shave.

Thumper - (Thump Gun) M-79 Grenade Launcher.

Thunder Road - Highway 13 from Saigon to Loc Ninh.

Ti Ti - (Pidgin English) Little bit or very small.

Tiger Balm - Vietnamese foul-smelling oil used to ward off evil spirits.

Tiger Beer - (Biere Larue) Vietnamese Beer (Tiger Piss), still brewed today.

Tiger Suit - Camouflage clothing.

Tight - To have a close friend.

Tits Up - (Tango Uniform) dead Body.

TL - Team Leader

TO - Tactical Officer.

TO & E - Table of organization and equipment.

To Dai - (Vietnamese) Booby trap area, ironically pronounce "to die."

TOC - Tactical Operation Center.

Toe Popper - Antipersonnel mine.

Tokay Gecko - Popular indigenous lizard with a mating call of "Faa Cue."

Tonkin - Region in North Vietnam near Hanoi named by the French.

Tooth Fairy - Dental technician.

Top - High-ranking NCO.

TOT - Time On Target, length of time for a planned barrage.

Tour of Duty - Length of time a soldier is assigned to an area or project.

Tracers (Green) - Communist bullets that leave a green phosphorus trail.

Tracers (Red) - U.S. bullets that leave a red phosphorus trail.

Trach - Tracheotomy.

Tracks - Any military vehicle with tracks: Tanks, APCs, etc.

Trench Monkey - Member of the U.S. Army.

Triangle Listening Post - Permanent or temporary fortified position near enemy lines to monitor activity.

Triage - Deciding the order in which to treat casualties.

Tricky Dick - Nickname of Richard M. Nixon, 37th President 1969 to 1974.

Trip Wire - Hidden wire that triggers a booby trap when disturbed.

Triple A - (AAA) WWII term for Anti-Aircraft Artillery.

Triple Canopy - Jungle plants basically growing up to three different heights, totally obscures the view.

Triple Threat - Soldier with Special Forces, Ranger, and Airborne training.

Troopers - Anyone (male or female) serving in the U.S. armed services.

Troops - Soldiers.

Tunnel-Rat - Infantryman who searched VC tunnels.

Turtles - Slow-arriving replacements.

Two-Digit Midget - One with less than 100 days before DEROS.

Two Step - (Bamboo Viper) If bitten, take two steps and you're dead.

Typhoon - Hurricane.

U - U-Shaped ambush.

U-2 - High-flying spy plane used in Vietnam, one was shot down over Russia in 1960.

UA - Unauthorized Absence, AWOL.

UH-1 - Huey, Bell Iroquois helicopter.

UN - United Nations.

Unass - Get off your ass and get moving.

Uncle Ben's Boys - Vietnamese people or VC.

Uncle Ho - Nickname for Ho Chi Minh.

Uncle Sam's Canoe Club - Combat river boats, AKA: Brown Water Navy.

Unf--k - To correct a problem.

Un-Hat - Take off your hat.

Uniform Hat - Formal olive drab Army dress hat with black rim and brass emblem.

US - Serial number prefix for conscripted soldiers, draftees.

USAF - U.S. Air Force.

USARPAC - United States Army Pacific.

USASTRATCOM - U.S. Army Strategic Command, Southeast Asia.

USAVN - United States Army Vietnam.

USMC - United States Marine Corps.

USN - United States Navy.

USNS - United States Navy ship.

USO - United Service (Serviceman's) Organization.

V - V-Shaped ambush.

VA - Veterans Administration.

VC - Viet Cong.

Vector - Having the direction as well as the magnitude of one point to another.

Venable, Joseph - 1st Infantry Division Command Sergeant Major, KIA September 13, 1968.

VFW - Veterans of Foreign Wars, military fraternal organization.

Victor Charles - Viet Cong, VC.

Viet Cong - South Vietnamese Communist forces.

Viet Minh - Predecessors to the Viet Cong.

Vietnam Conflict - The Vietnam War.

Vietnam Popular Forces - Local independent South Vietnamese forces, local militia defending their homes from the VC and NVA.

Vietnamization - U.S. policy to turn the fighting over to the South Vietnamese troops.

Ville - (Village) A group of American or Vietnamese hootches.
VN - Vietnam.
VNAF - Vietnamese Air Force.
VOCG - Verbal Order Commanding General.
VR - Visual Reconnaissance.
Vung Tau - In-country R&R location, also one of two places the 1st Infantry Division arrived in country in 1965.
VVAW - Vietnam Veterans Against the War. Held a huge 1971 rally in Washington, DC. Quoted as saying they had "identified the enemy and he is us."
WAC - Women's Army Corps.
Wacky Tobaccy - (Wacky Tobacky) marijuana.
Wakey - To wake up, or the last day in country before going home.
Walking Wounded - Casualty still able to walk without assistance. Also refers to all those mentally affected by the war but without physical injuries.
Walter Wonderful - Walter Reed Hospital in Washington, DC. Treated those seriously wounded and needing extended care.
Wannabee - Slang for "want to be."
War of Deception - The Vietnam War, or any other war for that matter.
War Powers Act - 1973 Act limiting the U.S. President's ability to deploy troops.
Ware, Keith - Big Red One Major General KIA September 13, 1968. Received the Medal of Honor during WWII. He was the first Major General killed in Vietnam.
Warrant Officer - (WO-1 to WO-4) Rank between Commissioned Officers and NCOs, they are technical specialists and leaders.
Wart Hog - A-10 Attack Aircraft.
Waste - (Wasted) To be killed in action.
Wasted - Drunk, high on dope, or KIA (killed one way or another).
Watcher - The enemy.

Web Gear - Canvas belt and shoulder straps used to carry equipment and ammo.

Weed - Marijuana.

Westmoreland, William - U.S. Commanding General in Vietnam 1964 to August 1968.

Wet Season - Vietnam's rainy season, from June to October.

WHA - Wounded Hostile Action.

Whiskey, Tango, Foxtrot - (WTF) What The F--k. Most people did not use the phonic words or the acronym, it was so much easier and emphatic just to say what you meant.

White Phosphorus - (Willie Pete) Phosphorus explosive that would even burn underwater.

Whitewalls - Military super sharp haircut, short crewcut top with both sides of head shaved.

WIA - Wounded In Action.

Widow Maker - Mechanical ambush or booby trap.

Willie Peter - (Willie Pete, Willie papa) White Phosphorus grenade, bomb, or shell.

WIMP - Weak, Incompetent, Malingering, Pussy.

WO - Warrant officer, technical leader.

WP - White Phosphorus.

World - Anyplace other than Vietnam, 99% of the time it meant the U.S.

WTF - What The F--k.

X-Ray Team - Communications relay team.

Xin Loy – (Vietnamese) Sounds like "sin-loy," sorry about that.

XO - Executive officer.

Yank - American soldier.

Yards - Montagnards, people from Vietnam's Central Highlands.

Yellow Alert - Standard warning to be cautious.

Zapped - To be killed.

Zipped In - Pinned down by enemy fire.

Zipperhead - Slang for Vietnamese peasant or Viet Cong.

Zippo - Cigarette lighter (usually engraved), or nickname for a flame thrower.

Zippo Mission - Search and Destroy mission in a village, basically assuming every hut belonged to a VC.

Zippo Raid - Burning a village suspected of harboring VC.

Zit - Slang for Vietnamese people.

Zulu - Casualty report.

> If you have taken the time to read the entirety of this Glossary, it will become apparent that it tells a much more poignant story than I have written. Although it contains many words best never used again, it is a brief safari into a mostly forgotten era. If you weren't there, just reading this Glossary will give you a little taste of the Vietnam experience, and some of these words will have an impact. If you were there, or anywhere else at any time serving our country and protecting America's ideals, God bless and thank you for your service. Depending on where and when you were stationed and what your duties were, the military jargon varied tremendously; so this Glossary will always remain a work in progress. If you are aware of a term or description that is not listed, please let me know. Hopefully this collection of definitions has proven to be an interesting trek back to the 'Nam.

Acknowledgements

MANY OF THE RESOURCES LISTED BELOW WERE USED TO RESEARCH THE HISTORICAL DATA AND EVENTS THAT WERE PART OF THE VIETNAM WAR ERA AND WERE STUDIED TO BETTER UNDERSTAND THE STORY OF HOW AMERICA'S INVOLVEMENT EVOLVED AS THE WAR PROGRESSED. OTHER RESOURCES WERE USED TO RESEARCH THE TYPES OF WEAPONS USED, THE TERMINOLOGY, THE GEOGRAPHICAL LOCATIONS, SOME OF THE PEOPLE INVOLVED, AND THE SAD STATISTICS THAT RESULTED FROM THIS CONFLICT.

THE ONLY HARDBOUND BOOKS USED FOR THE RESEARCH OF THIS BOOK WERE PUBLISHED BY THE UNITED STATES ARMY AS SOUVENIRS FOR TROOPS WHO HAD COMPLETED A TOUR OF DUTY IN VIETNAM. THESE BOOKS ARE NOW VERY HARD TO FIND; BUT, IF YOU SHOULD COME ACROSS ONE, I RECOMMEND YOU TAKE A LOOK. ONLY TWO OF THE THREE VOLUMES PUBLISHED CONCERNING THE 1st INFANTRY DIVISION WERE USED.

Hardbound Books:

- VOLUME 1 - THE BIG RED ONE'S HISTORY FROM JULY OF 1965 THROUGH APRIL OF 1967

- VOLUME 2 – THE BIG RED ONE'S HISTORY FROM MAY OF 1967 THROUGH DECEMBER OF 1968

- ALL THE OTHER RESEARCH WAS DONE ELECTRONICALLY ON LINE VIA THE INTERNET. TO PROPERLY IDENTIFY THEM, I HAVE LISTED THE INTERNET ADDRESSES BY THE NAMES LISTED ON THE WEBSITE AND UNDER THE HEADINGS OF HOW THEY WERE USED.

Terminology:

- VIETNAM VETERANS TERMINOLOGY AND TERMS -
  http://www.vietvet.org
- 1st BATTALION, 50TH INFANTRY ASSOC., VIETNAM ERA WAR "JARGON" - http://www.ichiban1.org/html/history
- 1st AIR CAV MEDIC, AIRMOBILE –
  http://www.1stcavmedic.com
- 1st BATTALION, 69th ARMOR -
  http://www.rjsmith.com
- WIKTIONARY -
  http://en.www.wiktionary.org/wiki

Big Red One History and Information

- FRED'S VIETNAM DAYS - http://dunlapsite.com/Dunlap/ VietNam/VietNam.htm
- SOCIETY OF THE 1st INFANTRY DIVISION - https://1stid.org/historyindex.php

People:

- VIETNAM VETERANS MEMORIAL FUND - http://www.vvmf.org/Wall-of-Faces
- THE PEOPLE HISTORY - http://www.thepeoplehistory.com

Everything:

- WIKIPEDIA, A TREMENDOUS RESOURCE USED TO RESEARCH ALL ASPECTS OF THIS BOOK: PEOPLE, HISTORY, TIME LINES, POLITICAL ACTIVITY & HISTORY, BATTLES, EQUIPMENT, TERMINOLOGY, ETC. - https://en.wikipedia.org/wiki

History:

- HISTORY.COM - http://www.history.com/this-day-in-history
- 1960'S FLASHBACK - http://www.1960sflashback.com

- NATIONAL ARCHIVES STATISTICAL INFORMA-TION –
  http://www.archives.gov/research/military/vietnam-war/casualty-statistics.html
- AMERICAN WAR LIBRARY -
  http://www.americanwarlibrary.com/vietnam

Equipment:

- THE HELICOPTER PAGE -
  http://www.helicopterpage.com

IT IS IMPORTANT TO NOTE THAT, OTHER THAN SOME OF THE TERMINOLOGY, NONE OF THE INFORMATION RESEARCHED FROM THE ABOVE RESOURCES WAS COPIED OR USED VERBATIM. I REDEFINED AND REWROTE EVERYTHING ELSE AND ONLY USED THE INFORMATION LEARNED TO AUTHENTICATE THE FACTS AND STATISTICS FOR USE IN MY STORY. I AM VERY GRATEFUL TO EACH OF THESE IMPORTANT RESOURCES AND HIGHLY RECOMMEND THEM ALL TO ANYONE LOOKING FOR MORE INFORMATION.

Made in the USA
Monee, IL
05 November 2021